WOMEN
AND
WORK

WOMEN
AND
WORK

A Psychological Perspective

Veronica F. Nieva
Barbara A. Gutek

PRAEGER

PRAEGER SPECIAL STUDIES • PRAEGER SCIENTIFIC

Library of Congress Cataloging in Publication Data

Nieva, Veronica F.
   Women and work.

   Bibliography: p.
   Includes index.
   1. Women--Employment.   I. Gutek, Barbara A.   II. Title.
HD6053. N48   331.4   81-2713
ISBN   0-03-055761-5 (hb)   AACR2
       0-03-062033-3 (pb)

Published in 1981 (hb) and 1982 (pb) by Praeger Publishers
CBS Educational and Professional Publishing
A Division of CBS, Inc.
521 Fifth Avenue, New York, New York 10017 U.S.A.

23456789 052 9876543

Printed in the United States of America

ACKNOWLEDGMENTS

We have benefited from the support of many individuals and institutions in the preparation of this book. We are indebted to the Institute for Social Research at the University of Michigan, the Advanced Research Resources Organization in Washington, D.C., the Urban Institute in Washington, D.C., and both the Institute of Industrial Relations and the Psychology Department at UCLA for institutional support. The superb library facilities at ISR were especially appreciated.

In addition, we wish to acknowledge the intellectual contribution in the form of ideas and comments on various stages and sections of the manuscript. We especially would like to thank Daniel Katz, Rob Quinn, and Pat Gurin at Michigan for providing feedback at the crucial early stages. Many other people also have read or commented on various sections and we appreciate their help. Several typists contributed their skills to this effort. We would like to thank them and acknowledge the help of Paul Phillips who organized, and Zulma Duran who typed the reference section in record time.

Finally, we would like to thank Steve, Rachel, and Christopher for being such terrific people.

PREFACE

The increasing participation of women in the employment world is met with widely divergent reactions. While some voices hail the push toward equal participation and equal rewards, others glumly predict the devastation of the basic fabric of the family and society. For some, women's increasing participation in paid work is seen as producing societal changes at a recklessly rapid rate; for others, changes have not taken place as rapidly as might be desired. There is disagreement on the reasons behind the perceived rate of change. Correspondingly, different measures are suggested to meet the perceived situation.

Behind the divergence in opinion and prescription are assumptions and beliefs about what women *can* and *want* to do. Do women really want to get jobs that typically have belonged to men? Do they have the necessary abilities to handle such work? Do they really want to work outside the home at all, or are they, as some arguments suggest, the victims of a new form of coercion forcing them into activities they do not really desire? On the job, why are so few women in leadership positions or skilled blue collar positions? How do token women fare?

Of late, there has been increasing curiosity about the validity of assumptions that have been generally accepted about women and work and greater interest in checking out myths against realities. As a result, research has burgeoned on a wide range of topic areas in a variety of disciplines. Psychologists and sociologists, for example, have conducted studies on questions regarding women's occupational choices and have compared their abilities, interests, and performance to those of men. Psychologists have looked at early acquired, relatively stable factors such as aspiration level, learned helplessness, and achievement motivation that affect women's behavior at work. Sociologists have compiled case studies on women in particular occupational groups, for example, social workers, attorneys, and college professors. Economists have examined trends in the labor force participation of women and have described the sex-segregated nature of the labor force. Organizational behavior specialists have looked into the unique barriers that women face in the day to day processes in work organizations: job selection, placement, and reward allocation. Family specialists, concerned with effects of women's work outside the home on their homes lives, have conducted studies of the impact of work on women's husbands, their children, and their mental health.

The many facets of the phenomenon of women and work make it understandable that relevant literature appears from such an array of different disciplines. Since the issues pertinent to women at work cannot be understood realistically from any single perspective, the first aim of this book is to make this multidisciplinary material available in one source, consolidating what is known about women and work, while retaining the scientific nature of the research reviewed. In sum, we intend to review the empirical and theoretical literature on the topic of women and work.

Although the data and commentary to be considered are multidisciplinary, the viewpoint that we take is primarily psychological. Readers primarily interested in a state-of-the-art economic, historical, or sociological analysis of women and work should consult one or more of the excellent books written recently by experts in those disciplines. Our analytic emphasis will be the individual woman, and the environment will be considered to the extent that it influences her options and decisions. We are both psychologists with specializations in social and organizational psychology. Our learned bias is to study the individual woman, her choices, decisions, behaviors, and problems. After all it is her actions that form the basis for the larger macrolevel processes. Nevertheless, we cannot ignore the larger context in which her actions are based. We will try, therefore, to bridge part of the gap between the macrolevel processes that concern economists, sociologists, and legislators, and the psychological processes within the individual women. We will therefore borrow from economists, sociologists, historians, and demographers to present a more complete picture of the topic. However, the bulk of the research we review was done by social psychologists and organizational behavior researchers.

We are conscious of some of the limitations of this book. First of all, although we speak in general about working women, we are aware that, in reality, we are dealing only with women engaged in paid work. We have decided not to discuss the other population of women who work without pay within the context of the home, although we will deal with family life and the homemaker role as they affect women's role in the labor market. There are specific topic areas that we have left out on purpose — for example, women in unions, poor and disadvantaged women, and working women outside of the industrialized Western world. We chose those areas that, in our judgment, have the greatest general relevance to the understanding of women who work, particularly from the viewpoint of social and organizational psychology. Our intention is to be as empirically based as possible, and we review the data available on the issues that we cover. However, there are areas in which very little empirical data exist. Necessarily these sections consist of much higher proportions of our thought and speculation than tested fact. The inconsistencies in data availability are reflected in some unevenness in the treatment of different topics in the book.

We are not concerned with critiquing individual studies or with evaluating the state of the methodology used in research on women and work. We do recognize, however, that studies vary greatly in quality, and try to take that into account in our discussion.

We hope to speak primarily to individuals directly involved in research in the area of women and work. This book is appropriate for use in upper-level university courses in the social sciences, women's studies, and organizational behavior. It is also relevant to practitioners who deal with women who are potentially or presently working: guidance counselors who provide early input into vocational decisions in educational settings, and those who provide guidance to women already employed. The book is also relevant to policy makers for whom the focus on empirical realities, the disclosure of areas of ignorance, and the discussion of alternative routes for change would be useful in the formulation of policies and programs based more on fact than on myth, and for the general public interest in women and work. We hope that those practitioners, policy makers, and lay public interested in sifting through many studies will find the results rewarding.

In general, this book reflects our exposure to open-systems theory. While we wish to focus on the individual woman, we know that her behaviors and attitudes are embedded in larger social, economic, and historical systems. The short introductory chapter provides some social, historical, and economic context for the study of women and work. Having "set the stage," we then focus mainly on the individual woman for the rest of the book.

Chapters 2 and 3 follow a developmental sequence, moving from processes of career choice to determinants of the actual decision to work. For women, more than for men, trying to combine work life and a family life is problematic. In Chapter 4 we discuss research, much of it fairly recent, about the relationship of work and family life. Here again our basic reliance on systems theory concepts is evident. "Women and work" needs to be studied within the context of women's lives and within the context of the larger socioeconomic system. We then focus on particular issues that women face in the work situation: integration into the workplace, performance evaluation, motivational factors, leadership, and the reward structure.

The final chapter will be more speculative in nature, relying on our own insights and predictions, as well as the theories, hypotheses, predictions, and speculations of other students of the women-and-work scene. Here we present four models or ways of viewing women and implications of those models for social change in areas important to women who work.

Overall, the book is divided into selected areas pertinent to the lives of working women. While the areas are conceptually distinct, however, several psychological themes recur throughout. Sex-role stereotyping and the demand of sex-role-congruent behaviors, for example, characterize career selection, organizational recruitment, performance evaluation, and leadership styles. These psychological issues are discussed when necessary in each topic area, but they are discussed most extensively in the area where the most research is available.

In the past several years, our knowledge of, and thinking on, the topic of women and work has increased and matured. This book represents four years of first-hand research, teaching, thinking, discussing, as well as reviewing and synthesizing literature on women and work.

Veronica F. Nieva
Barbara A. Gutek

CONTENTS

1
THE CONTEXT OF WOMEN'S WORK

Women have always worked, of course. Before the Industrial Revolution, women and men were both concerned with family sustenance and maintenance. For most of their work, women, like men, received no wages. Women were considered assistants to their husbands or fathers, or sometimes partners in business. When they were paid for their work, they were paid less than men, about half of male wages in the Middle Ages, for example (Boulding, 1976). As long as all income was considered family income, the system was not necessarily oppressive for women. However, when women chose not to be or were not part of a family with a male head, they suffered.

The division of labor into a male work sphere and a female family sphere described by Parsons (see Parsons and Bales, 1955) is thought to be a product of the Industrial Revolution. When work changed to paid employment, left the home, and moved into factories and offices, men followed. Women were supposed to stay at home not only to care for the home and children but also because meekness, modesty, and submissiveness, valued feminine character- istics, might be threatened in the work world. Giele (1978) pointed out that productive work that women did in the home gradually extended to work outside the home in the form of domestic and other jobs such as textile and clerical work. But it was a slow process and was not readily accepted. Often employers made special provisions to attract female workers. For example, when Francis Cabot Lowell started a textile mill in 1821, he had to organize living conditions that resembled supervised boarding houses for the young, single women he hired (Kessler-Harris, 1976). In the middle of the nineteenth

1

century, women entered the fields of teaching, nursing, and clerical work, all areas that were perceived as having womanly functions. For example, in developing the field of nursing, a spokesperson of the American Women's Education Association proclaimed that the "care of the human body in infancy and sickness was one of the true professions of women" (Baker, 1964). These jobs were viewed as appropriate for single women.

In 1890, only 2.5 percent of married women were working. By 1900, 25 percent of all women were in the labor force (Smith, 1979). Over 5 million women were working, an increase of over 1 million in ten years. By 1910, almost 7.5 million women were working (Flexner, 1974). The percentage of women working remained relatively stable until World War II, which had a tremendous impact on women's employment. Women from a variety of backgrounds were hired for skilled jobs and union jobs from which they were previously excluded. Since then, although there have been fluctuations, primarily the pressure to move out of the labor force (to make room for returning male war veterans) and into the suburbs in the 1950s, women's employment rate has continued to increase at a steady pace. The reasons for the increase are many: improvements in and acceptance of birth control, more favorable attitudes toward women working, increase in life expectancy, patterns of marriage.

> Since 1947, when statistics began to be collected on a regular basis, the participation rate of women has increased in all but four years, but never by more than 1.5 percentage points in one year (Smith, 1979, p. 2).

By 1978, nearly 50 percent of all married women and 40 percent of all women over 16 years of age were working; by 1990, about 55 percent of women 16 and over are expected to be working (Smith, 1979).

The history of women's participation in the labor force shows a great deal of resistance and reservation expressed by segments of society including many women. At various times women who worked were viewed as immoral, unfeminine, negligent mothers, or objects of pity. They were often not taken seriously by their employers, colleagues, significant others, or society in general. Working has been viewed as making women unattractive to men and contributing to missing out on motherhood and/or marriage. No doubt, the increase in paid employment of women has helped to dissipate these attitudes and less negative attitudes in turn encouraged more women to work.

The growth of the female labor force has not been even. At the turn of the century women workers were either young unmarried women or mothers whose husbands had deserted them. In the past 80 years, the growth of female labor force participation has increased more in married women and mothers. In the past the shape of the distribution of working women by age showed the highest rates of participation among young women with a sharp drop when women reached the childbearing and marriageable age. Participation gradually increased as the children grew and left home but never reached the same level as it did for young unmarried women. Today that U-shaped curve is much flatter. In 1978, 60 percent of women 16-54 years of age were working, but so were 55 percent of all married women, 66 percent of married women with no children under 18, and 42 percent of married women with children under six (Smith, 1979).

The prediction of increasing numbers of women working is not just a result of increases of married women or mothers working. Women are also changing their family arrangements in ways that suggest a higher employment rate. More women are heads of households now than in the past. Between 1970 and 1978, the number of women aged 25 to 34 who had never married rose by 111 percent and the number of women who divorced but did not remarry rose 170 percent (U.S. Bureau of the Census, 1978). These women are even more likely to work than married women, and married women are more likely to work in the future than they did in the past.

All of this growth in the role of employment for women is in the face of a general slowing in growth of the U.S. labor force. The growth rate for the whole labor force was an "unprecedented 2.3 percent" in the 1970s (Flaim and Fullerton, 1978). A sharp drop in the birth rate in the 1960s is one reason for the slowing in increase of the labor force in the 1980s. Flaim and Fullerton project three possible paths of labor force rate from 1980 to 1990, but all three of them involve increasing work participation for women.

SEX SEGREGATION OF JOBS

Although women are entering the labor force in increasing numbers, the kinds of jobs they are taking are fairly limited. Women are more likely to be in white collar clerical positions than men (38 percent to 6 percent) and also in service occupations (10 percent to 5 percent). They are less likely to be in blue collar skilled (3 percent to 19 percent), blue collar semi- or unskilled (27 percent to 35 percent), and white collar professional, technical, and managerial occupations (21 percent to 35 percent) (EEOC, 1972). Oppenheimer (1968) specifically examined the occupations that are predominantly female and noted high stability of percentage of women in various fields since 1900. Oppenheimer defined a female occupation as one that has at least 70 percent female workers. Of the 17 female occupations in 1900, 14 were still female occupations in 1960. Over half of all women were in jobs that were at least 70 percent female in 1960. By 1977, two-thirds of women were in stereotypically female jobs (Barrett, 1979).

The identification of specific occupations as female is well documented and well known at a general level. About 35 percent of all women and 42 percent of women aged 20 to 24 were in clerical work in 1977, more than in any other single job classification (Barrett, 1979). Professional women's jobs include teacher, nurse, librarian, social worker, and the like. Some jobs are sex-integrated at a general level but sex-segregated at the work group level. For example, the job classification of waiter/waitress is sex-integrated overall, yet any particular establishment is more likely to hire either waiters or waitresses. Clothing sales represents a slightly different case. Men sell shoes and men's clothing whereas women sell other clothing items. Laws (1979) pointed out that what is considered a female job may even vary between sites of one company. For example, she noted that at the time the Equal Employment Opportunity Commission filed suit against AT&T (Wallace, 1976), a job known as "frameman," a male job paying between $7,500 and $8,500, was called a "switch-room helper" in Detroit, was a female job, and paid a maximum of $7,000.

Why women are in so few occupations is a matter of interest to social scientists. Oppenheimer (1968) postulated and found evidence for several factors associated with female occupations. "Cheapness plus availability" and "cheapness plus skill" are two characteristics of women's jobs. Thus, jobs that pay less and combine low wages with a need for a ready supply of workers or skilled workers are female dominated. To support the argument that women's jobs are those requiring a cheap skilled work force, Oppenheimer compared the average income and median education of women in female occupations to the average income and median education of the average male worker. Women's jobs *all* had female workers who had more education than the average male worker and lower incomes than the average male worker. The average woman in a female occupation made 59 percent of the average male worker's salary in 1960. The general low salaries of women workers relative to men is one of the most outstanding characteristics of women's jobs and is a topic that will be covered in greater detail in Chapter 9.

A third reason for sex-labeling of jobs is that some jobs require traits that are considered attributes of one sex or the other. These traits may be skill-related, such as weaving or typing, or they may be much broader, such as sex appeal. A related factor is tradition: Work that has "always been done by a woman" will be viewed as a female job. Many men are loath to engage in work traditionally done by women. Such work may be viewed as low status or even emasculating. Bem's (1980) gender schema theory of sex-typing suggests that not only men, but also many women, will assume that any job in which women predominate is somehow more appropriate for women than men.

Another factor is prejob training. Men's jobs often require extensive training that may be provided by the employer. Women's jobs are either relatively unskilled or they require skills that the woman acquires on her own time at her own expense, a point emphasized by Lyle and Ross (1973) as well as Oppenheimer (1968). Employers do not train people to be secretaries, receptionists, medical technologists, or dental assistants, but they do often train machinists, mechanics, and repair workers as well as provide additional training to managers and engineers.

Yet another factor differentiating male from female jobs is whether career continuity is important. Women's jobs are often those that permit relatively easy entry and reentry. Teaching, nursing, and clerical work are usually in this category. Barrett (1979) included several other characteristics of female occupations. Women's work involves vicarious rather than direct achievements. The secretary achieves through the manager, the research assistant through the researcher, the nurse and medical technologist through the physician. Women's jobs also have limited upward mobility (Barrett, 1979). At some point the supervisor is male. School principals are male, as are office managers and heads of social service agencies.

All of these characteristics of male and female jobs encourage the development of two labor markets — a male labor market and a female labor market. Economists like Piore (1970) and sociologists such as Schrank and Riley (1976) have discussed the existence of two labor markets. Piore's discussion of primary and secondary labor forces focuses not on women alone, but on all groups who do not have access to the primary labor force. The primary labor force is characterized by stability, high wages, on-the-job training, substantial fringe benefits, and steady promotion, whereas the secondary labor force is characterized by lack of the above (Power, 1975). Women, recent immigrants, young people, old people, and minorities are all clustered in the secondary labor force.

Schrank and Riley (1976) specifically discussed male and female labor markets. The two are characterized by different "shapes." The male labor force covers the whole spectrum of job prestige. Jobs that are very low in prestige such as unskilled laborer are dominated by males, as are the highest prestige jobs. Female jobs, in contrast, occupy a narrower prestige spectrum. Women's jobs are clustered at the low end of a prestige continuum.

Male and female jobs are also differentiated by their range of tasks. Men's jobs include a variety of tasks whereas women's jobs are clustered in a few task areas. Jobs that are at least 70 percent female account for relatively few of the Dictionary of Occupational Titles' categories in contrast to the number of job titles dominated by men.

How separate or distinct the male and female labor markets are is covered in research by Duncan and Duncan (1955) and more recently by Staines et al. (1979) and Laws (1979). Laws pointed out that in 1970 jobs were so sex-segregated that "69 percent of the men would have to change occupational groups in order for the distribution of men and women in each of the major occupational categories to be the same as in the labor force as a whole" (p. 27).

Using national sample data from the 1969 Survey of Working Conditions and the 1972-1973 Quality of Employment Survey, Staines et al. (1979) classified the occupations of the 1,271 respondents according to the percent female in their occupation and then compared the distributions for males and females. What is most apparent and compelling about these results is the strength of three findings. First, the majority of men work in jobs clearly dominated by men and the majority of women work in jobs where the majority of other workers are female. For example, about 60 percent of men work in jobs that are 90 percent or more male. Second, the relationship is stronger for men than for women.

That is, more men are working in male-dominated jobs than women are working in female-dominated jobs. Third, very few men or women work in occupations that are integrated with respect to sex. Jobs that have about half male and half female employees are an infrequent occurrence.

Since there are so few sex-integrated jobs, one might argue that those jobs are inherently unstable and are in the process of becoming male jobs or, more likely, female jobs. The bank teller and secretarial jobs, for example, were male jobs at one time. As more women entered these fields, men left, probably for a variety of reasons, which include decrease in prestige caused by the presence of women (Touhey, 1974), change in the emphases in the job (change from guardian of your money to service giver in the case of bank teller), decrease in promotion probabilities, and erosion of salaries and fringe benefits. Computer programming may follow the bank teller pattern. It was a male-dominated job when it emerged about 20 years ago and today it is an integrated job. In the future it may become a female-dominated job.

IMPLICATIONS

The facts that women are latecomers in the world of paid employment, that they are not automatically assumed to belong to, and be part of, the labor force, that they are likely to be in low-paying jobs with other women all affect how women choose jobs, integrate work with family life, behave on the job, and are evaluated on the job. The fact that jobs are sex-segregated, in particular, is an important contextual factor that must be remembered when looking at all research on women and work. Research comparing men and women on job satisfaction or needs at work are flawed unless they control for occupational type and level. Studies of career choice that ignore the realities of the labor force leave much to be desired. Studies of psychological dynamics — fear of success, attributions about success and failure, commitment to work — all need to acknowledge the fact that men and women are in different jobs with different characteristics.

When job context is ignored, the researcher runs the risk of making attributions to the individual when they should be made to sex-segregation of jobs, a structural factor. One well-known example is the belief that women value hygiene (or extrinsic) aspects of jobs, such as friendly coworkers and comfortable surroundings, over motivating (or intrinsic) aspects of the job, such as challenge or achievement (see Herzberg et al., 1957). One may find such results if one compares female clerical workers with male engineers but not if one compares male and female engineers. The correct inference is that engineers (who are male) like intrinsic rewards more than clerical workers (who are female).

On the other hand, we cannot ignore the fact that there are relatively few female engineers. The fact that women generally occupy second-class status at work as well as in politics, science, and the arts strongly influences their behavior.

Why women occupy a second-class status in the world of work is hotly contested and will be dealt with throughout the book.

Regardless of beliefs about the origins of women's differential status compared to men, it is clear that women have a long tradition of doing different jobs than men. These findings provide an important context in which to study the individual woman, her choice of career, and behavior on the job.

SUMMARY

Women did not join the paid labor force as readily as men after the Industrial Revolution. A few single young women entered paid employment with reluctance or when they were suffering financial hardships. Women have gradually increased in numbers in the labor force. Today about half of all women work — married women with small children as well as single young women. Women workers are channeled into relatively few jobs in which women predominate. These female jobs are characterized by low wages, high skill levels, and "feminine" tasks or skills. The job context in which women work affects their work behavior. If job context is ignored, one runs the risk of interpreting research incorrectly, most likely by making unwarranted internal attributions.

2
WOMEN'S CAREER CHOICES

The process by which women eventually become linked up with a specific occupation can be viewed as containing two components. First, women make some kind of career or life-style choice, usually in their late teens or early twenties. This process involves learning general and/or specific skills that will make them employable in one or more occupations. This process is not just a career choice but it is also a choice about the importance of a career (see Angrist and Almquist, 1975; Osipow, 1975; Zytowski, 1969).

Several researchers have developed typologies of career choices in women. Barnett (1971) identified three approaches women use to choose a career. The first type she labeled internalizers. These young women set their own goals and were able to plan clearly through the years ahead. The second group, the most numerous, were the identifiers. These young women have more confused goals and make immediate career goals as outgrowths of relationships with other people, such as professors with whom they identified. The third group of young women were labeled compliers. They did not have clear plans and tended to choose whatever was available at the last minute. Only the internalizers showed career patterns similar to the idealized version of men's career choice, although Lunneborg (1978) found that the style of choosing a career was similar for the

Earlier versions of this chapter were presented at the American Psychological Association meeting, August 1978, and published as a chapter in B. Gutek, ed., *New Directions for Education, Work and Careers: Enhancing Women's Career Development* (San Francisco: Jossey-Bass, 1979).

two sexes. Women are as likely as men to use planning rather than intuition in choosing a career, but most women are heavily influenced by factors other than their own preferences. They apparently do not have clear preferences in college or feel it is inappropriate or unwise to make a clear choice in college.

Based on their four-wave panel study of 87 college women, Angrist and Almquist (1975) also proposed a typology of career choice. They isolated five types: careerists, who make up 18 percent of their sample; noncareerists, 33 percent of the sample; converts who become career oriented as they progress through college, 22 percent; defectors who lose their career aspirations, 13 percent; and shifters, the 14 percent of the sample whose career aspirations vacillate throughout the college years.

As the typologies of career choice suggest, the choice of a career also involves making decisions about the probability of getting married and of having children. Will she choose a career or a job that will be subordinate to wife and mother roles or not? (Angrist and Almquist, 1975) The areas of work and family life are not independent of each other, particularly for women. The interdependence of work and family roles becomes more apparent in Chapter 4.

After women "choose a career," they decide whether or not to become gainfully employed. There is a second set of determinants, less psychological and more often economic in origin, involved in choosing to take a job. This decision is made in the context of the educational preparation and the family situation in which a woman finds herself.

We can view the process of becoming linked to an occupation as a modified funnel process. Women first pick a general career orientation — clerical work, professional work, part-time unskilled work, housewife — and acquire any necessary skills, usually at an educational institution. Lyle and Ross (1973) pointed out that women are more likely than men to learn skills through schools or training institutions and are less likely than men to receive on-the-job training or be enrolled in apprenticeship or other company-sponsored training programs. Therefore, although they choose a career, they may have little idea of what day-to-day life in that career would be like. Nevertheless, through the career choice process, women narrow the range of potential occupations available to them.

The second stage involves the decision to take a job, a process that is different for women and men because men are expected to take a job whereas women may stay out of the labor force. Because women more often tailor their careers to their husbands' needs, the two steps of choosing a career area and selecting a particular job may not flow as smoothly for women as for men. As more and more women work at paid employment and both spouses have to consider the other's career, decisions about taking a particular job will be more similar for women and men.

Linking up with an occupation is a reciprocal process, although career choice and job selection appear to be a one-way process in the literature with women doing all the deciding. Organizations, however, also select. They hire or do not hire women for specific jobs based on tradition and beliefs about jobs to which women are best suited. These hiring decisions accumulated over time eventually affect the type of career a woman selects and also affect her decision to take or not take a job.

Research on the career choice process comes from several directions. One type of research concerns general attitudes about the appropriateness of various careers or activities for males and females. As long as prevailing attitudes prescribe certain jobs for each sex, both sexes will experience limited career options. In fact, however, the scope of female career options has been more severely limited than for males because fewer occupations have been labeled by both sexes as appropriate for women as for men (Clark, 1967; Siegel, 1973; Nelson, 1963).

The majority of women are clustered into relatively few occupations (compare Slocum, 1966; Oppenheimer, 1968). Changes in general attitudes about the appropriateness of various occupations for women will be an indicator both that women are exercising wider options in their career choices and that there will be a change in norms that will legitimize those career choices.

A second approach taken by researchers in the study of women's career choices is in looking at career preferences, primarily of college women. In particular, there has been a lot of interest in women who are pioneers (Rossi, 1965a) or role innovators (Tangri, 1972), that is, women who choose nontraditional careers, and how they differ from women who choose traditional occupations or who are interested in full-time homemaking.

A third direction of research on career choice among women uses a retrospective approach, analyzing the factors affecting the career choice of women who are already in a given occupation. Most women still plan to marry (deBoer, 1977) and may remain somewhat flexible in their career choice until/if they marry on the assumption that they will have to subordinate their work interests to their family responsibilities. Bardwick and Douvan (1972) argued that it is adaptive for women to remain flexible in their career plans if they wish to marry. This flexibility implies a late commitment to a career. It also suggests that another approach to studying career choice than asking preferences of college women is desirable. Retrospective studies asking female subjects already in a career what influenced their career decisions is one alternate approach. Retrospective research is subject to criticism but does provide additional information. Retrospective studies on this topic are mainly concerned with the differences between the pioneers and more traditional women and with the factors that influenced pioneers to enter a nontraditional occupation.

ATTITUDES ABOUT SEX-ROLE APPROPRIATENESS
OF OCCUPATIONS

The view that particular jobs are appropriate only for males or females begins early in life. In fact, children appear to be more stereotyped in their beliefs than older persons. For example, Shepard and Hess (1975) looked at attitudes toward sex-role appropriateness of various occupational activities among four age groups — kindergarten children, eighth graders, college students, and adults — and found that kindergarteners were the most stereotyped. Subjects increased in liberality, defined as the lack of sex-role stereotyping of occupations, through college but became more stereotyped again in adulthood. Other studies (Looft, 1971a; 1971b; Kirchner and Vondracek, 1973; Siegel, 1973; Iglitzen, 1972; Schlossberg and Goodman, 1972) also show strong stereotyping of occupations among preschool and elementary school children. Similar results were found among ninth graders with boys significantly more conservative than girls (Entwhistle and Greenberger, 1972). Shepard and Hess (1975) pointed out that children must learn these views at home since they occur before children are exposed to the school environment.

While the stereotyped attitudes may be introduced in the home, other factors also affect views of occupations. Weitzman et al. (1972) noted the role of stereotyping of tasks and occupations in children's stories. Many researchers noted the role of school textbooks (Wirtenberg and Nakamura, 1976; Ahlum, 1974; Bernstein, 1972; Saario, Jacklin, and Tittle, 1973), and schools in general (Ahlum, 1974; Feshbach, 1975; Saario et al., 1973) in perpetuating stereotypes of appropriate occupations for women and men.

Vocational counselors have also been criticized for contributing to occupational stereotyping. Thomas and Stewart (1971) found that high school counselors think students who select sex-atypical careers are more in need of counseling than students who select sex-typical careers. Medvene and Collins (1974) report that vocational counselors are relatively conservative in the types of careers they see as appropriate for women (Abramowitz et al., 1975). Further, male counselors, who are more numerous than female counselors in high school, are generally more conservative than female counselors (Pressley, 1974; Bingham and House, 1973; Thomas and Stewart, 1971). In addition, Vetter (1973) and Vetter, Stockburger, and Brose (1974) are critical of the materials used by guidance counselors. Like textbooks, these materials reinforce sex-role stereotypical behavior and underrepresent females in examples and illustrations.

Although numerous studies show a consistency in the appropriateness of various jobs for each sex, the results vary with the design of the study. For example, question wording and format affect results of studies on attitudes. When subjects are asked to indicate *whether* a job is appropriate for women rather than to specify *which* sex is more appropriate for a given job, there is less stereotyping. Medvene and Collins (1974) asked students, nonworking women, members of a woman's caucus, and classified employees if various occupations were appropriate for women. All the high prestige male jobs (for example, banker, lawyer) and some of the less prestigious jobs (for example, truck driver, soldier, mail carrier) were judged appropriate for women by a majority of subjects.

An interesting and subtle approach to the problem was taken by Nilson (1976). She found that occupational incumbents who violated sex-role expectations were awarded lower social standing than persons who followed sex-role expectations with respect to selecting a job. Nilson found that men who were in feminine occupations were penalized more than women who were in male occupations in her random sample of 479 Milwaukee adults. Although it might be appropriate for a woman to be a banker or a man to be a nurse, adults in general will accord lower social standing to the female than the male banker and to the male than the female nurse. There is also evidence that women who choose sex-atypical careers are viewed as less likable than their male counterparts (Suchner and More, 1975).

Since there are fewer sex-typical occupations available to women than to men (Siegel, 1973) and because "women's jobs" in general have lower prestige and monetary rewards than male-dominated jobs (see Corcoran and Duncan, 1979), women would give themselves more and better options if they felt free to select male-dominated occupations. Men have less to gain in terms of money, prestige, security, or challenge by selecting feminine jobs. However, some studies find that men and women are in fairly close agreement about the appropriateness of various jobs for each sex. For example, Shepard and Hess (1975) found that over four age groups, there was at least 90 percent agreement between the sexes on the sex-role appropriateness of 28 of the 43 occupations they studied. Only three tasks — painting a picture, being a teacher, and writing a book — were viewed as appropriate for both sexes. Shinar (1975) also demonstrated that sex-role stereotyping of 129 occupations was consistent for college students of both sexes. A study of adults in Utah showed similar results (Albrecht, 1976).

Other studies showed that women have weaker stereotypes about occupations than men. They are more likely than men to say an occupation is appropriate to either sex. Shepard and Hess (1975) found a significant sex difference between eighth grade, college, and adult respondents. Likewise, fifth-grade girls in Iglitzen's (1972) study were less stereotyped than fifth-grade boys in their assessment of the appropriateness of various occupations for the two sexes. Women also penalize those who are in sex-atypical occupations less than men (Nilson, 1976).

These studies vary in the rigor with which they are conducted, the size of the sample, and subjects in the sample. There is no clear, compelling evidence that women are substantially less stereotyped than men at this time, but that result may change with more women interested in atypical careers.

Although these beliefs about the appropriateness of various jobs for men and women show up across ages and sexes, it is not clear how much these attitudes actually affect one's career choice. The stereotypes are very strong among children. Presumably these strong early stereotypes of children have some impact on later career choice, although early career preferences tend toward dramatic, adventurous, and exciting jobs (for example, policeman, fireman, ballet dancer), and few people follow through on their initial career inclinations. It is also conceivable that a woman might view medicine as a career for men but still want to become a physician. Nevertheless, stereotypes that persist across age, sex, and social class might be expected to affect career choice. It is important to remember the context of this high consensus about which jobs are appropriate for males and which are appropriate for females when examining the career choices people make. A choice is not really a choice in the presence of strong norms that limit the types of behavior considered appropriate.

WOMEN'S CAREER CHOICES: PREFERENCES

Most of the literature on career choice use college students and really assess their preference for one occupation, usually including homemaking, over another. The "career choice" literature does not deal with *selecting* a career or a job. The actual selection of a job or occupation depends on many factors besides one's stated preferences in high school or college and this is even more true for women than men. One's initial preferences can be altered by many things, for example, ability or opportunity to acquire requisite skills, the labor market, one's other life circumstances, attitudes of significant others. The research on career choice then should be interpreted as reported preferences and should be recognized as only one factor that eventually determines the selection of a job or career.

Many of the research studies of career choice are grounded in theories that view career choice as a matching process, although they vary somewhat in their emphases. As Hall (1976) noted, there are a number of factors that can be considered in relation to job compatibility: interests, self-identity, personality, and family and social background. Super's (1957) theory relies on the importance of self-identity. For him, choosing a career is finding an occupation compatible with one's identity. Holland (1973) matches personality to occupation. He proposes six types of occupational environments and six types of personalities: realistic, investigative, social, conventional, enterprising, artistic. As an example, an artistic person is best suited to an artistic occupation. Roe's (1957) theory rests more on early background factors as determinants of career choices. Childhood experiences and childrearing patterns influence a young woman to choose a career compatible with needs established during her youth.

In reviewing the literature on career choice, one result stands out. Most women choose traditional, female-dominated occupations and they do so at all ages. Siegel (1973) found that 20 of 29 second-grade girls wanted to be either a teacher or a nurse. Similarly, Looft (1971b) found that 25 of 33 first- and second-grade girls wanted to be either a teacher or a nurse. O'Hara (1962) found that two-thirds of the choices of fourth-, fifth-, and sixth-grade girls were teacher, nurse, secretary, or mother. Other researchers using subjects who varied in age through college also found that female students choose occupations that conform to sex-role expectations (Nelson, 1963; Bailyn, 1959; Clark, 1967; Shuval, 1963; Slocum and Bowles, 1968).

Stereotypically male and female jobs vary on a number of dimensions (for example, prestige, person-centeredness, amount of physical strength needed) but there has been little research that attempts to isolate those factors that make traditionally feminine careers attractive to women or traditionally masculine careers attractive to men. The usual explanation is sex-role congruence (Shuval, 1963; Siegel, 1973), a plausible though superficial explanation. Other factors have been explained, although not in sufficient detail to permit definitive causal statements.

For example, Barnett (1975), who was interested in the relationship between prestige of occupation and career choice among males and females from ages 9 through 17, found that both sexes avoided occupations of high prestige at nine years of age but older boys preferred high prestige jobs. Unfortunately, sex-role stereotype of occupation was not controlled in this study; undoubtedly, there is a positive relationship between male sex-role stereotype and prestige of the 15 occupations Barnett studied. It is unclear from these results whether girls learn to avoid prestigious occupations simply because they are prestigious or because they are viewed as masculine. Feldman's (1974) study of female graduate students also shows that females avoid high prestige positions. Feldman concluded that female graduate students are more likely to be enrolled in fields that are lower in power, privilege, and prestige and that women faculty are less likely to aspire to prestigious academic positions regardless of their abilities. Since women are less likely than men to attain positions of power and prestige, their expectations reflect reality. Whether or not women would adhere to these positions if the probability of obtaining prestigious positions were greater is unclear.

Another factor that has been shown to differentiate males and females is interest in working with people. Using a sample of 146 adults who visited a vocational guidance clinic in Tel-Aviv, Weller, Shlomi, and Zimont (1976) found that women expressed a greater preference than men for person-centered occupations. Again, such studies should look at person-orientation controlling sex typicality of job choice to find out if women are actually more concerned with person-centered jobs, per se, or with choosing a sex-typical job that happens to be person-centered.

CAREER PIONEERS

Women who select sex-atypical occupations have been called pioneers (Rossi, 1965a) or innovators (Tangri, 1972) and have been the subject of numerous studies on women's career choices. Many of these studies follow from theories of career choice and assume that choosing a career involves finding a match between one's personality of self-concept and one's job. Since most girls have "feminine" personalities, they are best suited to "feminine" jobs.

Women who expressed interest in masculine occupations were then viewed as frustrated and dissatisfied (Lewis, 1968), were not supported in their career choices, and often were counseled out of these occupations and into traditional female occupations. The assumption of maladjustment on the part of women who select nontraditional careers is not supported by research. Angrist and Almquist (1975) looked at two hypotheses about why young women select sex-atypical occupations. The first, a deviance hypothesis suggesting that these women are very different from traditional women in terms of dating, extra-curricular activities, and the like, received little support from their data. An alternative hypothesis stressing the effects of enriching experiences on career choice received more support from the data. These women were interested in a social life leading to friendships and marriage as well as an academic life leading to a career. A similar causal model study by Sedney and Turner (1975) also showed that young women who choose atypical careers need not be regarded as deviants needing counseling.

Numerous studies have examined the determinants of nontraditional career choice in women. The studies vary on which group is compared to career pioneers. Some studies compare traditional with nontraditional career choice; other studies compare a choice of homemaking with choice of non-traditional careers.

Researchers in this area of career choice are imprecise in their use of traditional or homemaking orientation (Levitt, 1972; Surette, 1967). The characteristics and goals of the innovators are relatively clear and concise in the literature. They are women who have selected high prestige, high commitment, sex-atypical professional and managerial careers — but should women who want to be homemakers be categorized the same as women who select a traditional female career, for example, in nursing or social work? A future social worker may be just as committed to her career as a future lawyer, although many people incorrectly assume women select careers such as social work just because they have low career commitment. Although most researchers compare two groups of women, the literature suggests there are at least three groups: those committed to nontraditional careers, those committed to traditional careers, and those committed primarily to the homemaker role.

In order to organize the research, we have divided determinants of career choice into proximal and distal factors. Proximal factors are those with a rather immediate influence on the career preferences of high school or college women. Examples of proximal factors are college or high school grades, inter-ests measured during school years, support from faculty, or test scores. Distal factors are more remote in time and place. Examples are early childhood experiences or childbearing patterns in the home. Stable personality factors such as self-concept are included with distal factors since they are acquired early in life.

Proximal Factors

In an early study, Rezler (1967) was interested in describing the character-istics of the "atypical pioneer girl," thereby enabling counselors to recognize her early in high school and to support her in her chosen career. She studied proximal antecedents of career choice (for example, test scores, grade point average, preferred subjects in high school). She found that pioneers could be distinguished from women with more traditional interests in several ways although it was not possible to distinguish among different kinds of pioneers (for example, physicians from physicists or mathematicians). Pioneers, compared to traditionals, had higher computational and scientific interests but were not more intelligent. They were, however, more intellectual, got better grades, and scored higher on both parts of the Preliminary Scholastic Aptitude Test and the California Test of Mental Maturity. The pioneers could not be differentiated from the traditionals on the basis of hobbies, stability of vocational goals, or best- or least-liked subject in school.

Distinguishing between career-oriented college women and "work-oriented" women who selected traditional occupations, Richardson (1974) focused on the importance and value of a career. Career-oriented women were highly career motivated and perceived the career role as an important part of their adult lives. Munley (1974) found that pioneers had higher academic achievement. Richardson (1974) found that work-oriented women tended to choose tradition-ally feminine occupations, were more certain of their career choices than career-oriented women, and were lower in career orientation. Furthermore, the author suggested that career-oriented women were more concerned with intrinsic rewards from a job whereas the work-oriented women were interested in both intrinsic and extrinsic rewards.

It is somewhat incongruous to find that women go into medicine and law for intrinsic satisfactions but become secretaries or health technicians for money or other extrinsic rewards. Lipman-Blumen's (1972) discussion of vicarious achievement through husbands resolves the conflict. Several researchers (Turner, 1964; Astin, 1979) noted that women who seek material ambitions do so through their husbands. Women do not choose clerical work or low-level tech-nical occupations for the material rewards. They choose those occupations that they feel are compatible with marriage and, when considered as a supplement to a husband's income, will result in a high level of material comfort. Here is more evidence that women select a life style when they state a career preference. While men elect business or professional careers at least partly for the resulting extrinsic rewards, women still view the road to material well-being through a husband.

Women who choose professional occupations do so primarily for intrinsic satisfactions associated with those jobs. They apparently believe they will not receive extrinsic rewards or if they do, it will be through their husbands. Lack of interest in extrinsic rewards, however, may deter women from following through on career preferences. Astin (1978) found that women who worked continuously for eight years after college tended to endorse extrinsic values while those who never worked within eight years of college graduation preferred intrinsic to extrinsic rewards.

One of the dimensions underlying much of the literature on traditional versus nontraditional career choice is masculinity-femininity. The early assumption was that innovators were more masculine than traditionals. Munley (1974) found that career orientation was significantly negatively correlated with basic homemaking interest, but he found no relationship between career orientation and a masculinity-femininity dimension. This finding, though somewhat puzzling, is consistent with other research (for example, Hoyt and Kennedy, 1958; Rand, 1968). Rand (1968) found that homemaking-oriented women were not more feminine than career-oriented women but that career-oriented women were more masculine than homemaking-oriented women. Rand concluded that career-oriented women expand their definition of femininity to include components usually labeled masculine. In this way, career-oriented women can retain a feminine self-image and pursue a nontraditional career at the same time. Tipton (1976) came to a similar conclusion. He suggested that any relationship between masculinity-femininity and homemaking-career orientation was due to a rejection of masculine characteristics by the homemaking-oriented women; career-oriented women do not reject femininity as measured by the California Personality Inventory.

These findings are consistent with Bem's (1974) notion of androgyny. The career-oriented women have both feminine and masculine characteristics in their personalities. They are androgynous. In fact, in a study explicitly comparing androgynous and sex-typed individuals, Allgeier (1975) found that androgynous college women placed more importance on being competent at work and had higher educational aspirations than sex-typed women.

Liberal attitude is related to preference for nontraditional jobs. Tipton (1976) used Spence and Helmreich's (1972a) Attitudes Toward Women Scale to differentiate students with conventional attitudes from students with liberal attitudes toward women. He then compared the two groups on their vocational interests and found that male and female college students with traditional attitudes toward the roles of women scored higher on the Conventional Occupational Theme scale of the Strong-Campbell Interest Inventory than students with less traditional attitudes. Women with traditional attitudes scored higher on stereotypically female occupational scales and males with traditional attitudes scored higher on stereotypically male occupational scales. Tipton found that there is considerable diversity among women with contemporary attitudes toward women but that one commonality is their high scores in verbal orientation, a factor they shared with men having contemporary attitudes.

Another proximal factor that influences career choice is expectations of and support from people in the high school or college environment: faculty, teachers, and significant others. Both Tangri (1972) and Dickerson (1974) found faculty support to be related to career orientation. Angrist and Almquist (1975) noted that some female students are more susceptible to faculty influence than other students. Significant others are also important. Nontraditional women receive more career support from boyfriends than traditional women (Trigg and Perlman, 1976). There is also evidence that women do not get a great deal of support. For example, Dickerson (1974) found that in general female students' levels of expectations for their own careers were higher than faculty expectations for them. This finding is especially significant in view of the consistent findings that women do not evaluate their achievements as highly as men (Deaux, 1976a). Women's expectations for themselves tend to be low, but faculty expectations are even lower.

Distal Factors

Besides differentiating career-oriented or pioneer women from traditionals on proximal criteria, other researchers have looked at distal characteristics that might influence career orientation. The possibility that mothers might serve as either positive or negative role models was studied by several researchers. Mothers' behavior and attitudes are important. Tangri (1972) found a positive relationship between both mother's education and employment and her daughter's choice of an atypical career. Likewise, other researchers found that daughters of working mothers were more career oriented than daughters of nonworking mothers (Altman and Grossman, 1977; Siegel and Curtis, 1963; Astin, 1967; Vogel et al., 1970; Almquist and Angrist, 1971; Baruch, 1972) although Lipman-Blumen (1972) did not find this relationship.

Other aspects of maternal attitudes are also related to daughter's career orientation. Altman and Grossman (1977) found that career orientation in daughters is related to perceived maternal dissatisfaction with the feminine role among their sample of college seniors. Lipman-Blumen (1972) also found more contemporary attitudes among college-age daughters whose mothers were dissatisfied with their homemaker role. Using a sample of British women, Fogarty, Rapoport, and Rapoport (1971) found that daughters of happy housewives and unhappy working women were less likely to have careers than daughters of unhappy housewives or satisfied career women. These similarities in attitudes of mothers and daughters would suggest that mothers serve as role models for their role-innovating daughters. However, Tangri (1972) and Lipman-Blumen (1972) found that role innovators did not identify particularly strongly with their mothers, or their fathers, for that matter.

Other researchers were influenced by Roe's (1957; Roe and Siegelman, 1964) theory that early life experiences determine career choice. They focused on both parents as influencing agents. For example, Kriger (1972) concluded that more protective or restrictive parental attitudes result in greater homemaking orientation in young women. Oliver (1975), relying directly on Roe's theory, suggested that career-oriented women would perceive their parents as less accepting, less concentrating, and more avoiding. Oliver further hypothesized that career-oriented women would be more identified with their fathers than homemaking-oriented women. Oliver found that career-oriented subjects perceived significantly less father acceptance, but not less mother acceptance, than homemaking-oriented women and identified with their fathers more than homemaking-oriented women, contrary to Tangri's (1972) and Lipman-Blumen's (1972) findings. The other hypotheses were not supported. This study found only limited support for Roe's theory among female subjects as had earlier studies (for example, Grigg, 1959; Utton, 1962; Roe and Siegelman, 1964; Green and Parker, 1965).

Another theory of careers that has been examined as it applies to women is Super's theory that postulates that occupational choice is congruent with self-concept. Self-concept is relatively stable from early childhood and can be viewed as a distal characteristic. Richardson (1975) examined the self-concept as either consistent with homemaking orientation or career orientation to see whether a congruent self-concept predicts career orientation. She found that college women who perceive themselves as similar to their image of a home-maker were not career oriented. However, women who perceived themselves as similar to their image of a career woman were not necessarily career oriented except if they had a clear role differentiation between career role and home-making role or had high self-esteem.

Astin (1979) noted that self-concept plays an important role in career choice and suggested that high self-concept facilitates high career aspirations. Brief, VanSell, and Aldag (1979) likewise concluded that differences between the sexes in self-concept mean that women will be less likely to select male-dominated occupations.

A number of researchers have focused on need for achievement and need for affiliation as predictors of career choice. Early research on social needs suggested that women do not have needs for achievement the way men do but that their affiliative needs predominate (compare Hoffman and Maier, 1966; Stein and Bailey, 1973). This early position has been modified and research in the area of women's achievement needs has continued. For example, using nursing and medical rehabilitation students (traditionals), and medical and dental students (nontraditionals), Trigg and Perlman (1976) found that women choosing nontraditional careers scored higher than women choosing traditional careers on need for achievement and lower on affiliative needs, findings that are generally consistent with other studies (Tangri, 1972; Kriger, 1972; Hoyt and Kennedy, 1958). The importance of achievement motivation for women's work behavior is covered in more detail in Chapter 8.

A host of other psychological characteristics have been found to be related to high career aspirations in women. They include a sense of internal control (Turner and McCaffrey, 1974), involvement with masculine reference groups (Almquist and Angrist, 1971), presence of female role models (Almquist and

Angrist, 1971; Tangri, 1972), intraception and endurance (Hoyt and Kennedy, 1958), positive evaluation of female competence (Baruch, 1972), belief that men will not reject competent women (Farmer and Bohn, 1970; Hawley, 1971; Tangri, 1972), and fear of success (Horner, 1968). In addition, Wagman (1966) found that career-oriented women were more theoretical and less religious than homemaking-oriented women on the Allport-Vernon-Lindzey Study of Values.

CAREER CHOICES: RETROSPECTIVE STUDIES

A general issue concerns the time *when* women make career choices. Although Astin (1968) found that interests of ninth-grade girls predicted their twelfth-grade interests, Angrist and Almquist (1975) found that only 15 percent of women felt decided about their future occupations through all four years of college. These authors report a stability coefficient of only .37 for their measure of career orientation over the four years of college. Harmon (1970) concluded that women's careers cannot be predicted from career choice expressed at age 18 and that expressed career choice of college women has already undergone substantial change, especially if they have considered a non-traditional occupation (Harmon, 1971). Furthermore, only a small proportion of women work uninterruptedly after college. Astin (1978) found that only 24 percent of a national sample of women who entered college in 1961 had worked at least eight years in 1974.

Hennig and Jardim (1977) studied the careers of 25 successful female managers. All 25 held line positions as presidents or divisional vice-presidents of nationally recognized firms. The authors cited a number of family background factors common to the 25. All came from upper middle class business families and were only or oldest children. All had fathers who encouraged them to achieve. Mothers also encouraged them until adolescence, when they put greater emphasis on social interaction and less emphasis on competition and achievement. These women tended to identify with their fathers and since they were graduating from college during the depression, their fathers got them their first jobs. These findings are inconsistent with statements of career preferences of college women that show minimal influence of father's role. None of these women married young; the half who eventually did marry did so only after their mid-thirties when their careers were well established. Hennig and Jardim did not think that marriage hindered these women; in fact, they concluded that marriage and increased emphasis on fun and personal appearance allowed some women to increase their self-esteem and become more innovative and imaginative on the job.

Standley and Soule (1974) studied women in architecture, law, medicine, and psychology and found that most of them came "from prototypic upper-middle class American homes" (p. 247). Their finding that 57 percent were the oldest girls in the family is consistent with Hennig and Jardim's findings. Over half of these women expressed great interest in "boyish" activities as children, as had Hennig and Jardim's sample. And these women remembered their parents as having valued and emphasized achievement and competence. These authors also found a strong affinity between fathers and daughters. Sixty percent of subjects thought they were their father's favorite child. Over half respected their fathers more than their mothers. Although both parents were committed to academic excellence on their daughter's part, they were less interested in seeing their daughters pursue a career. The authors noted that few parents gave career advice and concluded that parental priorities turned to more traditional values once their daughters received their academic credentials. Vetter and Lewis (1964) also found evidence that parents wished for academic excellence in daughters but were less interested in having them work toward a career.

Several researchers studying career choice among high school and college women have suggested that fathers play a crucial role (Heilbrun, 1969; Oliver, 1975), whereas other data from college students are not in agreement (Tangri, 1972; Lipman-Blumen, 1972). Data on women who have achieved high status occupations suggest that fathers are important as role models and sources of support and encouragement for achieving daughters (Hennig and Jardim, 1977; Standley and Soule, 1974). The weaker evidence for the role of the father in career choice studies of college women may be due to the instability of career choice decisions in that population. It is also possible that among women choosing careers 15 to 35 years ago, fathers' support was important because there were so few mothers in high status occupations to serve as role models. For young women choosing a career within the last ten years, mothers' support, and their attitudes and behavior may be more important. Another possibility is that fathers' support is more important in "making it" in a nontraditional career than it is in choosing a career. A father's influence may be greatest after the daughter has selected a nontraditional career. Then she may use the father as a role model and rely on his expertise and advice. He may also help her find a job as Hennig and Jardim's (1977) subjects reported.

Morrison and Sebald (1974) also did a retrospective study of career choice, using a sample of 39 pairs of subjects who were either executives or "nonexecutives," matched on age, education, years of employment, and type of organization. What differentiated their groups were aspects of need for achievement, need for power, need for affiliation, and mental ability. The executives had higher needs for achievement and power, greater mental ability, and lower need for affiliation. Parental attitudes and behavior did not differentiate these two groups of women. A problem with Morrison and Sebald's study is that one can just as easily attribute differences found in the subjects to job differences as well as to personality differences. In other words, having an executive job may bring out achievement motivation, whereas a nonexecutive job may suppress such motivation so that two people with initial equivalent levels of achievement motivation may differ as a function of their jobs.

A study by Baruch (1967) got around this problem. She looked at the effect of achievement motivation on subsequent employment. Using a sample of 137 Radcliffe alumnae, she found that achievement motivation as measured by the Thematic Apperception Test (TAT) was related to number of years out of college. There was a dramatic drop in achievement motivation for those women out of college ten years with a resurgence in achievement motivation 15, 20, and 25 years out of college. She found a significant relationship between achievement and career patterns for married women 20 or 25 years out of college and a nonsignificant trend for women 15 years out of college. Her explanation is that once women establish their families, they are free to follow their own motives. Baruch failed to replicate her findings using national sample survey data collected at the Survey Research Center, University of Michigan (Gurin, Veroff, and Feld, 1960). She did find some supportive evidence among the most educated group of women, who had attended at least one year of college, though they were hardly as select a group as the Radcliffe alumnae. She concluded that lower class women are constrained by economic conditions at home and in the labor market and that these forces overwhelm their own motives. Need for achievement emerges only as a predictor of career involvement among women free to choose if and when they want a career. These findings are not inconsistent with Morrison and Sebald (1974), who did not have lower socioeconomic class women in their sample.

Although there are few retrospective studies of factors that affect career choice, there is some consistency among conclusions. Whether the same patterns of childrearing and family background are necessary or even desirable today in light of the women's movement and widespread social and economic change is not clear. There is also another problem of all retrospective studies — reliance on memory. Women who achieve in careers may remember achievement emphasis in childhood more than women who do not have a subsequent career.

SOME ISSUES AND PROBLEMS

A number of issues and problems emerge from a review of the litearture on women's career choice. Here we review the way in which career choice is measured and what career choice means, shortcomings of theories of career choice emphasizing "matching" personalities to jobs, and problems of emphasizing career choices of women in college.

One issue has to do with the way in which career choice is measured. Turner and McCaffrey (1974) noted a big difference in subject responses depending on whether they asked about career preferences or career expectations. They found that many white women who prefer to have a career in fact expect to be a homemaker. These researchers found the opposite pattern for black women. They also found less congruence between preferences and expectations for black than white women. The same pattern may hold true for working class women. By their own admission, college women are not necessarily going into the careers they choose or prefer. Only 16 percent of Turner and McCaffrey's white sample expected to engage in full-time paid employment. Career expectation may be a better predictor of occupation than career preferences or career choice.

This brings up the general point mentioned at the beginning of the chapter about the meaning of career choice. Angrist and Almquist (1975) noted that when college women choose a career, they are more realistically selecting a life style. A college woman who says she prefers a teaching career may be expressing strong commitment to and interest in teaching or she may be reflecting sex-role expectations, viewing teaching as an ideal job to fall back on in the event that support from her prospective husband vanishes. Much of career choice literature should be interpreted as preferences expressed in the context of feeling obligated to express an opinion. Some of the expressed preferences can be dismissed much as the career aspirations expressed by the women in the *Playboy* centerfold or Miss America contest are usually dismissed. The longitudinal research of Angrist and Almquist (1975) confirms this. More importantly, the external constraints faced by a woman in implementing a career "choice" often mean she will never have a chance to pursue a career of interest. The career choice literature needs to be considered in a broader social psychological context. Career counseling of women also needs this broad perspective (see Newman, 1979).

Much of the women's career choice literature relies heavily on career choice theories, which are predominantly concerned with matching some aspect of the person to some aspect of the job (Hall, 1976). The theories tend to stress the personality, self-identity, or family background of the person choosing a career. The view that certain personalities are suited only to certain jobs tends toward conservative decisions, toward counseling boys and girls into traditional jobs. If one takes the position that personality is flexible and that different personality styles could function adequately and happily in the same occupation, then there would be little reason to avoid letting people follow their inclinations as long as they have the ability to succeed in their chosen field. Matching people's abilities to job requirements is a less conservative approach than matching their personality to job requirements and results in a wider choice of occupations for both sexes. Yet theories of career choice have been less interested in abilities or aptitudes than other socially conditioned factors such as self-identity or personality, or even childhood experiences.

Several of the problems and issues discussed above result from using college students almost exclusively as subjects in career choice research. A final problem of using students is that the research leaves out all nonprofessional career choices. While there has been a lot of research on the minority of women who select sex-atypical professional occupations, research is only beginning to accumulate on the minority of women who are choosing atypical blue collar jobs. How does a woman decide to become a carpenter or a plumber? Schreiber's (1979) research suggests that many women do not think of such jobs until someone mentions them. The majority of women are in nonprofessional white collar, clerical, and sales jobs. Research on how they choose these jobs is scarce.

Do these women even make a conscious decision or do they just fall into a job? How many people, professional or nonprofessional, just fall into a job? Finally, what about talented women of lower socioeconomic status who do not attend college? Folger, Astin, and Bayer (1970) found that while over 90 percent of high socioeconomic, high ability students enroll in college, only 66 percent of men and 50 percent of women with high ability from low socioeconomic backgrounds enroll in college.

The literature on the decision to work, to which we now turn, includes women from all socioeconomic groups and presents a quite different view of the larger picture of linking women to occupations.

3
FACTORS AFFECTING
WOMEN'S DECISION TO WORK

The way in which studies of career choice are presented often implies that women follow through on their career choices made in high school and college. Yet that seems to be a shaky assumption. There are a number of reasons why people may not engage in the careers they "chose." Perhaps there are no jobs available in that area. The job may not pay well enough. A person's interests may shift. A "golden opportunity" may arise in another area. The employer may be unwilling to hire an applicant, for example, a young mother with several small children, whereas an employer in another field may be more willing to do so. In addition, many women experience problems in trying to combine a job and a family. These problems and issues involved in combining work and family life are covered in greater detail in Chapter 4.

While the process of career choice may involve an attempt to match one's interests to a job (Holland, 1973), the actual determinants of work are quite different. In particular, while career choice may be primarily a psychological process, deciding to work may be more of an economic decision. In the case of married women, the decision to work may also be determined by the dynamics of the relationship of husband and wife. Research studies that have looked at husband's attitudes and behaviors or women's perceptions of what their husbands or future husbands want all suggest that the husband's attitudes toward his wife's working is very important (Winter, Stewart, and McClelland, 1977; Farmer and Bohn, 1970). Yet there are few studies that directly address this issue, perhaps because researchers have looked at women's career choices and decisions to work much in the same way in which they have examined men's career choices, that is, as a rational, logical outgrowth of personal desires and needs, ignoring the needs and desires of significant others or labor market considerations. This model may or may not be inadequate for men; it is surely inadequate for women.

Looking at research on women's decisions to work reveals that most of the literature focuses on married women's decisions to work or mothers' decisions to work. The decision to work by single women is viewed the same as it is for men: They need to work to support themselves unless they are independently wealthy, although they and their employers may view working as a temporary state that will end when they marry. For the married woman, the other option, being a full-time housewife, makes her decision to work clearly different from a man's. Economists have pointed out that the full-time housewife is a product of the Industrial Revolution. Prior to that period, women worked out of economic necessity. It is interesting, however, that the majority of women today still say that they work out of economic necessity. That is, if asked why they are working most women will respond, "for the money" (deBoer, 1977).* In a national sample of working people, Crowley, Levitin, and Quinn (1973) found that two-fifths of U.S. working women are economically independent of men, that is, they are single, divorced, widowed, and so on. The women who are only or even predominantly working to satisfy their own needs for self-expression or self-actualization are, like men, quite rare. Most people work as a means of livelihood and hope that in the process they will satisfy their own needs, work with pleasant coworkers, achieve some level of prestige and status, and so on. Nevertheless, women respond to questions about working for noneconomic reasons much the same as men. Among all workers, Crowley et al. (1973) found that 74 percent of working men and 57 percent of working women say they would continue working if they did not need to. In comparing men and women on this question, it is necessary to take into account factors like the types of jobs that men and women have, amount of self-identity tied to one's work role, and the like.

Two other factors are important in deciding to work: the availability of jobs and the willingness of an employer to hire a particular applicant. During conditions of high unemployment, everyone has difficulty finding a job and some job categories, for example, heavy manufacturing, may be harder hit than others, for example, professional or service workers. Sometimes the career one prepares for suffers from an overabundance of applicants when one is ready to take a job. Engineering, for example, tends to go through cycles of shortage and overabundance of applicants. Women who obtained elementary or secondary teaching degrees in the 1950s and 1960s and looked for jobs in the 1970s found themselves in a tight labor market.

---

*Hoffman (1974c) suggested that working for money may be viewed as a more acceptable, that is, more selfless, reason than working for self-fulfillment. Therefore, women are more likely to respond when asked that they work out of economic necessity than some other reason.

In addition, employers have traditionally hired men and women for different kinds of jobs. The extent of sex segregation and limited number of jobs in which women predominate were covered in the introductory chapter. Although a woman may decide she wants a job in construction, she may have difficulty getting such a job even under conditions of low unemployment and legislation that encourages the hiring of women in building trades. The dynamics of the career choice process discussed in Chapter 2 suggest that not many women will choose a career in the building trades. Nevertheless, the fact that most women are working first and foremost for the money yet end up in low paying jobs strongly suggests that employer willingness to hire women is an important factor in the jobs they get.

In sum, in women the decision to work differs from the career choice process in several important ways. First, the career choice process is largely a ' psychological phenomenon, whereas the decision to work is largely economic. Second, the career choice process involves all women, although most research focuses on college students, whereas the decision to work is primarily addressed and considered to be an issue for married women. Third, career choice is viewed as involving only the person, and her wishes, needs, and future life style, whereas the decision to work involves the actual needs and wishes of a husband and/or children. Fourth, women choose a career assuming that their choice will be available, whereas the decision to work takes place in the context of some level of job availability and employer willingness to hire female applicants.

UNEMPLOYMENT AND UNDEREMPLOYMENT

The decision to work may not always be realized. Women have higher unemployment rates in general than men (Niemi, 1974, 1975; Barrett and Morgenstern, 1974; Barnes and Jones, 1975) in high prestige occupations such as psychologist (Shepela, 1977), as well as lower prestige occupations, and there is evidence that the gap in rates of unemployment between the sexes is increasing (Niemi, 1975; Ferber and Lowry, 1976). Female heads of household are also unemployed for longer periods of time than male heads of household (Moen, 1979). Furthermore, these relatively higher unemployment rates by women are not being treated seriously. For example, "Thomas F. Johnson, research director of the American Enterprise Institute, suggested that the White House should . . . shoot for subtotal targets [in unemployment] such as 3.5 percent for adult men and perhaps 6 percent to 8 percent for women" (Bell, 1972, p. 18). The assumption seems to be that women's employment is not as crucial as men's and therefore a higher rate of unemployment by women than by men should be tolerated, an assumption that is not borne out in fact (see Crowley et al., 1973).

A number of reasons have been proposed to account for the relatively higher unemployment rates among women than among men. Among the factors that have been suggested to account for these findings are lack of specific occupational skills on the part of women, extensive movement of women into and out of the labor force, geographic immobility of women (Niemi, 1975), the fact that it takes longer for women to find a job than it does men (Barrett and Morgenstern, 1974), and discrimination against women (Ferber and Lowry, 1976). Ferber and Lowry (1976) found that when occupational distribution, job search time, geographic mobility, and movement into and out of the labor force were controlled, discrimination was an important determinant of women's higher unemployment rates.

The concept of the "discouraged worker" (Schweitzer and Smith, 1974) has been used to describe the effect of continued unemployment. Schweitzer and Smith hypothesized and found evidence that people who had been unemployed for a long period of time eventually tend to stop looking for a job. Since women must look longer for a job than men on the average, they may be more likely than men to quit looking for a job.

Although some women who wish to become employed are unable to find a job, other women settle for jobs for which they are overqualified. Underemployment, the condition of being overqualified for one's job, is just coming to the attention of social scientists (O'Toole, 1975), yet significant numbers of women have probably been underemployed for years. In general, there is very little research in this area, although some studies suggest that, for example, the average secretary is often qualified for a more challenging and responsible position (see Majchrzak and Gutek, 1977), or that gifted women often find themselves either unemployed or in mundane occupations. In their famous longitudinal study of gifted people, Terman and Oden (1959) found that 86 percent of the men in their sample achieved prominence in professional or managerial occupations. At age 44, 61 percent of the women were full-time housewives. Of those women who were employed, only 11 percent were professionals; 37 percent were nurses, librarians, social workers, and noncollege teachers; over 25 percent were secretaries, stenographers, bookkeepers, and office workers. Surely, this is impressive evidence that women have experienced underemployment for a number of years.

THE DECISION TO WORK

There are a number of factors that influence whether or not a woman decides to take a job. We will divide them into three groups: characteristics of the woman, attitudinal factors, and situational factors. Characteristics of the woman include demographic characteristics of education, age, and race as well as personality factors. Situational factors include attitudes and behaviors of her husband and children, her mobility, and previous experience. In the studies reviewed in this section, most apply only to married women and many refer only to mothers.

Personal Characteristics

Age

Women have the highest employment rates when they are in early adulthood and again after their children are grown. More women from ages 16 to 24 are deciding to work now than ever (Grossman, 1975). Especially among women who are of childbearing age, however, there has been a tremendous increase in employment during the last 60 years, a fourfold increase according to Mahoney (1961). More than half of the women from 25 to 54 were employed in 1974 with there being very little difference between women aged 25 to 44 (prime childbearing years) and women aged 45 to 54. Fifty-two percent of women 25-44 were employed in 1974 compared to 55 percent of the older group (Klein, 1975). In sum, age determines whether or not a woman will decide to work less now than in the past.

Education

Many researchers report that a positive relationship exists between amount of education and probability of engaging in paid employment among women (Finegan, 1975; Mahoney, 1961; Sobol, 1973; Dickinson, 1974; Bell, 1974; Hoffman, 1974d; Molm, 1978). For example, Finegan reports on his study utilizing a sample of the 1960 Census that adjusted labor force participation rate of married women "rises steadily from about 20 percent for wives with less than five years of schooling to 38 percent for those with a high school diploma, to 47 percent for those with a college degree, and finally to 61 percent for those who attended graduate school" (p. 30). Several researchers (for example, Sobol, 1973) have noted that the increasing level of education attained by women could be related to higher rates of labor force participation in the future.

Another factor suggests that, in the future, women's education may be an even stronger predictor of labor force participation, or at least number of years employed. Women in college are choosing majors, for example, the business major, that require continuous employment. Furthermore, women are choosing majors in areas where there are job openings as the shift from majoring in education to majoring in business indicates (Scherrei, 1979). In 1969, over 35 percent of women in college were majoring in education, whereas in 1978 less than 10 percent of women chose education. Business majors increased over 10 percent from 1969 to 1978.

Race

Turner and McCaffrey (1974) found that more black college women than white college women expect to work in the future. These expectations are borne out in fact. The labor force participation rate of black women is higher than that of white women. For example, Finegan (1975) found that for urban wives aged 14 to 54, 47 percent of black women were working in comparison to 35 percent of white wives. After adjusting for a number of other relevant factors — wife's education and age, other family income, presence of children of specific age groups, and employment status of husband — the difference diminished but still left about a 7 percent difference in employment rates.

Other

Other personal characteristics, personality traits, might be expected to influence whether or not a woman decides to work. No doubt individual difference variables do have some impact on decision to work, but there are few personality characteristics that exert a strong enough influence to emerge as important factors across diverse types of employment, as Hoffman noted:

> It is not meaningful to try to describe the personality characteristics that distinguish working mothers. The pattern is too widespread and the group too heterogeneous. However, comparisons between working and non-working mothers in the same situation, with comparable education and family incomes, at the same stage in the family cycle, with the same number of children, and with equal opportunities for employment, should reveal personality differences. Unfortunately, few such studies have been made . . . (Hoffman, 1974c, p. 49).

Attitudinal Characteristics

Women's attitudes toward women and mothers working have become more liberal. For example, the National Longitudinal Study showed that among white women aged 35 to 49, attitudes favorable to market work increased by 9 percentage points over a five-year period. In 1972, 32 percent of respondents favored married women with children working outside the home, up from 23 percent in 1967 (Parnes et al., 1975). In addition, women who are working have more favorable attitudes toward market work than women who are not working (Mahoney, 1961; Hoffman, 1974c), and their husbands also have more favorable attitudes toward women working than husbands of nonworking wives (Parnes et al., 1975). The relationship between own attitudes toward working and actually taking a job were stronger for more affluent women.

In fact, Molm (1978) hypothesized that a woman's attitudes toward female employment do not affect her employment status but rather the reverse is true: Working outside the home leads to less restrictive attitudes about women's roles. Using national sample data collected in 1970, she found a weak causal relationship between employment status and attitudes but no effect of attitudes on employment status. The two-stage least squares analysis also included other relevant variables such as presence of children, educational attainment, and husband's income.

These results, along with the Parnes et al. (1975) data suggest that attitudes are related to work behavior only if the woman has a choice about working or not and then the direction of the relationship may be the reverse of what is expected. Behavior influuences attitude more than attitude affects behavior according to Molm (1978).

Hall and Gordon (1973) also supported Molm's hypotheses. They looked at the relationship between working status and satisfaction. They hypothesized that women who choose to work or choose to be full-time housewives would be more satisfied than both women who worked but preferred to be housewives and housewives who preferred to work. Their hypothesis, that satisfaction would be related to the extent to which women did what they actually wanted to do, was confirmed only for housekeeping and volunteer activities, but not among employed women. Their sample, mostly college graduates, was a group of women on mailing lists of women's organizations and college alumnae clubs in the New Haven, Connecticut area. Although these women might be expected to have a high degree of choice in whether or not they want to work, that choice was not related to their satisfaction.

Situational Factors

Perusal of a number of factors that influence whether or not a woman works suggests that situational factors are probably more important than the woman's own characteristics or her attitudes. Several clusters of situation characteristics can be delineated. One cluster concerns the woman's husband, whether or not he is employed, his occupation, his income, and his attitudes. A second cluster has to do with a woman's children, whether she has any, and if so, how many and at what ages. Also, does she need childcare and what is its availability? A factor related to both husband's work status and children is the woman's mobility. As Mahoney (1961) states: "The decision of married woman to seek employment outside the household involves some adjustment by all members of the family since the welfare of the family as a unit may be substantially affected by such a decision" (Mahoney, 1961, p. 565).* Finally, the woman's own previous work experience is a determinant of her decision to work.

Husband Variables

Using a suburban New Jersey sample of wives, Weil (1961) found that a strong determiner of wife's decision to work was whether or not the husband had a positive attitude toward his wife's working outside the home. Another

---

*The decision of a married man to take a job also has implications for the family's welfare, yet there has been less emphasis placed on the role of the family in husband's than in wife's decision to work.

factor is husband's employment status. If a woman's husband is unemployed, she is more likely to take a job than if he is employed (Mahoney, 1961; Finegan, 1975). This is even more likely if there are children under the age of six present in the house (Finegan, 1975). Decision to work by the wife is negatively related to her husband's occupational level. The greater the prestige and responsibility attached to her husband's job, the less likely it is that the wife will work, although this relationship is fairly weak (Mahoney, 1961). The stronger relationship is between husband's income and wife's decision to work (Dickinson, 1974; Bell, 1974; Finegan, 1975; Mahoney, 1961). Finegan (1975) noted that in his 1960 census sample, among women whose other family income (all income except the woman's salary) is under $4,000, there was a labor force participation rate of 45 percent compared 10 percent for women whose other family income was over $15,000 per year. Bell (1974) found that blacks do not follow this pattern. Husbands of black women who work have higher incomes than black women who do not work outside the home. Dickinson (1974) noted that single mothers are forced to work for relatively low wages in the absence of alternative incomes.

A very careful and imaginative study by Winter, Stewart, and McClelland (1977) shows the magnitude of the husband's effect on the wife's labor force participation. Using a sample of 41 college graduates (class of 1964), Winter et al. found that level of wives' careers in 1974 could be predicted by power motivation of their husbands as measured in 1960. In fact, there were an impressive number of "husband variables" that were related to wife's decision to work and kind of job she chose. Career level, the dependent variable in this study, was measured by a four-category variable: nontraditional lifetime careers, traditional lifetime careers, series of brief jobs, no work outside the home. Although the dependent variable is a broader concept than decision to work, it still shows the importance of husband's input. Table 1 shows that husband's motives, family social status, college experience, and contemporary situation all relate to level of wife's career.

The regression coefficients show that low power motivation, high social status of husband's family, and high satisfaction with college are the most conducive to a high level of wife's career involvement. In fact, the eight variables in Table 1 produce a multiple correlation of .77, accounting for 59 percent of the variance in wife's career level. A number of current husband variables were also related to wife's career level. High wife career involvement was positively related to, among other things, husband's having intrinsically interesting work, a pleasant work environment, work that makes "unreasonable" demands, the general feeling of having too much to do, describing oneself as hectic; and negatively related to the husband's feeling settled, orderly, and traditional.

TABLE 1
Husband's Motives, Background, College Experience, and Contemporary Situation Variables Associated with Wife's Career Level

	Relationship to Wife's Career Level[a]	
	---	---
Husband Variable	Correlation	Standardized Regression Coefficient
Motives		
N Power	-.42**	-.26*
N Affiliation	.31*	.15
Background	.21	.13
Social status of family of origin	.39*	.39***
College experience		
Senior year grade point average	.38**	.15
Reported satisfaction with college[b]	.33*	.38**
Contemporary situation		
Business executive	-.33*	-.15
Conservative political views[c]	-.38*	-.07

Note: The largest N for this table is 51, but it is reduced for some variables because of missing data.

[a]Using a four-point scale taken from Steward and Winter (1974); see text for explanation.

[b]Average of answers on a five-point scale, for freshman through senior years to the question, "How satisfied are you with your _____ year at Ivy?"

[c]Response to this question in 1974: "How would you characterize yourself politically? Check one of the following: far left / liberal / independent / conservative / far right / apolitical / other." The last two choices were eliminated, and answers transformed into a five-point scale.

  * p .05.
  ** p .01.
*** p .001.

Source: D. Winter, A. Stewart, and D. McClelland, "Husband's Motives and Wife's Career Level," *Journal of Personality and Social Psychology,* 162.

Children Variables

A second group of situational variables has to do with the woman's children. Women who have children are less likely to work than those who do not have children and the more children she has, the less likely she is to work (Mahoney, 1961; Gramm, 1975; Sobol, 1973; Hoffman, 1974d; Waite, 1976; Waite and Stolzenberg, 1976; Stolzenberg and Waite, 1977; Collver, 1968; Molm, 1978). For example, using 1960 census data, Finegan (1975) found that among urban women with children under six, 15 percent were working in comparison to a labor force participation rate of 55 percent for women who have no children under fourteen. The presence of teenagers facilitates the decision to work (Hoffman, 1974c). Finegan (1975) found that women who had children under six and teenagers (aged 14-17) were more likely to work than women who only had children under six (22 percent to 14 percent). Walker (1970) reports that in families with no younger children, teenage children of working mothers did about 30 percent of household tasks.

While the relationship between decision to work and number of children is well documented, the causal direction has been a matter of some discussion (for example, Collver, 1968; Bumpass and Westhoff, 1970; Hoffman, 1974d; Smith-Lovin and Tickamyer, 1978). It has been suggested by population planners that offering more jobs for women will lower the birth rate. This argument rests on the assumptions that decision to work causes a reduction in number of children and that this decision is made before women already have children (or very many children).

Waite and Stolzenberg (1976) state the four possible hypotheses about their relationship between decision to work and number of children: labor force participation causes a reduction in fertility; absence of children facilitates the decision to work in paid employment; labor force participation and fertility cause each other; other factors cause both decision to work and decision not to have children. Their analyses, based on nonrecursive models, showed support for the first three hypotheses but found that decision to work had a greater impact on decision to have children than the other way around. A later study (Stolzenberg and Waite, 1977) reported that the negative relationship between decision to work and to have (more) children was much stronger among 27 to 29 year olds than among women aged 19 to 20.

> To explain this finding, we advanced the Learning Hypothesis. According to the Learning Hypothesis, the inverse effect of work plans on fertility expectations increases as women age from 19 to 29 because their knowledge of the demands of motherhood and their information about the labor market improve during that time. . . . (Stolzenberg and Waite, 1977, p. 780).

Among college-age women, there is only a weak relationship between desire to have children and desire to have a career. Indeed, studies of career choice reviewed in Chapter 2 show that most young college women plan to have children and to work. The realities of the demands of doing both apparently facilitate moving either in the direction of children or work as the woman ages, that is, Stolzenberg and Waite's (1977) Learning Hypothesis. Molm (1978) supported their findings with a causal model analysis. She found a strong causal relationship between presence of children under six and wife's employment status using national sample data. Smith-Lovin and Tickamyer's (1978) causal analyses also support the hypothesis that the presence of children lowers the probability of taking a job. Their results suggest that the presence of children is the more important factor over taking a job. Clearly the debate over the causal relationship between work and children is not over.

Since many young women want to both work and have children, the *sequence* with which they begin these two endeavors may be very important for their subsequent behavior. If a young woman who wants to have a career and children marries in college or soon after college, moves to a city where her husband is employed, and immediately has one or several babies, her chances of establishing a career or even getting a job are substantially less according to the data than the woman who marries, works, and does not have children for a while. In fact, the longer she works, the less likely she is to have children or additional children.

The dynamics are somewhat different for the young woman who selected a life style centered around husband and children. That is, the relationship between fertility and working is moderated by whether or not the woman wants to work. Hoffman (1974d) reports studies by Whelpton, Campbell, and Patterson (1966) and Ryder and Westoff (1971), which found that women who enjoyed or wanted to work expected to have fewer children than women who worked because they had to. And Havens and Gibbs (1975) found that the more committed a woman is to a career, the stronger the negative relationship between decision to work and decision to have children. Hoffman (1974d) further points out that the relationship between decision to work and decision to have children might be weakened if there were better childcare facilities or if other structural changes were made that would facilitate having both children and a career. Since most younger women want to do both, one might anticipate a weakening in the inverse relationship of working and having children if doing both were not such a burden for women. As it is, however, doing both *is* a burden. The woman who wants to have a career will probably lessen her burden by having fewer children. The woman who wants a family will quit her job when and if she can. The woman who wants both may end up devoting most energy to the role she acquires, and gets involved in, first.

Mobility

Another factor that concerns a woman's decision to work is her mobility. It is common knowledge that married women have less geographic mobility than men. Not only are women usually constrained by the location of their husband's jobs, but they are also expected to pack up and follow him if he is transferred or takes another job. Long (1974) looked at the effect of wife's working on family mobility. He found that families in which the wife works are more likely to move short distances but less likely to move long distances. He concluded that migration of the husband has a negative impact on the career development of the wife.

Perhaps one reason corporations periodically move managers is to ensure loyalty to the corporation by both the husband and his wife (see Kanter, 1977a). If she is moved frequently, it will be difficult for the wife to have her own career and she may show more interest in, and support for, her husband's career. As more and more wives have their own careers, the corporation may have to find desirable jobs for both spouses. The long-term effect will surely be a decrease in the number of work-related moves couples make.

Previous Experience

Finally, a strong determinant of wife's decision to work is her own previous experience (Parnes et al., 1975; Mahoney, 1961; Polachek, 1975; Weil, 1961; Waite, 1976). Parnes et al. (1975) found a strong relationship between work status prior to marriage and work status after marriage in their longitudinal study. Eighty-one percent of respondents who did not work one or more years between completion of school and marriage also did not work at least one year between first marriage and birth of first child. On the other hand, 54 percent of white women and 43 percent of black women worked one or more years before marriage and after marriage but before birth of first child.

Changes in Determinants

In her discussion of determinants of the decision to work by mothers, Hoffman (1974c) noted motivators and facilitators of decision to work but also some obstacles to working. In our discussion, we could conceptualize previous work experience, high education level, and own positive attitudes as facilitators, whereas the presence of children, high husband income, and occupation are obstacles. Waite (1976) looked at changes in determinants of labor force participation over a 20-year period, 1940 to 1960. She found a significant decrease in importance of those predictors classified as inhibitors or obstacles but no change · in the effects of the facilitators or motivators. In particular, the presence of young children and the woman's age were less inhibiting in 1960 than in 1940. The influx of mothers with young children into the labor force is certainly one of the biggest social changes in recent years, promising to have long-range impact on childrearing patterns and the attitudes, interests, and personalities of the next generation of Americans.

SUMMARY

In general, married women who decide to work tend to be fairly young or beyond the childbearing age, have relatively high levels of educational attainment, be black, have a sense of personal competence, have favorable attitudes toward women working, have a husband whose income is not too high, have no children, and have previous work experience. These are all rather general statements and the majority of working women do not actually fit this profile.

While these are factors that contribute to a woman's decision to work, there are other ways one can examine the process. For example, a demographer's analysis of the situation is that women work because the demand for "women's work," that is, occupations with 70 percent or more female employees, has increased dramatically. The supply of young, single women is not sufficient to fill the demand so older, married women with children enter the labor force (Oppenheimer, 1973).

The demand for "women's work," the age, race, sex of the female applicant, and her husband's and children's circumstances all set the context for the reasons women themselves give for taking a job. A woman may say that she wants a job to use her skills that are becoming rusty, for example. This may mean that she has few children or they are teenagers, her husband supports her working, and his income is relatively low. Another woman may say she is working for the money. A different constellation of contextual factors are associated with her verbal report of why she is working.

While the literature on career choice concerned a number of psychological characteristics that influence career choice, the research on determinants of labor force participation focused on demographic characteristics. There are several reasons for this difference in emphasis. Career choice is determined by the individual woman, her needs, interests, and life-style choice. Decision to work involves a number of constraints so that psychological characteristics may not emerge or might be dwarfed in importance by the constraints that women face both from the employer and her family in her decision to take a job.

A second reason for the difference in emphasis is that career choice studies are largely done by psychologists but decision-to-work studies are largely done by sociologists and economists. Psychologists are often unconcerned about their sample so they use college students, a most accessible group of people. Economists and sociologists, however, are often concerned about generalizing their findings to adult Americans and use the Census data or other large data sets for their analyses. These data sets do not have measures of psychological variables, but they do have a large amount of demographic and economic data. The contextual factors that determine career or life-style choice must be studied as well as the attitudes and verbal reports that go with the contextual factors related to labor force participation. A more complete psychological picture of the process of becoming attached to an occupation would then emerge.

4
COMBINING WORK
AND FAMILY LIFE

People do not work in a vacuum. A woman's family is assumed to be more important to her than her work. For women, family life encompasses the roles of wife and mother. In order to understand women's behavior at work, it is important to understand the effects of this other important arena. We need to understand the interdependence of work and family roles, an area of interest that is relatively new (see Gutek, Nakamura, and Nieva, 1980).

A NEGLECTED AREA OF RESEARCH

Combining the roles of work and family has recently received a great deal of attention from researchers and the popular press; but this has not always been true, largely because traditionally work and family were viewed as complementary spheres each belonging to one sex only. This tradition, which had both biosocial and cultural origins, was made explicit by Parsons in his discussion of instrumental (male) and expressive (female) roles (Parsons and Bales, 1955) and was reinforced by the research of Bales on task leaders and socioemotional leaders (Bales, 1950; Bales and Slater, 1955). Bales' research was viewed as empirical proof of Parsons' theorizing although Bales' research used only male subjects.

On the whole, society still perceives the role of homemaker as the woman's domain (deBoer, 1977). Society in general still perceives the work role as male although that belief is undergoing faster change; women are more likely to enter the labor force than men are to become full-time homemakers. Nevertheless, men who abdicate the breadwinner role are neither admired nor tolerated by most segments of our society.

As long as it is presumed that women exclusively or even predominantly occupy the homemaker role and men occupy the breadwinner role, there is little interest in these two roles occupied by the same sex. Such a presumption is powerful even though there is little basis in fact. At present, only 6 percent of Americans live in the idealized family situation of working husband, nonworking wife, and two children (Pifer, 1978).

There is a second, more pragmatic reason why there was little research focused on the interdependence of home and work in the past. The two areas of interest are studied by different academic disciplines. Organizational and industrial psychologists and sociologists and management scientists study work behavior, whereas family behavior is more often studied by developmental psychologists or marriage and family sociologists. In the past there has been little professional collaboration among these groups. Today, while there may still be little collaboration, there is at least a greater acknowledgement of the contributions of the various fields. Topics such as dual career couples are being studied by both organizational and social psychologists and marriage and family sociologists (compare Morgan, 1980; Bryson and Bryson, 1978).

Coinciding with a tremendous increase in number of women in management careers (see Scherrei, 1979) is the emergence of research on women in management (for example, Gordon and Strober, 1975; Terborg, 1977; Hennig and Jardim, 1977). One outcome of this interest is a concern with how women managers will integrate their private, family lives with their work responsibilities. Other academic women interested in the topic (for example, Kanter, 1977a & c) have also called attention to the interdependence of home and work. Even though research on the interaction of work and family accumulates, there is still limited appreciation of the effects of family role on work role for either sex. For example, articles presenting overviews of women and work rarely mention family life as a factor affecting women's work behavior (see Terborg, 1977).

In addition to the current attention by industrial-organizational psychologists, the area of family and work is studied by developmental psychologists and marriage and family sociologists. The emphasis is on mother's employment, not father's, and these researchers are usually concerned with work in general rather than specific types of occupations or job characteristics. A weak feature of the family-oriented studies is that the work component is insufficiently defined. Women are divided into gross categories, that is, employed or not, employed part time versus employed full time. More recently, psychological variables such as whether the mother wants to work or not, whether she feels she has adequate childcare or not, and the like have been included as potentially important variables. There has been little interest in the type of job the mother or wife has, for example, how physically demanding it is, whether she is a supervisor or subordinate, whether she has adequate resources on the job, whether her chances for promotion are excellent or nil. At least, however, these researchers appreciate the interdependence of work and family life and are initiating research efforts in the area.

THE IMPORTANCE OF WORK AND FAMILY INTERDEPENDENCE

Over 50 percent of women are currently working. The large majority of women will work in paid employment sometime in their lives and this trend shows no signs of abating (Flaim and Fullerton, 1978). Young women, especially those interested in having a career, will readily admit that they are concerned about combining their work with a family. The majority of young women want to have both. They want role models; they want to learn strategies of combining the two areas of life; and they have been concerned with the effects of pursuit of a career on their children and their marriage. More recently, they want to know the effects of husband's career, his attitudes and behavior, and children on their own career development.

Work and family interdependence is important because these are the two areas of life that make the largest contributions to life satisfaction (Campbell, Converse, and Rodgers, 1976). These are the two areas of life that take up most of people's time. The research on the relationship between job satisfaction and life satisfaction in general shows that they are strongly related (Iris and Barrett, 1972). Furthermore, there is little evidence that people "make up" for their unsatisfactory jobs by getting greater enjoyment out of other areas of life. Rather, satisfaction with work "spills over" into family life (Staines, 1980; Rousseau, 1978). For example, Staines (1980) found more evidence for a spill-over effect than a compensation effect, stating that people "make up" for an unsatisfactory work life with a satisfactory family life (Staines, 1980; Rousseau, 1978). The way in which one negotiates the interdependence of work and family affects satisfaction with each of the domains as well as overall life satisfaction.

Yankelovich (1979) contends that a New Breed of American workers has emerged in the 1970s and that the meaning of work has changed as a result. New Breed workers, according to Yankelovich, place a very high priority on self-expression, achievement, and accomplishment at work. As a result, work takes on new meaning; it becomes more important in one's overall life goals. The New Breed are not all men. Hoffman (1979) suggested that decreasing family size has made work more important for women's lives as well.

Older women who felt the need to choose between the wife-mother role and a work role and made the traditional choice may regret their decision. Women who are homemakers interviewed by Barnett and Baruch (1979) reported that they wished they had accomplished more and had more ambition for themselves. They had felt compelled to choose either a career or a family. They would have benefited from knowledge about combining the two options that they had viewed as mutually exclusive. They are still interested in information about combining the two roles, as evidenced by the growth of centers for the continuing education of women on college campuses.

GENERAL EFFECTS OF FAMILY LIFE ON WORK

In Chapter 1 we discussed the fact that jobs are sex-segregated. Here we explore three hypotheses about the effects of family life on the kinds of work women do in the labor force. While people usually assume that women occupy certain jobs but not others because these jobs are somehow more compatible with their roles as housewife and mother, there is little research that addresses the topic.

We advance three hypotheses. First, jobs that are dominated by women allow women to accommodate their work demands to their family demands. These jobs would allow a woman to concentrate on her assumed greater interest in the wife and mother roles and to mold and shape her work responsibilities to fit these needs. The second hypothesis is that the presumed greater interest in family life is an excuse for assigning women the worst jobs. Only someone predominantly interested in family life would be satisfied with the poor working conditions, poor promotion possibilities, and poor pay that characterize some jobs. Hence, men avoid and women are encouraged to enter these jobs. The third hypothesis is that work roles are an extension of family roles. Women's jobs are characterized by the same tasks and responsibilities that wives and mothers have.

The evidence about women's jobs accommodating to family life is hardly overwhelming. The strongest case can be made for women's professional jobs and for clerical jobs. Teaching is probably the best example since teachers usually have the summer off, and prior to the oversupply of teachers, it was easy to move to follow a husband's job and still find another teaching position. Of course, one was unlikely to be promoted to principal. Clerical jobs are 12-month jobs but are still in supply and skills are readily transferable from one job to another. Other women's jobs, however, are not any more accommodative to family responsibilities than many male professional jobs. For example, is the job of social worker more accommodating to family roles than the job of probation officer? In the area of blue collar jobs, the rationale is even weaker. Women are less likely than men to belong to unions that promote fringe benefits and employee rights. Paid personal leave and a union steward to protect worker rights mean an employee can take work time to tend to family responsibilities, whereas the lack of union benefits often means the employee must give work priority all the time or lose her job.

Bailyn (1978) points out that both husbands and wives vary in how much their jobs accommodate to their family lives, whereas the kind of job the wife has does not seem to be a determining factor in ease of meshing the two domains of life. Pleck (1977) notes that for women, family life is *expected* to intrude on work life, but that is not the same as saying that work is designed to fit around family responsibilities. In fact, if work were really designed to fit around family responsibilities, there should be little or no need for family to intrude into the work arena.

While there is little evidence that women's jobs can be easily accommodated to family responsibilities, there is more evidence that family roles are used as excuses for assigning undesirable jobs to women. For example, Blauner (1964) found that women who worked in textile mills labored under poor working conditions. The fact that they did not complain much was attributed to the belief that women derive their greatest pleasure from the wife and mother roles and therefore are willing to tolerate tedious, boring, or difficult working conditions.

Nonunion, poorly paying industries such as textile work are often dominated by women. Dead-end, low-paying white collar positions are also women's jobs. Sales jobs that pay by commission such as insurance or appliances are usually men's jobs, whereas the low salary sales jobs with few promotion possibilities are women's jobs.

An alternate hypothesis about the origin of women's jobs is that women's jobs are not those that can be easily accommodated to family life but rather are those jobs that are an extension of the wife and mother roles. There is more evidence in support of this hypothesis. Many women's jobs are characterized by a service component as are the wife and mother roles.

In fact, providing service is an overriding theme in women's jobs. The largest single occupation of women, clerical work, is often primarily a service function. For example, there are estimates that secretaries spend about 20 percent of their time waiting for work and only a small percentage of their time actually doing tasks involving clerical and secretarial skills (Coopers and Lybrand, 1979). These assessments suggest that a portion of the secretarial job is to wait for and wait on the supervisor. Kanter (1977a) has also called attention to the similarity of the secretary to the wife role. Numerous researchers as well as secretaries and clerical people all over have recently begun protesting some of the more absurd aspects of service, for example, cleaning false teeth, as well as the more mundane aspects, for example, dusting the desk and fixing coffee.

Other jobs that are dominated by women also show a strong service component. Professional jobs dominated by women — nurse, teacher, social worker, librarian — all have a service-giving component to them. Nurses provide tender loving care to patients; social workers service the poor and needy. The growing service sector among occupations is also dominated by women. To some extent, service is a factor in most jobs but still one usually thinks of the physician providing expertise and the nurse providing tender loving care.

Only a few women's jobs really accommodate to family life. More realistically, the importance of family life is an excuse for putting women into undesirable jobs. Other women's jobs are an extension of the tasks and responsibilities of wives and mothers.

SPECIFIC EFFECTS OF A WOMAN'S
FAMILY LIFE ON HER WORK LIFE

Women's family life in general has an effect on the kinds of jobs women are likely to enter. However, an individual woman's own family life, especially the age at which she marries (Elder and Rockwell, 1976), also affects the particular kind of job she selects and what she might accomplish in that job.

One way that women respond to the demands of family life is to make adaptations in their labor force attachment. Women can choose an intermittent work style. This choice implies that family life is clearly more important than work life. Super (1957) and Cooper (1963) identified three types of career patterns that fit this adjustment mode: the one-role pattern, in which the work and domestic roles are sequential, the young woman working in a stop-gap job until she marries and leaves the labor force; the interrupted pattern, in which a one-role and a two-role pattern may involve taking time off to rear children and then return to uninterrupted employment; and unstable in-and-out of the labor force pattern that fits her short-term needs or personal whims.

Focusing on professional women, Bernard (1971a) discussed five interrupted career patterns involving various combinations of marriage, childbearing, career preparation, and career work. The pattern with the largest effect on women (and the modal pattern) is probably the early interrupted pattern of career preparation, marriage and children, and assumption of a career. Such a woman is out of the labor force in the crucial early stage of her posttraining career assumption, and often she finds that her skills are outdated when she is ready to begin a career in earnest.

The intermittant work style precludes women from setting goals with respect to her work life. Inderlied (1979) noted that "goal setting has also been consistently associated with career planning and aspiration and with effectiveness in occupational choice" (p. 34). Bryson, Bryson, and Johnson (1978) found that female psychologists married to psychologists were less satisfied with freedom to pursue long-range goals in comparison to their husbands. Shea et al. (1970) found that women who had been absent from the labor force for a while tend to return in lower status jobs. For example, women originally in profes-. sional and technical jobs tended to return in clerical and sales jobs.

A second response of a woman to family demands is to lower her career commitment. A woman who might like to become a physician decides to become a nurse instead both because there is less preparation and it is more acceptable for a nurse than a physician to move in and out of the labor force.

The concept of work commitment in women has been studied extensively and has been operationalized in several ways. Fogarty, Rapoport, and Rapoport (1971) and Sobol (1963) measured work commitment by length of time that a woman plans to work. In addition to using the time measure, Haller and Rosenmayr (1971) also used attitude about the appropriateness of mothers' working and willingness to work without financial necessity as measures of commitment. Haller and Rosenmayr (1971) found that work commitment varies by social class and previous experiences. Women who have a lengthy work history and a successful career have higher work commitment. Commitment to work breeds work commitment; but both Sobol (1963) and Haller and Rosenmayr (1971) found that women who had children also had a higher work commitment than married women without children, suggesting that being around children or already having the pleasure of having children increases a woman's interest in pursuing a career. As Bernard (1971a) and Rossi (1965b) wrote, however, it may be most difficult to resume a career after marriage and motherhood.

A third response to family demands is to choose a traditional job because it is viewed as more compatible with family responsibilities than a nontraditional job. Or because of her concern with fulfilling her future or present family responsibilities, a woman may not even find out the alternatives available to her and instead select a traditionally female job. In Schreiber's (1979) study of women in nontraditional technical jobs, she found that few women had chosen those jobs. Rather, they were more likely to have learned about the jobs "on the job" or been recommended for them. They did not learn about or plan for these higher paying jobs on their own.

A fourth effect of women's family life on her work life is that she may suffer a loss of career attainment. By career attainment we mean accomplishments, progress, or "moving up" in one's career. Because women's family lives are assumed to be more important than their work, they may not even be offered a desirable job in another location. Or it may be assumed that they do not want a managerial job or any more demanding job. Bryson, Bryson, and Johnson (1978) found that women who are psychologists and are married to psychologists were less satisfied than their husbands with rate of professional advancement.

In sum, the general effect of family roles on work roles for women is a sex-segregated labor force in which women are hired into jobs that are low paying, low prestige, and generally undesirable and/or jobs that are extensions of the wife and mother roles. On a specific level, family roles may reduce a woman's involvement in the labor force, lower her career commitment, steer her into a traditional career, and reduce her career attainment. Laws (1979) notes that there has been a great deal of concern on how working affects a woman's marriage and family with relatively little evidence that working necessarily harms the children, the marriage, or the husband. On the other hand, there has been less concern with the effects of marriage on a woman's work life and the effects seem to be greater. Marriage is more harmful to a career, according to Laws, than working is to a marriage.

EFFECTS OF WORKING ON FAMILY LIFE

The effects of a mother's working on her family life have been well documented by several authors (for example, Nye and Hoffman, 1963; Hoffman and

Nye, 1974; Cochran and Bronfenbrenner, 1979). Although there is a wealth of information available on effects of mother's working on children, that topic is outside the scope of this book. Reviews of the literature on children include Hoffman (1974a), Hoffman (1979), Etaugh (1974), and Siegel and Haas (1963).

Here we concentrate on cumulative and day-to-day effects of working on the woman. Four cumulative effects are covered: the increased sense of competence and well-being that accrues from working, increased power in the marriage, increased or decreased marital satisfaction of the wife, and the increased work load that comes from adding outside employment without giving up many of the housekeeping and childrearing responsibilities and support for husband's career.

There is evidence that working has a rehabilitative effect on mental health, measured in terms of psychological distress. Bernard (1971b; 1972) showed that working women have less than expected frequencies of such symptoms, in comparison to housewives who showed more than expected frequencies. The right to take a job and be released from the boredom and isolation of housework would be expected to contribute to the happiness and self-fulfillment of women.

Barnett and Baruch (1979) argued that working increases a woman's sense of well-being. Women acquire an increased sense of competence through working for pay. The financial independence that comes with having a job also increases one's sense of being adult and capable. These effects on the woman in general also affect her behavior in the family. Her increased sense of confidence may make her more assertive in decisions about childbearing. She may demand greater respect from her children and husband or refuse to cater to their needs. Her increased financial independence allows her to spend money on things she values, perhaps on a housekeeper or music lessons for the children.

Safilios-Rothschild and Dijkers (1978) and Blood (1965) point out that having an independent financial base gives women more power within the marriage. Couples who both work are more likely to share in decisions about major purchases than couples where only the husband works in paid employment (Heer, 1958; Blood and Wolfe, 1960; Geiken, 1964). In some cases, the financial independence means the wife no longer receives an allowance or has to ask for permission to buy things. It also gives her the option of leaving the marriage. In fact, one probable effect of higher employment among women is a rising divorce rate (Sawhill, 1976), although more recent research suggested that divorce is more likely to occur only under certain conditions such as the wife earning more than the husband (Hofferth and Moore, 1979).

A third effect of interest is the way in which working affects the woman's marital satisfaction. Early research (for example, Blood and Wolfe, 1960) suggested that the wife who worked decreased her husband's marital satisfaction and presumably her own in the process, but much of this research is fraught with problems, not the least of which is how marital happiness, marital satisfaction, or marital adjustment are operationalized (Laws, 1971).

Later research suggests that the mere fact of a wife's working has very little effect on marital satisfaction or adjustment without taking into account other factors (Staines, 1980; Hofferth and Moore, 1979). For example, Campbell, Converse, and Rodgers (1976) found that employment outside the home neither "enhances [n]or diminishes a marriage, at least as the wives see it" (p. 425). Staines et al. (1978) agree. They found no differences between wives who work outside the home and housewives on four measures of marital adjustment. These authors did find two differences between working and nonworking wives, but with the strongest effects for women with preschool children and women with less than a high school diploma. These women were more likely to report that they had thought about getting a divorce and that they wished they had married someone else. Later research (see Hoffman, 1979) suggested that when both husband and wife support the wife's employment, marital satisfaction is increased.

A fourth area in which women are affected by their employment is in the increased work load they bear. While they take on a work role that may be intermittent or may involve well over 40 hours a week, they do not give up the home responsibilities of childcare and housework. Women have an expanded set of tasks. Working wives and husbands do not share household tasks. In an intensive study of organization of the household day among a cross-section of urban families, Berk and Berk (1979) found that in two-thirds of the wife-employed families studied, husbands made no contribution to after-dinner chores over husbands of nonemployed wives. Walker (1970) found that men average only 96 minutes of household work a day, including 12 minutes of primary childcare. Robinson and Converse (1966) found that among working couples with children, husbands averaged 1.3 hours more free time each weekday and 1.4 hours more on Sunday compared to wives. Hedges and Barnett (1972), reviewing the literature on working women and division of household tasks, concluded that "family roles of men and women may have changed less than has often been suggested" (p. 11). Wives clearly spend more time on paid and unpaid work than their husbands. However, they think they should be doing more. Bryson, Bryson, and Johnson (1978) found that female psychologists married to male psychologists were less satisfied with the time they have for domestic activities than their husbands.

Besides continuing with their housewife and mother chores, working women do not abdicate their role of supporter of their husband's job (Gutek and Stevens, 1979; Bryson et al., 1976). Women expect to move when their husbands have a better job offer, expect to attend his company parties, may discuss his business problems (Kanter, 1977a), and the like.

Besides these cumulative effects of employment on family life, there are also day-to-day effects. Kanter (1977c) discussed a variety of day-to-day work factors that affect family life and Schein (1978) organized them into four factors. The time it takes and the flexibility involved affect family life. Schein (1978) pointed out the extreme case of work patterns from 9 to 2 and 5 to 8 in countries such as Mexico, Spain, and Greece, which means fathers rarely see their children. The amount of travel to and from work is another factor. The longer the commuting time, the less likely the worker is to be home at all or be able to come home for school awards for the children, take children to piano lessons, and the like. A third factor is the amount of income and prestige the career garners for the worker and the family. A family that can afford vacations together and can hire people to provide household services often compensates for long working hours of the mother or father. A fourth effect is the physical and emotional condition of the worker when he or she comes home. Pleck (1979) called this work spill over.

Pleck (1979) researched the area of work interference with daily family life and found that over one-third of a national sample of working people reported at least moderate interference of work on family life. Parents, compared to nonparents, reported significantly more day-to-day interference between work and family life. The specific kinds of interference reported vary. Whereas husbands were more likely to report excessive work time, single (female) parents were more likely to report schedule incompatibility, and employed wives reported both excessive work time and schedule incompatibility as well as some spill over in the form of exhaustion, irritability, and preoccupation. Thus, on a daily basis, women also experience effects of work on their family life. Pleck (1979) concluded that the women with the greatest scheduling problems, schedule uncertainty, excessive work load, or work spill over might leave the labor force. Or they might alter their work lives by lowering career aspirations, selecting traditional jobs, and so on, as mentioned above.

INTEGRATING WORK AND FAMILY LIFE

Problems of integrating work and family life are more severe for women than men because women have traditionally been assumed to be available during the day to care for children, chauffeur children, let in the plumber, run errands, and do the housework. As a result, Hall (1972) noted that working women have simultaneous role demands from work and family whereas men have sequential role demands. This situation leads to more role overload on working mothers and wives than on working husbands and fathers. Hall's hypothesis is consistent with Pleck's (1977) hypothesis that for women, the family role is allowed to intrude into the work role, and for men, the work role is allowed to intrude into the family role. The fact that men's family responsibilities are sequential to their work responsibilities, that is, that they have no family responsibilities until their job tasks are complete, is an indication that work role is allowed to intrude into family role.

Bailyn (1978) discussed accommodation: "the degree to which work demands are fitted into family requirements" (p. 159). Both husbands and wives can be located anywhere along a continuum of extreme accommodation to extreme lack of accommodation although the modal high accommodation person is a woman who is guided by family needs rather than work requirements. The typical low accommodation person is a man whose work commitments do not accommodate in the least to family matters.

The concept of role conflict has been used to discuss the problems that women have in integrating home and work responsibilities (Hall and Gordon, 1973; Hall, 1972). Rapoport and Rapoport (1969) wrote that role conflict resulting from physical overload can be intensified by social-psychological overload of four types: normative conflict, sex-role identity maintenance, network management, and role cycling.

One way women can lessen various kinds of role conflict is to eliminate some roles. Remaining childless or single can reduce role conflict for women. Women in demanding careers, especially, may choose these options. For example, Rebecca (1978) studied voluntary childlessness as a conflict-reducing mechanism. Women who work are less likely to have children and are less likely to be married. For example, female psychologists are less likely to be married than women in general (Cuca, 1976). Herman and Gyllstrom (1977) found that women faculty, administrators, and clerical workers were all less likely to be married than their male counterparts.

Another way to lessen role conflict is to combine work and family roles, in either a traditional manner, for example, family farm, "Mom and Pop" business, or in a newer manner, for example, husband-wife law firm (Epstein, 1971) or a husband-wife consulting operation (Schein, 1978). At the very least, the commuting time between the two is eliminated and the family members have control over the work schedule.

Research results in general suggest that the more responsibilities a woman has around the home, the more work-family conflict she will experience. Staines et al. (1979) found that women with small children are less adjusted to their marriages. A woman can lessen those responsibilities by sharing more of the housework and childcare with her husband, but this option is not often chosen, both because the wife and especially the husband are not prepared for equal division of responsibilities. Andrisani and Shapiro (1978) found that conflicting demands between home and work result in lower job satisfaction for women and the presence of young children exacerbates the problem. Yet most women are not prepared to give up primary responsibility for childcare.

Nor are most husbands willing to take on a greater share of family responsibilities. The tasks they do take on are those that are the least threat to their masculinity. They prefer to play with children and "help out" with light housekeeping chores. Working wives are interested in having husbands increase their involvement in household responsibilities. For example, Staines et al. (1978) found that working wives, particularly those with less than a complete high school education, wished their husbands would contribute more "around the house."

Not all husbands are equally remiss in helping around the house. Weingarten (1978) found that husbands who have similar employment histories to their wives do a greater proportion of family work than husbands with dissimilar employment histories. And Perucci, Potter, and Rhoads (1978) found that husbands who have an egalitarian sex-role ideology were more likely to partic- ipate in housework and childcare than husbands with a traditional sex-role ideology. Perucci et al. (1978) further found that time available to both spouses and resources available to apply to housework and childcare were not predictors of husbands' involvement in family responsibilities. Husbands participate in family responsibilities to the extent that they begin doing so in a marriage and to the extent they believe they should contribute. Wife's availability, number of children, or work responsibilities do not seem to be factors affecting the amount of time husbands spend on household tasks. The amount of money she earns relative to her husband is also not a predictor of his involvement with family tasks (Farkas, 1976).

Most often, the solutions to role overload are ones the woman selects on her own. She often tries to solve the problem by lowering standards for her "housewife" role. She can also reduce her social life. Other solutions are to clearly compartmentalize roles with an effort toward not letting one role inter- fere with another or to try to become better organized, more efficient, and a "superwoman" (Hall, 1972). The latter choice, to become superwoman, has been highly touted in the media but is not a viable solution for the majority of women. It sets impossible standards for women and leads to feelings of failure that are not justified. This choice also leaves the whole role conflict and overload problem on women's shoulders.

Men do not have to make such choices, at least they did not in the past. As men in general take on more family responsibilities, some men too may opt for a childless or single life in order to devote more time to work.

While it is possible to discuss integrating work and family life in general, the general discussion does not cover all possible work-family groups. There are some unique problems and issues faced by particular groups. Based on the belief that integration of work and family in general is too broad to cover all specific cases (Gutek, Nakamura, and Nieva, 1980), we focus on two specific groups: dual career couples and single parents.

Dual Career Couples

Dual career couples have special problems integrating work and family life, as noted by both organizational psychologists (for example, Hall and Hall, 1978) and family psychologists (for example, Rapoport and Rapoport, 1978). A dual career couple is usually defined as two people who are involved in a permanent relationship and who are each involved in a full-time career. A dual career couple can be contrasted with a two-worker couple or two-job family in which both people are employed but not in careers that require development, persistence, and nurturance. Sometimes one or both of the persons are in a "two-person" career (Papanek, 1973); that is, a career that is so time-consuming that both husband and wife are expected to make contributions. Examples are minister, corporate executive, elected official, or ambassador. If one or both spouses are in a two-person career, they will need to work especially hard to coordinate their two careers with their family life.

Among the problems faced by the dual career couple is the kind of careers they wish. If they want to minimize the friction or competition between work and family, they might wish to share a job, as some Norwegian couples have done (Gronseth, 1978). Job sharing has also been promoted in the United States on the West Coast (Arkin and Dobrofsky, 1978). Yet this option is clearly an unusual form of combining work and family and not easily obtained. Even if couples can find a job to share, or find someone else willing to share a job and an employer willing to hire two people for one job, they face problems of living on one salary, advancing in a career, and living in a world that expects husbands to work full time. Job sharing may not be viewed as unconventional, of course, as the couples who live separately and commute on weekends or less often, depending on the distance between their jobs (see Farris, 1978), or even couples who choose to live apart for periods of time for attending a training program, going to school, taking a short-term assignment, or just organizing their lives (Douvan and Pleck, 1978).

More usual is for the two people each to pursue a career while living in the same home and dividing, in some way deemed equitable to both parties, the housekeeping and childrearing chores. Problems here are finding a job and dealing with problems of the wife being more successful.

In general, three results are clear in the literature on finding jobs for dual career couples. First, both spouses' careers are affected by the other's career (Bryson et al., 1976). Men as well as women usually have to pass up a job offer or accept a less desirable job in the interest of preserving the relationship. The second finding is that women's careers are affected more than men's are. That is, women more often than men accept a less desirable job or go without a job for a while or do not accept an attractive job offer in another location in the interest of maintaining the relationship with their husbands.

Wallston and her colleagues (Wallston, Foster, and Berger, 1978; Berger, Foster, and Wallston, 1978; Foster, Wallston, and Berger, 1980) have conducted research on the role of having a feminist orientation on strategies for finding jobs for dual career spouses. They hypothesized that a feminist orientation on the part of both spouses would result in more egalitarian decisions. They found that feminist orientation was a predictor for the initial decision to look for a job (for example, we will accept the best offer between us), although strength of career orientation was a more important factor. Furthermore, feminist orientation was not a predictor of final decision. Their results constitute the third well-documented finding. The constraints of the labor force and work environment overpower the initial decision strategies of the spouses. Husbands are more likely to be offered good jobs than wives; they are also offered higher salaries and wives feel more responsible for childcare. These pressures combine to induce couples to make traditional career choices. Foster et al. (1980) found that 60 percent of women and 52 percent of men in their study made traditional career choices.

Hall and Hall (1978) noted that there are different problems for the dual career couple job hunting at the beginning of the career than at midcareer. For example, in the early stages of their careers, both people may be reluctant to approach an organization as a "package," but when both become established in their careers, they are less reluctant to do so. Finding a job is also more problematic in the beginning because both people are highly career committed and may not have developed a strong commitment to the relationship. They may also have little experience in coping with conflict and have little control over what is available in the job market.

Another problem of dual career couples is handling the wife's success. Since men are expected to be as or more successful than their wives, a wife's success can lead to problems in the relationship. It is quite possible that between two career-committed spouses any dramatic difference in success can lead to marital problems. Traditionally, the wife's success has been viewed as more problematic than the husband's. Safilios-Rothschild and Dijkers (1978) discussed the problem in the case of Greek couples. They found that women who are successful often continue in a very subservient position within the marriage. Thus the husband's masculinity is less threatened. They also suggested that this effect may be less pronounced where financial hardship is not a problem and where the marriage is based on an "interpersonal perspective" that allows both partners a search for self-realization. In a national sample survey, Richardson (1975) found that wives having higher occupational prestige than husbands was not related to lower marital satisfaction. Richardson suggested that such conflicts are resolved in the dating stage or the couple breaks up. It is also possible that marriages split up because of differential occupational prestige and the intact marriages consist of husbands who do not find wives' success a threat.

Single Parents

Single parents must combine the roles of worker and parent by themselves. This category is almost exclusively female, although there is a good deal of interest and attention drawn to fathers who have custody of their children. Women who are single parents, unlike career couples, do not have the problem of finding two jobs nor of negotiating differential success. Their problems are often economic (for example, inadequate incomes to provide for the family [Corcoran, 1979]) and psychological (for example, inadequate social support to handle all the problems of work and parent roles [Giele, 1978]). Single parents do not prepare for their roles in the way dual career couples do because people do not aspire to become single parents. It is a status one acquires. Single parents, therefore, are often ill-prepared to assume the roles of solo parent and solo worker. Because they are ill-prepared, they may be exploited on the job, being assigned the worst jobs or being sexually harassed at work. Their economic vulnerability prevents them from leaving the job. Single parents report lower job satisfaction than other working women (Gutek and Hotchkiss, 1978). Unsatisfying, poorly paying work combined with all the childrearing and housekeeping chores lead to low life satisfaction (Campbell, Converse, and Rodgers, 1976) and role overload.

Like dual career couples, single parents may face different work-family conflicts at different stages of being a single parent. Many single parents remarry, often within two years. Their solution to the conflicts is to return to a less conflicted situation — marriage. In fact, Ross and Sawhill's (1975) study of single parents is called "Time of Transition" because they view single parenthood as a transitory state. Nevertheless, the problems of adjusting to divorce, learning job skills, adjusting to the work environment, and the like may diminish as the woman acquires the competencies needed for the single parent role. She may then feel satisfied with her ability to handle both roles alone. Because having a career and supporting a family increase feelings of competence and well-being (Barnett and Baruch, 1979), the single parent adjusted to the single parent role may have a strong sense of self-realization and accomplishment.

SUMMARY

Because work and family often make simultaneous demands on women, understanding the way women behave at work depends on their situation of their family environment. The mere fact that parental and housekeeping responsibilities are expected to intrude on their work life means that women will have a different work experience than men, who do not anticipate such an intrusion into their work responsibilities. The most general effect of the interdependence of work and family roles for women is the existence of a sex-segregated labor force. Jobs that are dominated by women are extensions of their wife and mother roles and often exacerbate the conflict between the two spheres of life rather than reduce it. In addition, the interdependence of the two roles and the expectation that family role is the most important of the two also affect the work experiences that women will have.

Women's employment also affects her family situation, overloading her with work, but also increasing her self-confidence, feelings of independence, power in the marital relationship, and, under some circumstances, her marital satisfaction as well. People vary in the level to which they accommodate their jobs to their family lives. Dual career couples, in particular, face the problem of accommodating each career to their relationship without either of them sacrificing their career commitment. The realities of the labor market and current society often mean that they ultimately make rather traditional decisions. Single parents have other concerns around earning enough money and finding a flexible enough schedule to fulfill all the parental responsibilities to the children.

Having recognized the influence of family experiences on work experiences of women, we now turn to some of the particular kinds of experiences women have at work.

5
INTEGRATING WOMEN
INTO THE WORKPLACE

Although women have always been present in the workplace, they have tended to occupy a different occupational world than that in which men live. As we noted previously, women have been confined to a few overcrowded spheres. Women's work occupies the bottom of the occupational wage and prestige ladders and even within those rungs, women rarely occupy positions of authority.

When women try to function outside of the positions deemed appropriate for them, they confront problems typical of those befalling any newcomer desiring entry into an established setting — problems of acceptance, perceptions of deviance and role conflicts, confusion regarding appropriate and effective rules of behavior, and obstacles to mobility within the situation. Like other newcomers, expectations for their behavior in the work context are shaped greatly by rules attached to the other statuses they possess.

Even for newcomers who possess characteristics similar to those of the majority membership, the acceptance or "breaking-in" period can be difficult. Newcomers must be able to create a role at work that simultaneously satisfies the demands of the work organization, of their work peers and supervisors, and of themselves. While mastery of the technical demands of the job is an essential task for the newcomer, it is often the simple part of the breaking-in period.

Integration into the culture of the workplace is more complicated. It involves learning the subtleties in the organization's culture and climate, including necessary "adaptive skills" (Fine, 1967) — the new values, attitudes, and self-images most likely to lead to organizational rewards — often without the benefit of formal organizational assistance. These adaptive skills are learned in interpersonal interactions with the veterans in the work setting (Schein, 1971) and informally arranged systems of apprenticeship in which a veteran becomes responsible for the fate of a new employee. Thus, "an individual learns the behavior appropriate to his position in the group, through interaction with others who hold normative beliefs about what his role should be and who reward and punish him for correct or incorrect actions" (Brim, 1966, p. 9).

For a woman entering into previously male domains this process can be extremely problematic, since her mere presence — regardless of her behavior — is the source of difficulty (Harragan, 1977). Her male peers resent her very presence, which threatens the established friendship and pecking order of the male work environment (Wolman and Frank, 1975), and violates "hunting-group" norms (see Tiger, 1972) of toughness and nonemotionality. The woman is alone in a male world. She is often lost, unable to use her experience as a guide for behavior in the face of a male turf that defines and interprets rules in ways that do not tally with her experience. Because she is different, she tends to be isolated, unable to use her peers to help her understand the norms and requirements of a world that is new to her.

THE ROLE OF INFORMAL NETWORKS

Informal interactions with one's peers and superiors are critical to success at work because so much of the true requirements of the work situation are not codified into formal rules and regulations. The importance of these interactions transcends the particulars of the work setting. In bureaucracies, professional associations, and the assembly line alike, informal work groups heavily influence what and how things are done.

The Peer Network

Many authors have discussed the exclusion of women from the social networks of the workplace. The "old boy network," the "white male club," and the "stag effect" are among the labels invoked to describe such exclusion (Bernard, 1964; Terry, 1974). Exclusion can come about as a result of overt ridicule and social rejection. For example, Rossi (1970a) quotes a grade school teacher who started out in an architectural firm: "I never wanted to teach grade school children, which I am doing now. But I found so much prejudice and resentment against me in my job in an architectural firm, where the men refused to take me seriously and I couldn't take it." Such overt ridicule, however, is becoming increasingly socially unacceptable, and exclusion is usually the result of much more subtle processes.

In fact, overt ridicule and other forms of active exclusion are seldom necessary for the exclusion of women. Kanter (1977a & b) suggests that the entry of a new type of member into a group becomes the occasion of emphasizing the characteristics of the group that differ from those of the new member. In a study of one of Fortune 500's firms, Kanter found that in the presence of women, men highlighted what they could do, *as men*, in contrast to women. Compared to instances in which only men were present, there were increases in sexual innuendos, off-color jokes, and prowess-oriented "war stories." The men would preface such conversation with apologies addressed to the women — before invariably going ahead. Kanter interprets such occurrences as ways of making clear the expected cultural rules under which women were to be allowed to interact with the group.

As one consequence, oftentimes women withdraw from situations that they anticipate might be uncomfortable. Bernard (1964), for example, found that the women scientists she surveyed were less aggressive than men in actively seeking formal communication, even by mail, although they took advantage of opportunities, when they were offered to them, as much as the men did. Epstein (1970b) found that some of the women lawyers she studied avoided joining colleagues at lunch. She quotes one: "Sometimes the natural thing to do would be to join an associate and client at lunch if you were a man, and you feel, 'Well, I'd better not. It might be awkward for them. They might want to talk about something and might feel constrained' " (p. 176).

When women do not exclude themselves, men may exclude them. Certain activities are moved away from public settings to which everyone has access to more private ones from which they can be excluded — the bar, the men's room, the golf course, and private gatherings. When this happens, peer interaction is limited to the official occasions and meetings held at work, where only formally acceptable news and opinions are expressed for the public record.

Exclusion from such opportunities for informal interaction implies exclusion from settings where much information is shared and decisions are made. Informal networks are the repositories for much valuable information. Crucial trade secrets are not accessible to newcomers until they are accepted (Becker and Strauss, 1956). Information about unofficially recognized organizational events is often unavailable through formal communication and is available only through these networks. Because women are frequently left out or leave themselves out of these informal sites for negotiation, they can be astonished at the apparent speed by which some formal decisions are reached at the conference table, failing to understand that these formal sessions are merely charades to play out formal rituals after the heart of the matter has already been established.

In many cases, inclusion in informal networks is necessary to career success. Individuals who aspire to mobility within their work organizations must be able to utilize their peer networks for exchange of information and other favors. Informal linkages become increasingly important at higher levels in the organization, where information sharing and decision making are greatly entwined with the social networks. Individual performers who cannot or do not develop the capacity to build the connections and alliances necessary for success at higher-level jobs may find themselves stagnated at a prematurely low career plateau. The importance of acceptance is highly accentuated in many professions where the informal networks carry within them much of the new knowledge in the process of formulation. Bernard (1964) cites Sir Alfred Egerton on this point: "Of the total information extant, only part is in the literature. Much of it is stored in the many brains of scientists and technologists. We are as dependent on biological storage as on mechanical or library storage" (p. 303).

Exclusion from the informal networks also results in women's isolation in the workplace. They cannot associate with the men who are their peers and superiors, yet they cannot be too closely identified with the women in subordinate and traditionally female positions. In fact, the price of even peripheral inclusion by the dominant male group often includes the willingness to turn against one's own, to ignore disparaging remarks made about women in general, and even to contribute one's own comments that are derogatory to them. Women operating outside their traditional roles are encouraged to think of themselves as exceptions superior to their general class. Women who identify with males and denigrate other females who aspire to positions similar to those they occupy have been labeled "Queen Bees" (Staines et al., 1973).

The Protégé System

The protégé or mentor system is a special case of the general social networks through which individuals get assimilated into the system. A promising young man is taken under the wing of an individual higher up, to be trained, developed, and given special advice, inside information, critical experiences, and social status by association with his mentors (Becker and Strauss, 1956; Epstein, 1970a & b; Wells, 1973). The practice is a carryover from medieval days, when a beginner in a craft was apprenticed to a master craftsman. The protégé system has its special value in cases where learning the appropriate values at work is as important as learning the tasks (Caplow, 1964).

In addition to providing access to information and contacts, the sponsor often plays the important function of role-model to the protégé, providing crucial guidance on how to behave in a variety of situations, what attitudes are important, and what aspirations to form. The mentor, or "coach," sees to it that the recruit is properly groomed and advised or cared for in the "breaking-in" period, guiding the learner along a series of noninstitutionalized steps leading to full organizational membership (Strauss, 1968). Sponsors also provide means to bypass the hierarchy to short-circuit official procedures by informal interaction.

Women are rarely sponsored in this manner (Epstein, 1970a & b). While many potential mentors would be happy to have a woman assistant, the mentor (usually male) often finds it difficult to accept her as his protégé — that is, someone who would most likely be his successor and potential peer. Often the mentor makes assumptions about her relative lack of career commitment and drive that may produce reluctance to engage in a long-term professional involvement (Epstein, 1970a & b). For a sponsor, a protégé gives a sense of continuity of work and assurance that the protégé will build on the foundation already laid. A woman who is presumed to have an unreliable career commitment cannot be depended upon for this.

In addition, many women are not as sensitive as their male counterparts to the need to link themselves with someone in the organization who could teach and protect them and further their progress in the workplace. Many women, such as the managers studied by Hennig and Jardim (1977), assume that their superior competence and technical ability are the true determinants of advancement, and that for excellent performance, they will be noticed and rewarded by their superiors. They wait to be chosen, relying on beliefs about the effectiveness of the formal structure and the way things ought to be. For example, Schreiber (1979) found the biggest worry of women entering into previously all-male technical jobs was whether or not they would be able to do the job. Many of their male counterparts, in contrast, are concerned with informal ties of loyalty and dependence, which can make the critical difference in an employee's life and movement at work.

There are exceptions, however. While it is usually difficult for most women to obtain the sponsorship of critical individuals at work, an occasional one does come under the protective wing of an influential sponsor. Often the woman possesses characteristics culturally associated with the dominant male group, and it is this that brings her to the attention of the sponsor (Laws, 1975). She is then brought into the male network to some extent, where she is provided attention, rewards, and credentials that are not available to other women. Thus she assumes the role of the *token*, and she becomes increasingly different from the rest of the women in the workplace.

The relationship between the sponsor and the token provides benefits for both of them that help to cement the relationship. The woman token is offered access and power that is withheld from the majority. She is provided an avenue for potentially influencing the course of events and exercising her talents and abilities (Rich, 1979). The cost of this special treatment is usually an increased distance from the wider female condition and an increased identification with the dominant male group. The token is usually willing to pay this price.

Tokenism has even greater advantages for the sponsor. Tokenism serves to salve the sponsor's conscience. It allows him to maintain a progressive and egalitarian self-image, while doing little to alter conditions substantially for the subordinate female class. It gives the appearance of providing access to recognition and reward to any truly deserving woman, while actually operating to maintain the traditionally discriminatory reward system. By its very nature, tokenism restricts the number of people from the nondominant group who will be allowed inclusion, and severely limits the system they enter (Laws, 1975). These restrictions, which distinguish the token from the true protégé, are not overt. In most cases, they are veiled by the promise of general mobility advertised by the sponsor-token relationship.

ROLE PROBLEMS

Women who defy the boundaries traditionally defined for them at work tend to experience difficulties in assessing how to behave on the job. Because they are new, general rules for their behavior have not yet been established firmly. Most of the rules concerning male-female interaction have been formulated solely for social-sexual behavior. Often there are competing norms simultaneously defining the "right" way to be and all too often, patterns that characterize women's more traditional and familiar roles are inappropriately carried over to the work context.

Role Conflict and Ambiguity

Women employees in a male setting face the basic challenge of finding a comfortable fit between the often disparate demands of their sex roles and their work roles. Performing successfully in the female sex role and in the work role can be seen as a mutually exclusive, zero-sum game. If a woman is successful at work, she becomes, almost by definition, less successful at being a woman. Thus women become subject to the "damned if you do, damned if you don't" syndrome experienced by people with negatively evaluated statuses (Merton, 1957, p. 426). In her study of female lawyers, for example, Epstein (1968) described complaints by opposing male lawyers that women attorneys often win by using feminine "wiles"; other women lawyers were told that because they did not use "wiles," they were masculine.

The expression of assertiveness, a trait that is considered to be out of character for the female role, is another difficult issue for women. A woman typically runs the risk of alienating her male environment if she comes on too strong and of being totally ignored and suppressed if she comes on too weak. In their study of women in high-level positions, Fogarty et al. (1971) quote a senior woman in a large international organization on the pitfalls awaiting women in industry.

> I think that people in authority can be either authoritarian or permissive, and the authoritarian line doesn't go well with women. Men have an easier approach — but authority tends to produce the extremes in women. They find it difficult to be relaxed. Women have had to fight so hard that they tend to be less relaxed, more anxious, more rigid (p. 47).

The expression of the set of behaviors that have come to be called "femininity" is also a problematical area. Fogarty et al. (1971) suggest that women had better chances of being accepted in the male world of work if they did not underplay their femininity. Along the same lines, other researchers (for example, Kanter, 1977a & b) have found that behaviors that characterize the dominant male culture — for example, swearing, telling dirty jokes — are not seen as acceptable behaviors for women.

On almost all occasions when conflicts between the woman's sex role and work role occur, it seems that her sex status becomes excessively salient, to the consequent underemphasis of her occupational status. In this way, women share similar fates with others who possess statuses (for example, age or race) that have been defined as inappropriate to the occupational status (Epstein, 1970b). Thus a woman worker soon learns that if she steps outside of the few areas that have been defined as appropriate to her sex, she will find herself walking on a tightrope where signals for appropriate behavior are ambiguous and often contradictory. In contrast, for individuals with the appropriate statuses, the path to success is clear — the messages on how to move from being a recruit to a full member are direct, instructive, and motivating.

The results of experimental studies concerning conformity (for example, Hollander, 1958; Nord, 1969; Wiggins, Dill, and Schwartz, 1965) are relevant to the general question of deviance from prescribed behaviors appropriate to one's sex role. These studies show that one *earns* "idiosyncracy credits," or the right to violate certain norms, by first exhibiting conformity to the group. The basic notion is that of an even exchange between one's "credits" of competence and conformity and one's "debits" of rule violation. Because a woman working in a male environment is in violation of tradition, she is expected to contribute much more by way of conformity to other role prescriptions in order to be "allowed" to function in that environment. This exchange notion also suggests that women may be able to "bank" their credits, such that they suffer less from norm violation after some time in a group. Wahrman and Pugh's (1974) experimental study of the effects of sex on nonconformity shows support for this contention. They found that the earlier a female subject exhibited nonconformity, the less influence she had over her male partner and also the more pleased he was to be rid of her. In contrast, nonconformity enhanced the influence and desirability of male subjects.

The Spill Over of the Female Role into the Workplace

Interactions between men and women may be simplified by the carry over of other gender-based roles into the workplace. One such aspect of the female role has been called the "stroking" function by Bernard (1972). In society at large, women are expected to be the suppliers of socioemotional support rather than the direct achievers. Epstein (1976) suggests that the spill over of the female helping role into the occupational setting operates to keep women in peripheral positions — women who have talent and training are often pushed into sex-role niches where, although they are "allowed" to contribute, their work is not identified as their own. Women frequently become fixed in sex-role associated help and service roles and do not move on to independent command roles. Schrank and Riley (1976) call this phenomenon the "dependency status" characterizing many women's jobs. In such jobs, performance is assessed on the assistance extended to another rather than on the demonstration of skills that suggest a capacity to assume a higher ranking job. Although this apprentice role is typical for men, too, for them the apprentice phase is only one status in a sequence leading to a ranking status position (the protégé system), whereas for women the apprentice status is often the end of the line. The positioning of women into helper roles acts to absorb them into the established structure, thus benefiting from their contributions without having to pay in rank, salary, and recognition.

Further, by performing the stroking function, women are disqualified from activities that require fighting, competing, and challenging. Women are excluded from normal group processes such as competition for leadership, jockeying for power, and the establishment of a pecking order. When they try to become a regular group member and to compete fully for status, they run the risk of being labeled bitchy or manipulative (Wolman and Frank, 1975).*

Other types of role spill over are found in interaction between men and women at work. A common one is the assignment of women to the role of prizes in the competition among men. Although functioning in this role may ensure attention from the men in the group, it may arouse tensions among the competitors and thus, indirectly, may be a source of resentment among the men. Needless to say, the type of attention obtained in this role is not that which focuses on the woman's abilities or achievements. Yet another familiar role is that of the helpless female, called the "pet" (Kanter, 1977b), whom the men could protect (especially if she was also attractive) and whose shows of competence receive special mention because of their unexpected nature.

The spill over of the female role into the work situation is usually neither relevant nor helpful to the task at hand. Yet women accept it as the price for inclusion, and the roles are comfortable ones, familiar to the women since early childhood. On the support function Epstein (1976) says, "Quite on the contrary to feeling exploited, women are grateful to have their ideas noted, and indeed used, in a world where they expect their statements to be glossed over, their comments to go unheard and their contributions to be downgraded" (p. 190).

---

*It is not clear to what extent the noncompetitive styles that women show in groups (for example, Borah, 1963; Vinacke, 1959; Shomer et al., 1966) can be interpreted as female behavioral preferences or as results of group pressures as the Wolman and Frank study would suggest. Aries (1976) found that male groups tended to focus much more on dominance issues than women's groups.

Even the roles of sex object or helpless female may provide the only means to secure some kind of attention from the power-holders at work.

Sexual Roles at Work

Women are not alone in having role-related problems in their unaccustomed positions. Men, too, have problems with the spill over of other aspects of the female role into the work situation. In particular, the fear of sexuality invading the workplace is a potent factor blocking the integration of women. That the opportunity for sexuality on the job emerges so frequently as an argument against the entry of women is somewhat surprising, given the fact that women have been around most work settings, albeit in peripheral roles. Nevertheless, anecdotes about resistance to female presence in traditionally male environments abound in the popular press. For example, stories on the sex-integration of the military forces are often characterized by accounts of social-sexual liaisons between the men and women that threaten the hierarchical order of the system. The introduction of women into other occupations such as truck driving brings visions of men running off with the women with whom they work.

The sexuality that women bring with them is feared because of its potential to disrupt established relations between colleagues at work, of stirring up sexual rivalry among the men, or of interfering with their personal relationships. In his research on sexual relationships of couples who work together, Quinn (1977) noted that more negative consequences were reported than positive consequences. The typical relationship involved a male in a superior position and a female in a subordinate position. The general negative consequences observed were a tendency for the man to be distracted from his work; take long lunch hours, breaks, and business trips; and delegate too much responsibility to the woman involved. The woman was perceived as obtaining increasing amounts of confidential information, one source of power, as well as an increase in real power unwarranted by her organizational position. A sexual liaison is viewed as one way a woman may gain power in an organization. Thus, the woman is viewed as temptress and disruptor, with the emphasis not on men's difficulty in adapting to women at work but rather women's disruption of the male work arena.

While the popular concern has been with women who exploit their sexuality to gain favoritism or power, a new concern has recently emerged. Men who exploit women's sexuality often engage in, or set the stage for, sexual harassment, a term popularized by Farley (1978) and MacKinnon (1979).

As it is most narrowly defined, sexual harassment occurs when a woman is expected to engage in sexual activity in order to get or keep a job, to be promoted, or acquire a desirable job, or to avoid being fired or put in an undesirable job. Between 85 and 90 percent of working people recently surveyed on the West Coast define such behavior as sexual harassment (Gutek et al.,

1980). Farley (1978), however, defines sexual harassment more broadly, to include all unwanted sexual behaviors or comments. It occurs when a woman's sex role overshadows her work role in the eyes of male supervisors, peers, customers, or clients; her work receives less attention than her gender. It occurs when she feels no control over the situation, when she is not interested in the initiator, and when her job depends on sexual acquiescence. Recent regulations of the Equal Employment Opportunity Commission (EEOC) have adapted this broad definition of sexual harassment (Reeves, 1980). The West Coast worker survey (Gutek et al., 1980) showed that many people concur with this expanded definition. The survey showed that 27 percent of women and 11 percent of men considered positive comments of a sexual nature to be sexual harassment and 63 percent of women and 48 percent of men considered negative comments of a sexual nature to be sexual harassment (Gutek et al., 1980).

There appears to be no consensus on the set of behaviors that define sexual harassment. Another approach to definition was taken by the recent EEOC regulations, which suggested that effect on recipient was an important criteria by which sexual behavior is labelled as harassment. Behaviors are considered as harassment if they negatively affect the work fate or performance of the employee. Estimates of the occurrence of sexual harassment defined this way may vary from almost nonexistent to over 90 percent of women having experienced it at some time, but data to date suggest that 10 to 15 percent of women have quit a job because of sexual harassment (Gutek et al., 1980). Benson and Thomson (1980) argue that sexual harassment has both short-term and long-term effects on women. In the short term, women adopt a strategy of pragmatic avoidance, keeping away from situations where they might encounter harassment, even though the contact may be desirable for one's job. Women also suffer a loss in self-confidence and disillusionment with male colleagues and supervisors. Both of these effects inhibit the integration of women at work. In the long term, career commitment in women is lowered and gender inequality is reinforced in the workplace. Benson and Thomson's (1980) analysis suggests also that sexual harassment constitutes an abuse of power; it is an attempt to devalue a worker by emphasizing her sexuality and ignoring her work role. In its more extreme forms, sexual harassment is an indication of misogyny or a pathological need for power.

Although women are not necessarily the only objects of sexual harassment, they are much more likely to be victims than men (Gutek et al., 1980). The typical structure of sexual relationships makes it likely that men act as the initiators, rather than recipients, of sexual contact. In addition, males are more likely to be in positions of authority and dominance and women easily fall into "ingratiating, flattering and deferential manner which projects sexual compliance" (MacKinnon, 1979, p. 22). The stereotypical case of sexual harassment involves a male supervisor and a female subordinate (Farley, 1978; Benson and Thomson, 1979), although a customer or coworker on whom one depends can also exert unwanted pressure toward sexual activity.

It is clear that the effects of placing sexuality over work role are overwhelmingly negative, with respect to integrating women into the workplace. Men's fears that women will use feminine wiles to seduce male employees reduce the probability that women will be accepted into the work group. Men may retaliate against women's invasion of traditionally male arenas in the form of sexual harassment. Harassment further erodes the trust and informality that facilitate women's integration.

Margaret Mead (1978) suggested that a work taboo, similar to an incest taboo, is needed before real integration of the sexes at work will come about. However unlikely that idea is to become reality, it has merit. Potential problems in implementing it, however, can be foreseen. Many women and men view work as a setting for meeting potential sexual partners (Schriesheim, 1980). When work absorbs a great deal of time and energy, or, conversely, when work is extremely boring and monotonous, there may be increased incentive to use the workplace for friendship and sexual purposes (Gutek and Nakamura, 1981).

An alternative to placing a total taboo on sexuality at work is the development of conditions that eliminate only its negative aspects for women. One factor that is important in working toward this end is achieving clearer understanding of sex roles and work roles and making behavior more situation-appropriate. Gutek and Nakamura (1981) suggest that separation of the two roles is more likely when there are balanced sex ratios within job categories, since single-sex jobs tend to perpetuate sex-role behaviors. Further, this separation would be facilitated by an organizational climate that restricts the extent to which sexuality — in the form of sexual jokes and comments, sexually revealing clothing, or the encouragement of exaggerated "masculine" (particularly in terms of a "macho" image) or "feminine" (particularly in terms of helplessness, vulnerability, and subservient flattery toward males) behavior — is emphasized or tolerated, and that strongly discourages the use of organizational resources, rewards, and punishments to further all sorts of personal aims, including sexual.

THE EFFECTS OF SEX RATIOS

As long as women are in the minority within the particular context of their workplace, they will tend to be isolated from and in conflict with their male colleagues. In this, as in other situations, it is difficult to separate the effects of being deviant from the effects of being female. Based on her study of one of the Fortune 500 firms, Kanter (1977a & b) suggests that the relative number of men and women in the work setting is a critical factor in determining interactions and processes that take place in groups composed of different types of people.

One major effect is visibility. Outside of their traditional positions in the workplace, women are highly visible. Their presence is immediately noted, although this does not mean that their achievements are similarly prominent, since the attention directed at them arises from their deviant characteristic – their gender. As Kanter (1977a & b) notes, male colleagues would tend to forget information about a woman's credentials and expertise, while remembering her dress style and appearance.

Experimental support for the importance of solo status in how one is perceived has been found by Taylor and her colleagues (1978). College students who watched slides of a group discussion in which racial composition was varied (that is, six white men, three blacks and three whites, or five whites and one black) remembered more about the solo black and noted the solo black as making more of an impression than any other group member. A related study using mixed sex groups also found that tokens, whether male or female, were regarded as more prominent on a variety of dimensions than a comparable individual in a more sex-balanced group. Further, Taylor and her colleagues found that solo status tended to produce more extreme evaluations, in both positive and negative directions. Thus they concur with Kanter's conclusion that imbalanced membership results in visibility for the solo. Constructive, intelligent behavior would tend to be more noticeable in a solo, as would negative, stupid, or mistaken behavior.

Visibility has built-in performance pressures. In the limelight, mistakes are more evident and less forgivable. Visibility results in different rules being applied to women and men. Thus, women have to be more careful to avoid mistakes or even the appearance of negative attitudes or behavior. Additional performance pressures stem from the fact that women are burdened with representing their category, not just themselves. Token women are asked to speak for the "women's point of view," and their acts are interpreted in terms of how well women in general would do in this new role.

Performance pressures also emerge in contradictory forms. Although women have to do well for themselves and "for all women," they may not do *too* well. Visibility carries with it the possibilities of backlash. As the achievements of a few are greeted with exaggerated publicity, male fears of being bypassed or of being humiliated by a "mere woman" are aroused. Backlash may also manifest itself in suspicion about the legitimacy of any of the achievements or qualifications of the visible female, particularly where there are official (though not necessarily real) goals to achieve greater equity in the distribution of rewards. Women who are hired through affirmative action programs must face the suspicion that they were hired only because they are women and that more qualified men were available but passed over. This is not necessarily true, of course, but the affirmative action employee's efforts and accomplishments may be ignored because she lacks legitimate claim to the job. The result is a high performance pressure atmosphere that many women (and men) would prefer to avoid. As a result, women sometimes decline affirmative action positions when that is feasible.

In addition to the visibility effect, Kanter also suggests two other effects of imbalanced sex ratios — polarization and assimilation. Polarization is the exaggeration of differences between members of the dominant group and the out-group and of the similarities within the dominant group. Such effects have received consistent support from experimental studies, which show that when objects have been categorized into groups, the perceiver tends to overestimate the degree of similarity among members of a group and to overestimate the degree of dissimilarity between groups (Hamilton, 1976).

Often it is only the confrontation with individuals who are "different" from the dominant group that makes dominant group members self-conscious of their own culture and norms. This self-awareness is often uncomfortable for people who prefer to operate without the strain of habitual self-examination. However, this new awakening is also used to assert in-group solidarity so that the newcomer becomes the means for underlining the majority culture. In-group male behavior such as the expression of off-color jokes or tales of sporting prowess are exaggerated to delineate the "rules of the game" to the newcomer, rules that then become focal to her inclusion as one of the group. Under these conditions, women would have the choice of accommodating to male interests, language, and style, or to remain isolated, since there would be too few others to begin to develop a different "counterculture."

The third outcome of imbalanced sex ratios suggested by Kanter is assimilation — the distortion of individual characteristics to fit preexisting stereotypes about their category as a group. Assimilation is "statistical prejudice," which tends to caricature newcomers in ways that allow dominant group members to use known modes of action, for example, the traditional ways men treat women. Women professionals are familiar with efforts to treat them as though they were fragile and helpless or (in what appears to be a strongly contradictory perspective) as though their sole function was to be a service provider or support to their male colleagues. The phenomenon of assimilation is the same as that of role spill over previously discussed.

PRESSURES TOWARD SOCIAL HOMOGENEITY

The integration of women into the workplace is heavily influenced by pressure toward homogeneity, and certainly pressure toward social homogeneity is a factor that characterizes a wide range of situations, including many that are work related. Early studies of the workplace (for example, Roethlisberger and Dickson, 1939) revealed that workers set production norms for the group and violators were punished. Positive feelings, as well as organizational rewards such as pay and promotion, have been found to be heavily influenced by social homogeneity (Nieva, 1976).

Pressure toward homogeneity and similarity exist because they facilitate interactions in the interpersonal environment (Byrne, 1971). Social similarity makes one's environment more predictable and understandable, because the relevant others think, act, or look like one's self. The fact that others see the world as one does provides reinforcement and validation of one's hold on reality. In addition, in interacting with similar others, it is usually relatively safe to expect that the parties will like each other and thus be able to work out problems together (Byrne and Griffitt, 1969).

These pressures toward homogeneity tend to make the acceptance of female newcomers problematic. Women are seen as possessing different values, orientations, and experiences from the dominant male group. Thus they are regarded as unreliable, worthy of trust only in thoroughly subordinate positions (Lorber, 1975), and unacceptable as regular members of the group. Kanter (1977a) suggests that the pressure for similarity rises with increasing situational uncertainty. The problem of integration thus becomes more difficult as one progresses up the organizational hierarchy, where procedures are less specified, the need to communicate accurately and rapidly is magnified, and there is increasing dependence on human trust and discretion. Under such circumstances, the importance of similarities is heightened, as people require assurance that others on whom they have to depend share their values and perspectives.

In support of this argument a study of over 600 employees showed that the effects of similarity on subordinate rewards were significantly weaker for individuals with high-certainty jobs than for those with low-certainty jobs (Nieva, 1976). The same study showed that similarities between the supervisor and subordinates tended to be more critical for the favorability ratings received by female employees compared to those received by males, and that the effects of similarity were stronger when the supervisor and subordinate were of different sexes than when they were of the same sex. In general these findings support the argument that homogeneity on a variety of dimensions becomes increasingly important in conditions of ambiguity and uncertainty. Females are relatively novel in many situations, and their appearance introduces a great deal of discomfort and confusion regarding appropriate actions, values, and behaviors. The discomfort provoked by the lack of clarity in the situation stimulates greater dependence on the traits that are familiar and known. The importance of similarity to the favorability of ratings received by women and different-sex subordinates is consistent with the well-established finding that pressures toward conformity increase with increases in discrepancy (Festinger, 1952). A difference in gender is a very clear indication of a discrepancy that carries along with it implications for other discrepancies. Thus, for females and other deviants at work, it appears to be particularly critical to be able to assure the dominant group of similarity and loyalty to them.

DILEMMA OF THE FEMALE NEWCOMER

The female newcomer is, by definition, an anomaly in her work context. Her female status and the scarcity of others like her make her deviant, causing her internal pressures and creating ambiguity for the members of the establishment. Her position is characterized by ambivalence, which often results in her isolation.

Hughes (1944) and Kanter (1977a) neatly summarize the dilemmas of the token or newcomer with incongruent statuses. Newcomers are symbols of their category, yet exceptions to it — thus they are different, individual, and often alone, yet they are treated in terms of stereotypes and generalities. Although they are highly visible, "on stage," they are excluded from the "backstage" where the scripts are set. They cause disruption of interactions because they are few, leading to the conclusion that their number must not increase for the sake of the workplace, yet it is their scarcity that causes the disruption. Conflicting expectations are created for them — their female role often clashes with their work role; they are under pressure to perform, but not to outdo their male colleagues for fear of backlash; they are rewarded for being visible when it suits the establishment to have a symbol for public consumption, while being expected to blend in and become invisible among the dominant group members.

The pressures that affect female newcomers occur around people of any category who find few of their kind among others of a different type. They exist because the intrusion of unfamiliar elements into the work context creates uncertainty and disturbs its established and commonly held rules of order. In the face of the new type of member, pressures toward certainty and homogeneity cause distress both to the newcomer and to the in-group, creating a context in which the solution to discomfort is likely to be the continued or increased exclusion of the category perceived as the cause of distress. Thus without external intervention, imbalance is a self-perpetuating system.

6
THE EVALUATION OF
WOMEN'S PERFORMANCE

Among the critical processes affecting the fate of women in work organizations are the evaluation and reward allocation processes. Evaluation is a ubiquitous part of organizational life. Not only do organizations have formal policies and procedures concerning formal evaluations, but informal judgments are made constantly by superiors and peers regarding employee abilities, accomplishments, and potential. For both organization and employee, these are critical processes. They provide data about what is going on both to the formal organization and the individual employee (Porter, Lawler, and Hackman, 1975) and insure that valued behaviors are perpetuated within the system. Evaluation is critical to the employee since decisions regarding how tasks are allocated and those regarding various personnel decisions — career developments, promotions, pay increases — are made on the basis of the formal and informal assessments made by evaluation in the organization.

Given the centrality of both formal and informal evaluations in an individual's life within an organization, it is critical to examine whether women are evaluated in the same manner as men. Prejudicial evaluation has been cited as one explanation for the apparent failure of competent women to achieve as much success as men have. According to this argument, it is not so much the

Earlier versions of this chapter were presented at the Annual Conference of the Association for Women in Psychology, Pittsburgh, 1978, and at the Conference of the International Council of Psychologists, Oslo, 1978. An article based on this material was also published in the *Academy of Management Review* 5 (1980): 267-76.

inability or unwillingness of women to perform well that prevents their upward mobility in a wide range of situations, as it is the general lack of recognition that their performance meets. Although employee evaluation is supposed to be objective and merit-based, there is extensive documentation of frequent deviation from these ideals (for example, Kane and Lawler, 1979; Guion, 1965). With the recent focus on discrimination and equality of opportunity, there has been increased interest in examining a specific form of deviation: the operation of bias, particularly sexual and racial, in evaluation.

PRO-MALE EVALUATION BIAS

A landmark study showing evaluation prejudiced against women was conducted by Goldberg in 1968, a study that is important not only for its findings but also because it established a paradigm that has been used in many subsequent studies. Goldberg's study involved evaluating a "phantom other," a person who exists only on paper. Subjects were given a description of a hypothetical male or female with varying amounts of relevant or irrelevant information about the person and his/her performance. The subjects were then asked to evaluate the stimulus person on one or more dimensions. Since the stimulus persons are identical except for their sex, systematic variation in their evaluation can be attributed to their sex.

In the Goldberg (1968) study, 40 college women were asked to evaluate six professional articles in terms of writing style, professional competence, professional status, and ability to sway the reader. On all criteria, the articles attributed to John T. McKay were considered more impressive than the identical articles attributed to Joan T. McKay. The results were particularly striking because John was evaluated more favorably than Joan in all fields, including the "masculine" ones of law and city planning as well as the "feminine" ones of elementary school teaching and dietetics.

Since the Goldberg study, a variety of studies have demonstrated similar downgrading of women purely on the basis of sex. Male job applicants tend to be selected more frequently than equally qualified females for managerial, scientific, and semiskilled positions (Rosen and Jerdee, 1974; Shaw, 1972; Haefner, 1977b; Gutek and Stevens, 1979). The same pattern of results was found among the supposedly more enlightened population of college and university chairpersons. In response to descriptions of hypothetical psychologists, 228 chairpersons rated the men as more desirable than the women (Fidell, 1970). In addition, women tended to be offered jobs at the assistant professor level, while their male counterparts were offered jobs at the associate professor level.

Other studies showed that subjects tended to rank women lower than equally qualified males. For example, Dipboye, Fromkin, and Wiback (1975) found that of the top-ranking candidates for a hypothetical managerial position in a furniture store, 72 percent were male; a 50 percent split would have shown no bias, since characteristics of the hypothetical male and female applicants were identical. Dipboye, Arvey, and Terpstra (1977) essentially replicated these findings, observing that males were more likely to be hired than females and to receive higher initial salaries. Similarly, Terborg and Ilgen (1975) found that, although a female was hired as frequently as a male in an in-basket simulation of an engineering job situation, the female was offered a significantly lower starting salary than the male.

The male bias extends to selection outside the management context. Lao et al. (1975), for example, found that male applicants for scholarship funds were judged as more intelligent and more likable than their female counterparts. Likewise, Deaux and Taynor (1973) found that, in general, male applicants for a study-abroad program were favored over identical female applicants.

Pro-male bias has also been demonstrated beyond selection situations. For example, when identical professional articles and paintings were attributed to male or female sources, the "male" products were more highly rated than the identical "female" products (Goldberg, 1968; Pheterson, Kiesler, and Goldberg, 1971). Deaux and Emswiller (1974) showed also that male performance on a perceptual discrimination task was rated as more skillful than the equivalent female performance, whether the task be male-related (that is, discrimination of mechanical objects) or female-related (that is, discrimination of household objects). Another study (Taynor and Deaux, 1975) found parallel results for rating of responses to emergency situations. The study showed that when "Linda" and "Larry" responded in the same way to the situation described, "Larry" was judged as behaving in a more logical fashion than "Linda."

In addition to bias concerning the qualification and performance of males and females, studies also demonstrate that more global-affective reactions favor male workers over their female counterparts. A survey of workers in two Illinois towns, for example, showed a preference for working with males rather than females (Haefner, 1977a). Furthermore, while there was little distinction between barely competent men and women, workers clearly preferred working with highly competent men over highly competent women. Hagen and Kahn (1975) conducted a laboratory study that arrived at similar conclusions. In a role-playing game situation, they compared reactions to competent and incompetent women (defined in terms of the number of correct answers on a task) under conditions of competition, cooperation, or observation without reaction. While they discovered that everyone liked competent others more than incompetents — a finding that has been reported repeatedly by a number of studies (for example, Aronson, Willerman, and Floyd, 1966; Helmreich, Aronson, and LeFan, 1970) — they also found that males preferred competent females to incompetent ones when the females were at a distance (that is, in the observation condition). They did not have the same preference when they had to interact with females in any manner, whether cooperatively or competitively. In addition, the study also found that when deciding which members to exclude from a group, both men and women showed a greater tendency to eliminate a competent woman than a competent man.

CONTRASTING FINDINGS

In contrast to the studies showing evaluation bias favoring males, a number of studies have found that women received disproportionately favorable praise compared to men, given similar performance. For example, Jacobson and Effertz (1974) found that followers tended to rate the performance of male leaders as being worse than that of female leaders, even though the actual performance of both sexes was equal. They quote Samuel Johnson's remark on women preachers in the eighteenth century: "Sir, a woman preaching is like a dog walking on its hind legs. It is not done well, but you are surprised to find it done at all." Thus, the female's leadership performance, because it was so out of role, seems to have been given more value than the equivalent male performance. Abramson et al. (1977) found similar results, which they labeled the "talking platypus phenomenon." They found that female attorneys and paralegal workers were rated as having more vocational competence than identical males. Other authors have found higher ratings obtained by females than by males under similar conditions. Hamner et al. (1974) found that business students, watching a film of grocery stock workers, gave males lower task performance ratings than females, given the same performance level. The effect was magnified in the case of high-performing stock workers.

Also, a number of studies have found no differences in the evaluation of males and females. Frank and Drucker (1977), using an in-basket technique, found no differences in ratings of males and females on sensitivity, organization, planning, and written communication. Taynor and Deaux (1973) found no differences in the ratings of performance, ability, and effort given to male and female stimulus persons described as acting in an emergency situation. Hall and Hall (1976) also found no sex differences in ratings of ability, motivation, and overall task performance, using an extensive case study of a male or female personnel director. Likewise, Dipboye and Wiley (1977) found no differences in the evaluation of males and females.

THE PERCEIVED CAUSES OF PERFORMANCE

The process of evaluation includes not only the judgment of the worth of the performance being evaluated, but also the attribution of causality for that performance. Causal attributions of performance are important because they determine whether specific performances are seen as accidental occurrences or as consistently repeatable in the future. In turn, perceptions of causation and repeatability of performance are crucial because they can greatly influence decisions made (for example, promotion) about the person being judged.

Weiner et al. (1971) suggest that performance can be attributed to four major factors: ability, effort, task difficulty, and luck, which can be characterized as either internal or external, and as either stable or unstable. Performance is likely to be seen by others as repeatable if its perceived causes are either stable or internal, and in general, behavior is maximally predictable if its perceived causes are *both* stable and internal. Of the four proposed causes, ability fulfills the condition of maximum predictability in its combination of stability with internal locus of control.

Studies show that women who have been perceived as performing well may not receive credit for their performance, which tends to be attributed to factors other than ability. Deaux and Emswiller (1974) found that when women were perceived as performing as well as men on male-related tasks, their performance tended to be attributed to luck, an external factor, while the same performance for males tends to be attributed to skill, an internal factor. Similar results were obtained by Cash, Gillen, and Burns (1977). In addition, good performance was seen as more indicative of the males' general intelligence (Deaux and Emswiller, 1974) or ability (Taynor and Deaux, 1975) even when there was no difference in the evaluation of their performance. In both the Deaux and Emswiller (1974) and Taynor and Deaux (1975) studies, an interesting highlight emerged. Although differential attribution to skill and ability was found for good performance on male-related tasks, no such differences were found for performance on female-related tasks. Thus, sex-typing of the task seems important in making attributions about ability versus task difficulty. Feminine tasks seem to be viewed as inherently requiring less ability and effort than masculine jobs. Cash et al. (1977) found support for this notion.

Other attribution studies have compared attributions for male and female performance along the dimensions of stability (that is, effort [unstable] versus ability [stable]) and locus of control (that is, ability [internal] versus task difficulty [external]). Again, attributions tend to favor males. Good female performance is seen as due to effort, which is temporary, rather than to ability, which is permanent (Feldman-Summers and Kiesler, 1974; Etaugh and Brown, 1975; Taynor and Deaux, 1975), while the reverse is true for males. Similarly, female success in a school situation tends to be attributed to easy courses – an external factor – whereas male success tends to be attributed to ability – an internal factor (Feather and Simon, 1975).

The pro-male attribution bias persists in cases of ineffective performance. Etaugh and Brown (1975) and Cash et al. (1977) found that unsuccessful female performance was more frequently attributed to lack of ability than was comparable lack of success in a male. Cash et al. (1977) also found that unsuccessful performance by a male was more likely to be attributed to bad luck than the same performance by a female. Likewise, Feather and Simon's (1975) field study in a school setting found that lack of ability was used to explain female failure more than male failure, while course difficulty was used to explain male failure more than female failure.

These attributional conclusions can be explained in terms of congruence with expectations. Success or failure that is in line with expectations tends to be attributed to stable factors – that is, ability and task difficulty – while performance that is not in line with expectations tends to be attributed to unstable factors — that is, effort or luck (Weiner et al., 1971). Successful performance by females in masculine and demanding situations is often perceived as a freak phenomenon that, in all likelihood, will not be consistently repeated.

These findings imply that for women, the favorable evaluation of any single event can be limited greatly by the attribution of good performance to factors that do not suggest future predictability. This lack of future predictability resulting from the assumed causes of good female performance may make any single positive evaluation virtually meaningless. Thus, for any well-evaluated woman to have the same chances for success and mobility as her male counterpart, the link between performance and ability must be emphasized time and time again.

FACTORS AFFECTING THE EVALUATION OF MEN AND WOMEN

The studies reviewed indicate clearly the evaluation bias exists, but that its effects are not consistent across all situations. Examination of the evaluation situations in the studies reveals certain features that may reconcile some apparent contradictions and clarify the processes underlying some of the findings.

Required Level of Inference

Greater evaluator bias was found in studies on the evaluation of qualifications and on the causal attributions of performance than in the studies focusing on past performance. Of these areas, the evaluation of past performance requires the lowest level of inference from the evaluator, since the assessment is confined to the behavior or product exhibited, and no further speculation is required. In contrast, situations that call for judgments regarding a person's qualifications for a job require the evaluator to make an assessment for the future about which little information is available. Evaluators in hiring situations are asked to make inferences on how present information on an applicant or candidate (for example, education, past experience) would translate into future job behaviors in a new setting. Likewise, contexts that require judgments about the causes, and implicitly the value, of performance are situations that call for high levels of inference. It appears, therefore, that the greater the amount of inference required in the evaluation situation, the more likely it is that evaluation bias would be found.

Inconsistent results in the studies focusing on past performance can be reconciled when the required level of inference is taken into account. When ambiguity regarding performance criteria or the person's actual performance level is high, inference and stereotypic reactions are also high. Increasing clarity in the evaluation situation reduces the possibility for biased inferences. For example, the studies by Goldberg (1968) and Pheterson et al. (1971) showing pro-male bias called for the evaluation of written articles and paintings, for which criteria are highly ambiguous. Pheterson et al. showed that bias was minimized and evaluations of male and female paintings were equalized when situational ambiguity was minimized by the attachment of awards to paintings of both sexes. Another study (Deaux and Emswiller, 1974) found no sex differences in performance ratings when objective criteria were identified and performances were clearly portrayed as identical. Rosen and Jerdee (1974) also showed that increasing information reduces evaluation bias.

Terborg and Ilgen (1975) suggest that the effects of bias and stereotypes are most potent when little is known about the female and that stereotyping decreases as more information is obtained. Frank and Drucker (1977) use the same line of argument when, contrary to other studies in the area, they find no sex differences in in-basket evaluation. They suggest that their findings result from the abundance of managerial data that they presented to the evaluators for use in making their judgments. Likewise, Hall and Hall (1976), who also found no sex differences, suggest that their presentation of an actual perform-ance sample (rather than a brief resume) reduced the extent to which raters relied on sex as the basis of evaluation.

Without specific and concrete information about the merits of an individual relevant to the demands of particular situations, judges tend to resort to infer-ences based on what is generally known about the group to which the person belongs. Thus, the evaluation of any particular woman's abilities can be hindered by the operation of "actuarial prejudice" (Kiesler, 1975), a process whereby the perceived probability of success of any one person is reduced when the proba-bility of success of the group to which the person belongs is lower than that of other groups. Since most successful persons, thus far, have been males, a judge or evaluator makes a best guess that an unknown person is less likely to be a success if that person is female. The use of such actuarial probabilities as the basis for judgment implies that unless additional specific information is provided to change the probabilities for any individual woman, the judgments of success of performance will favor men. Actuarial prejudice is a response to ambiguity.

A similar phenomenon of inappropriate inferences made in ambiguous situations has been discussed in terms of "status characteristics and expectation states" (Berger, Cohen, and Zelditch, 1972). Expectation-states theory proposes that critical status characteristics (of which sex is one) tend to structure and dominate social interaction, becoming the basis for inferring an individual's characteristics and capabilities even in areas irrelevant to the particular status. Thus, because a person holds a female status, expectations regarding her ability or inability to perform certain tasks are activated, unless specific information to the contrary is provided.

Although it is clear that additional information is helpful in obtaining more accurate evaluations, the amount and type of added information required to counterbalance general expectations in specific cases is less obvious. Kiesler

(1975) pointed out that, to be effective, information must be relevant to the person's performance on the task in question. She suggested that increases in irrelevant information would only exaggerate the tendency to base evaluations on actuarial estimates because then judges would feel that they better understand the person. The importance of information relevance is highlighted by a recent study (Dipboye, Arvey, and Terpstra, 1977) that found that, in spite of extensive information provided about the stimulus persons, females were still evaluated less favorably than males. The information provided in this case consisted largely of nonperformance-related items, for example, extracurricular activities, career plans, and hobbies.

An even greater unknown than the amount and type of information needed for specific cases is the amount of actual shift in the general success rates of men and women that would be required to alter the actuarial estimates that people make. It is clear that change in society's general expectations, when such expectations are based at least in part on reality-based actuarial estimates, necessitates not only the elimination of subjective prejudice but also real changes in women's achievement levels. Frequently, this in itself is difficult, since less is expected of women than of men by others (Cash, Gillen, and Burns, 1977) and by themselves (Crandall, 1969; Frieze et al., 1975), particularly if the task at hand has been labelled as masculine (Stein, Pohly, and Mueller, 1975; Montemayor, 1972; Deaux and Emswiller, 1974). In addition, like their evaluators, women attribute their success to nonability factors (Feather, 1969; Feather and Simon, 1975; Bar-Tal and Frieze, 1977) and, therefore, have low expectations of success for their future performances. Like the students randomly labelled "disadvantaged" who were treated and eventually behaved as though they were truly handicapped (Rosenthal and Jacobson, 1968), women from whom less is expected – by themselves and others – often act to fulfill those expectations.

Sex-Role Congruence

In general, behaviors that violate societal sex-role expectations tend to be negatively regarded (Holter, 1971). The negative effects of sex-role incongruence on various types of evaluation have been noted repeatedly. For example, Lao et al. (1975) showed that assertiveness, a typically masculine trait, is negatively related to estimates of intelligence and likability in females, but not in males. Along the same lines, Costrich et al. (1975) showed strong penalties for role reversals in three role-playing studies. A submissive male in a group discussion was considered highly unpopular, and both passive males and aggressive females were considered as needing therapy more than their counterparts who fell in line with sex-role specifications. Shaffer and Wegley (1974) also demonstrated negative evaluations resulting from sex-role incongruence. They presented raters with competent stimulus females who differed along the dimensions of success orientation (a trait typically regarded as masculine) and sex-role interests (masculine or feminine). They found that a competent woman who was described as nonsuccess-oriented and who expressed feminine interests was judged as more desirable as a work partner than a competent woman who was described as success-oriented or had masculine interests. On the other hand, conformity to sex-role expectations is viewed positively and rewarded. Schein (1976), for example, found that hypothetical women in feminine occupations (for example, nurses or librarians) were perceived as better socially adapted than men in these same occupations. Individuals who stay within occupations with the appropriate sex-role assignment have easier access to such jobs than those who cross sex-role boundaries.

It is possible that the pro-male bias reported in many studies may actually reflect reactions to sex-role incongruence as much as bias per se. An examination of the studies showing pro-male evaluation bias reveals that the majority involved situations that, until the present, have been considered predominantly masculine domains, for example, situations for managers (Rosen, Jerdee, and Prestwich, 1975; Dipboye, Fromkin, and Wiback, 1975), engineers or scientists (Terborg and Ilgen, 1975; Shaw, 1972), and psychology professors (Fidell, 1970).

The sex-role congruence explanation for findings of evaluation bias receives support from a number of recent studies. Levinson (1975) had students respond to newspaper ads, most of which were sex-typed jobs with low skill and low education requirements (for example, pest control serviceman, delivery boy, salesman, receptionist, office clerk, telephone operator). Applicants who applied for sex-incongruent jobs were much more likely to be turned away. Employers showed clear-cut discrimination toward 28 percent of females inquiring about male jobs and 44 percent of males inquiring about female jobs. Only about one-third of the women applying for male jobs and one-fourth of males applying for female jobs did not experience any discrimination. Another study (Nilson, 1976) asked Milwaukee respondents to rank occupational prestige specifying the sex of the worker (for example, male banker, female physician, male nurse). The results showed the both males and females who were in sex-atypical jobs were ranked lower in prestige than their sex-typical counterparts, for example, a female banker was rated lower in prestige than a male banker. Likewise, Cash et al. (1977) found preferences for sex-congruent applications. Among applicants for masculine jobs (automobile sales and wholesale hardware clerk), males were seen as more qualified and received stronger hiring recommendations. The same results were shown for female applicants for feminine jobs (telephone operator and office receptionist). The rewards for sex-role congruence were also demonstrated in a study of the effects of sex applicant and type of job (personnel technician, a male job, versus editorial assistant, a female job) on decision to hire (Cohen and Bunker, 1975). The study showed that 150 campus recruiters involved in the study were more likely to choose males for the personnel technician position, and females were more likely to be chosen for the editorial assistant position.

All of these studies show that both males and females suffer in applying for sex-atypical jobs, although it is unclear which sex suffers more from sex-role incongruence. The Levinson (1975) study showed discrimination of greater proportions to sex-incongruent males than to sex-incongruent females, as did Nilson's (1976) study. On the other hand, Cash et al. (1977) suggested that females are more handicapped because men have more options than women. Men were seen as more appropriately placed in masculine and neuter jobs than feminine ones, whereas women were seen as more appropriate in feminine jobs than either masculine or neuter ones. Furthermore, as Cohen and Bunker (1975) pointed out, there tend to be more male jobs than female ones, and the male jobs also tend to be higher in status.

In addition, women suffer the effects of sex-role incongruence in other, more fundamental ways. For instance, many norms regarding desirable work-related behaviors are often not compatible with norms regarding behaviors appropriate to the female sex role. The most global of these potentially conflict-ing standards concerns general competence, which is expected on a job, but is not expected of women (Broverman et al., 1972). A woman who behaves in a competent manner disconfirms sex-role expectations and usually suffers one of two possible fates: she is disliked or excluded from the group (Hagen and Kahn, 1975), or her performance is discounted and attributed to chance (Deaux and Emswiller, 1974; Cash et al., 1977). Successful performance by females, particu-larly in masculine and demanding situations, is perceived as a freak phenomenon that is not due to their real abilities but to other unstable or external factors.

In addition to the conflict between competence and the female sex role, tension is also found between other traits considered desirable for the effective worker and those considered appropriate for women. Assertiveness, for example, is frequently a necessary attribute for success in many areas but is regarded nega-tively for women (Lao et al., 1975). Furthermore, while competitiveness in a man is enjoyed by other men, competitiveness in a woman results in her ostracism (Hagen and Kahn, 1975).

The effects of sex-role incongruence, however, are not always so clear cut. There is some recent evidence that the negative impact of sex-role incongruence on evaluations may be going underground and therefore may be increasingly difficult to detect. In a study by Spence, Helmreich, and Stapp (1975), reactions to a female stimulus person were different when the subjects were asked direct questions in an objective questionnaire and when they were asked open-ended projective questions modeled after the TAT. Responses to the objective questionnaire showed that, given equally competent females, the masculine one was preferred to the feminine one. This finding replicates an earlier one by Spence and Helmreich (1972b), which used a videotape of a competent woman's performance. When subjects responded to projective questions, however, a different picture emerged. In responding to questions such as: "What is happen-ing?," "What led up to the situation?," the general preference shifted from the masculine competent to the feminine competent. Spence et al. (1975) interpret their findings in terms of pressures from current social norms that profess outward egalitarianism without real changes in fundamental preferences. Thus, while there may be superficial acknowledgement that women can express masculine interests without a loss in attractiveness (reflected in the responses to objective questions), there are still underlying preferences for females who conform to traditional sex-role expectations. In support of this argument, another study (Kristal et al., 1975) showed that women with masculine interests were liked as long as they exhibited a pattern of femininity as measured on a personality test. The increasing social desirability of expressing nonsexist attitudes may make it necessary to go beyond direct questioning to more indirect probing methods like the projective techniques, if some of the conflicts involved in the shifting status of the sexes are to be adequately explored.

It should also be noted here that the detrimental effects of sex-role congruence are not universal and may operate more strongly in selection decisions than in evaluation of job incumbents who are clearly performing well. When women are actually seen as performing well in unexpected contexts, the incongruence may result in the reverse of what might be expected: the overevaluation of performance (for example, Hamner et al., 1974; Bigoness, 1976; Jacobson and Effertz, 1974; and Abramson et al., 1977). Taynor and Deaux (1973, 1975) use equity theory to explain such reversals. The equity model suggests that persons perceived as operating under constraints over which they have no control are usually perceived as more deserving of reward than individuals who are not operating under such constraints (Leventhal and Michaels, 1971). If being a woman can be considered a constraint under some circumstances, then a woman would be rated as more deserving of reward than a man for comparable performances.

Level of Qualification or Performance

Several studies suggest that the level of performance or qualifications may affect the manner in which bias operates. Whereas men have the edge over women when they are equally competent, women are judged as superior to men when the merits of both are clearly low (Deaux and Taynor, 1973; Feather and Simon, 1975). In addition, while males were evaluated more positively when they succeeded than when they failed, females were evaluated more positively when they failed than when they succeeded. Other studies show similar results, which imply that bias has maximally detrimental effects on women who are competent. For example, Haefner's (1977a and b) survey of employers showed that they made little distinction in selection between barely competent males and females, but they clearly preferred to hire highly competent males over highly competent females. Along the same lines, Rosen and Jerdee (1974), found that the pro-male bias was much stronger in the "demanding" jobs requiring decisive managerial action and aggressive interpersonal behavior than in "routine" jobs requiring clerical accuracy and dependable performance. Heneman (1977) reported similar results from a simulated selection of life insurance agents. While males and females received identical ratings for low and medium test scores, high-scoring females were rated much less suitable than high-scoring males.

Bias, then, appears to work in both directions. Competent males are rated more positively than equally competent females, while incompetent males are rated lower than equally incompetent females. This pattern of results can be reconciled by the notion of sex-role congruence. Since success at most demanding situations or occupations is generally expected of males and not of females, unsuccessful females are not as heavily penalized as unsuccessful males from whom more is expected; on the other hand, females are not rewarded for success in the same way that males are. Success, therefore, is viewed more positively if this success is consistent with sex-role expectations than if it is inconsistent (Feather, 1975).

SUMMARY AND CONCLUSIONS

Sex bias affects some evaluation situations more than others. Studies focused on the evaluation of qualifications in selection and promotion situations and research on the perceived causes of performance show fairly consistent bias in favor of men. Among the studies of sex effects in the evaluation of products or past performance, however, there are a number that show no sex differences or even pro-female bias.

Three factors affect the operation of sex-related evaluation bias. First, the level of inference required of the evaluator appeared to be directly related to the occurrence of pro-male bias. Bias tended to be found in situations where inferences about the causality of performance were called for, where extrapolation from available information to future contexts was required (that is, in selection and promotion), and where there was ambiguity concerning the focal female or the evaluation criteria. The more task-related information provided about the "evaluatee" and the greater the clarity about the criteria to be used in the evaluation situation, therefore, the less likely it is that "actuarial prejudice" would operate.

Second, sex-related bias may be a function of sex-role incongruency in the particular contexts in which the evaluation ratings are made. Incongruency can occur in two ways: by functioning either in situations defined as inappropriate to one's sex, or in ways that contradict prescriptions for sex-appropriate behaviors. Sex bias, therefore, may diminish should situations and behaviors become less sex-bound.

Third, the operation of evaluation bias appears to be affected by the level of qualification or performance involved. While females are evaluated less favorably than males when they are highly qualified or perform well, females are evaluated more favorably than males when both are not well-qualified or are unsuccessful performers. This implies a different reward system for males and females, one that rewards success and competence in males, on the one hand, and failure and incompetence for females, on the other. In sum, sex-related evaluation bias presents the greatest problem for successful or competent women, in situations where there is considerable ambiguity, and which involve sex-inappropriate situations or require sex-role-incongruent behaviors.

The validity of these findings depends, to a great extent, on the extent to which the "hypothetical person" paradigm used by most of the studies represents the realities of the evaluation situation. This paradigm typically allows only one point of information input, resembling many selection situations, and differing from evaluation of job incumbents where more opportunities for observation may be available to the evaluators. Thus, the conclusions derived from the research may be applied with less confidence to conditions that do not resemble those of the "hypothetical person" paradigm than to selection and evaluation situations in which the evaluators do not have extensive contact with the focal individual.

Research showing that sex does affect evaluation undoubtedly reflects the social conditions of the times in which they exist. As Gergen (1973) pointed out, social-psychological research is embedded in a historical context, and findings that may be true of one time period may not be replicated in another. While it is still too early to make any statements on the effect of history on this area of research, three of the four studies showing no sex differences in evaluation (Hall and Hall, 1976; Dipboye and Wiley, 1977; Frank and Drucker, 1977) are all fairly recent and may be interpreted optimistically as a trend toward increasing equity in evaluation.

A number of concrete measures can be taken to hasten the day when there is evaluation equity for men and women. Among the factors cited as affecting evaluation bias, the one that can be linked most directly to action, both by women and their evaluators, is the need to minimize ambiguity in evaluation situations. Women must make special efforts to make their work more visible to their evaluators. Toward this end, Epstein (1970a, b, & c) counseled women to become experts in some readily recognizable specialty. Such a move would highlight the ability requirements of a woman's performance and would minimize ambiguities regarding the causes of her work. Evaluators and employing organizations must work at clarifying objectives and task responsibilities to the greatest extent feasible and to implement methods, such as behaviorally based rating scales, that maintain focus on job-relevant behavior and minimize the opportunity for inference. Training workshops alerting employers to the operation of biases in evaluation have also been found to be effective in facilitating fairer judgments (Schmidt and Johnson, 1973). Clearly, these are all partial measures, and no single one will solve the problem of obtaining accurate evaluation of women's work.

7
WOMEN AND LEADERSHIP

Very few women occupy leadership positions in the workplace. The many stumbling blocks to women's progress at work, discussed in previous chapters, explain why, until very recently, women have been forced into work situations with very low opportunity and almost no real probability of overcoming traditional barriers to horizontal and vertical mobility. The recent influx of women into the labor force and the accompanying legal and social concern with increased sexual equity in the work setting, however, is beginning to result in increasing numbers of women in positions of leadership. Although still few, these women have become the subject of much interest. As relatively unknown quantities, they provoke questions about the functions they perform on the job, their acceptance by subordinates (particularly their male subordinates), and their impact on the quality of life at the workplace. Many such questions are tinged with apprehension that these new women leaders will behave very differently from traditional male leaders, in ways that will be detrimental to themselves and to the well being of other employees.

The study of women and leadership is relatively new. Although leadership per se has been researched heavily over the years, for a long time there was little or no interest in the impact of sex on leadership. Perhaps reflecting the

Earlier versions of this chapter were presented at the Annual Conference of the American Psychological Association, Toronto, 1978, and at the Annual Conference of the Association of Women in Psychology, Pittsburgh, 1978.

realities of the times, leadership research has been concerned largely with men leading other men, and occasionally with men leading women.

The bulk of research thus far on women and leadership follows two approaches that have typified much of the thinking on leadership in general. The first focuses on the personalities of leaders and assumes that leaders are a chosen breed with special characteristics. For those who think of leadership in terms of rare traits, the woman question is: Do women possess the traits necessary for leaders? There are widely held beliefs that women, the frail sex, do not possess leadership qualities. The second approach, which focuses on leadership style instead of personality, examines the relationships between sex and two major styles: consideration, which has a socioemotional focus, and initiating structure, which has a strong task orientation. Popular belief in this area suggests that female leaders would tend to behave more considerately than males, while the males would be stronger than the females. A third perspective on leadership is one that has been implicit in many definitions of the leadership concept, but for which very little empirical evidence as yet exists. This viewpoint holds that leadership is power, and that power accounts for the differences in subordinate reactions to male and female leaders.

WOMEN AND LEADERSHIP AS PERSONALITY

Traditionally, women have been seen by both sexes as undesirable superiors, unfit for positions of leadership (Haavio-Mannila, 1972). Several opinion surveys demonstrate the prevalence of beliefs about women's unsuitability for leadership roles. Gilmer (1961), for example, found that 65 percent of the male managers surveyed believed that female supervisors were inferior to male supervisors. The managers also believed that women were more neurotic than men and had higher absenteeism and more work-related problems than men. Similarly, Bowman, Worthy, and Greyser (1965) found that 51 percent of their male respondents thought that females were temperamentally unfit for management.

Women are seen as not possessing the necessary attributes for leadership. They are believed to be compliant, submissive, emotional, and to have great difficulty in making decisions (Broverman et al., 1970). They are characterized by qualities such as dependence, passivity, fragility, nonaggression, and noncompetitiveness (Bardwick and Douvan, 1972). Men, on the other hand, are seen as independent, objective, rational, aggressive, and competitive — characteristics not only appropriate to the healthy adult (Broverman et al., 1970) but also closely allied to the image of "successful middle managers" (Schein, 1973, 1975). Schein asked 300 middle managers to rate women in general, men in general, or successful middle managers on 92 descriptive terms. She found that the mean ratings of men and managers were significantly similar on 60 traits (for example, emotionally stable, aggressive, self-reliant, vigorous, desiring of responsibility, well-informed, and direct), whereas there was a significant resemblance between women and managers on only eight fronts (for example, understanding, aware of feelings, neat).

Writers in business administration have tended to encourage beliefs in the inappropriateness of women for positions of leadership. McGregor (1967), for example, describes the successful manager in this manner:

> The model of the successful manager in our culture is a masculine one. The good manager is aggressive, competitive, firm and just. He is not feminine; he is not soft or yielding or dependent or intuitive in the womanly sense. The very expression of emotion is widely viewed as a feminine weakness that would interfere with effective business process (p. 23).

Unfortunately, beliefs about women's inappropriateness for positions of leadership and management are not held by men alone. The perceived conflict between the image of women and the image of successful managers is just as real for women as for men (Schein, 1973, 1975).

Reviews of research into sex differences on personality traits presumed to be important or detrimental to leadership (for example, Maccoby and Jacklin, 1974) show that there is probably some factual basis, though limited, for stereotypical views about the dichotomous distribution of certain personality traits in the total population. The most consistent support of leadership-related stereotypes is found for aggressiveness; Maccoby and Jacklin (1974) concluded that males are, in reality, more overtly aggressive than females in a wide variety of situations and using many different measures. Other studies of sex differences on leadership-relevant traits show mixed results. The majority of studies on competitiveness, for example, have demonstrated no sex differences (for example, Komorita and Mechling, 1967; Miller, 1967; Speer, 1972). A similar pattern is found for compliance and influence-ability (for example, Nisbett and Gordon, 1967; Willis and Willis, 1970; Wyer, 1967). However, the few studies that have reported sex differences tend to support popular beliefs — males show more competitiveness (for example, Kahn, Hottes, and Davis, 1971) and less compliance (for example, Cook et al., 1970; Hollander and Haaland, 1965) than females.

More important than the studies on sex differences in the general population are those investigating differences between men and women who actually occupy leadership positions. In general, stereotypic notions on the distribution of traits in male and female leaders have not been substantiated. A study of 40 high school department heads, for example, found no significant sex differences in aggressiveness, suggestibility, professional knowledge, and sense of power (Roussell, 1974). Two studies conducted by Miner (1974) on department store managers and educational administrators also showed no consistent sex differences on various measures of managerial motivation. Strache's (1976) recent study of 22 male and 22 female university administrators, in fact, reported results opposite to those that would be predicted from the general stereotypes. Comparisons between the male and female administrators on five traits of managerial interest taken from the Cattell Sixteen Personality Factor Test (1973) — decisiveness, objectivity, emotional stability, warmheartedness, and passivity — showed the women as significantly less warmhearted, less passive, and more objective than the men. In each case, the women's scores were closer to the managerial stereotype than were those of their male counterparts.

Interestingly, when the supervisors of these administrators in the Strache study rated them on these same traits, the supervisors apparently responded according to general stereotypes. They rated the males as more objective than the males themselves scored, and they underrated the women on decisiveness, while overrating them for warmheartedness. Strache's findings show that stereotypes concerning the traits of women in general are applied to women in leadership positions even though such applications may be invalid. Although the women administrators in the study were actually more similar to the managerial model than their male colleagues, they were perceived as being less similar to the model than the males.

It is probably a useless exercise to try to determine whether women do or do not possess the personality traits "necessary" for leadership. Whether by the process of selection (if one believes that personality traits are stable and unchanging) or development (if one believes that traits can develop as a response to one's situation), or both, it seems that individuals, whether male or female, who occupy positions of leadership tend to possess the characteristics that allow them to cope well in their positions.

A more basic question concerns the validity of the interpretation of leadership as personality, on which the traditional beliefs regarding women's unsuitability for leadership are based. Although this perspective on leadership is still held by many people, reviews of research on differences between leaders and followers (for example, Bass, 1960; Gibb, 1969; Mann, 1959; Vroom, 1976) have come to the general conclusion that there is little utility to the oversimplified conception of leadership as personality. Few traits have been found to distinguish the leaders from the led, and large degrees of overlap between the personalities of leaders and followers have been discovered. In addition, because situational demands vary so much, there is little guarantee that personality traits that seem to make a good leader in one situation will be equally appropriate in another.

WOMEN AND LEADERSHIP STYLES

Male and Female Leadership Styles

The Ohio State studies on leadership (for example, Fleishman, 1957; Halpin and Winer, 1957) identified two factors on leadership styles — consideration and initiating structure — that have become the basis for much subsequent research on leadership in general, and sex differences and leadership in particular. This differentiation parallels that made by Bales (1950), who proposed categories of leaders who have a greater socioemotional orientation and those who are predominantly task oriented. Consideration includes supervisory behavior "indicative of friendship, mutual trust, respect, and warmth," while initiating structure includes behavior in which "the supervisor organizes and defines group activities and his relation to the group" (Halpin and Winer, 1957, p. 57).

Popular belief suggests that these two leadership styles are sex-linked — female leaders are considerate, supportive, and emotionally oriented, while male leaders are initiating, assertive, and task oriented. These notions emerged from a combination of forces. One influence came from personality-oriented research that shows that women are more concerned with interpersonal relationships while men are concerned with tasks (for example, Bardwick, 1971; Bass, 1965). A second influence was derived from sociological work on role differentiation in small groups (Bales and Slater, 1955). Bales and his colleagues originally proposed that two contrasting patterns of behavior — task-oriented behaviors and socioemotional behaviors — are mutually exclusive and undertaken by separate "specialists" in the group. Parsons and Bales (1955) applied this analysis to the nuclear family, stating that "the more instrumental role in the subsystem is taken by the husband, the more expressive by the wife" (p. 151). These associations were extended further, equating the expressive, socioemotional function with femininity, and the task-oriented, instrumental functions with masculinity.

Both the ideas of function specialization in groups (Bonacich and Lewis, 1973; Lewis, 1972) and the sex-linkage of these functions (Aronoff and Crano, 1975; Leik, 1963) have been subject to criticism. These criticisms focus on the nonexclusive nature of these functions and, consequently, on the invalidity of assigning separate functions to each sex. Within the context of the work organization, the evidence available thus far suggests that the beliefs in the existence of different task-oriented male and emotionally oriented female leadership styles are unfounded. Women in leadership positions function similarly to men in the same circumstances. This appears to be true of a variety of comparisons conducted across a range of situations. Day and Stogdill's (1972) field study, for example, compared subordinate descriptions of 38 male and 38 female supervisors in the U.S. Air Force Logistics Command. They found no significant differences between males and females on the 12 scales of the Leader Behavior Description Questionnaire (Stogdill, Goode, and Day, 1962), for example, structure, persuasiveness, consideration, production emphasis, and influence with supervisors. In a 1973 national probability sample, Hansen (1974) found no sex differences on subordinate perceptions of supervisor goal facilitation (a concept similar to task orientation and initiation of structure) and support (similar to socioemotional orientation and consideration) even when sex of the subordinate and job level were taken into account. Bartol (1973) likewise found no differences between male and female leaders in group maintenance and goal achievement behavior in a simulated management game. A later study of 75 supervisory and 127 nonsupervisory employees in a large government-operated psychiatric hospital (Bartol and Wortman, 1975) also found no sex differences on 11 out of the 12 Leader Behavior Description Questionnaire scales.

Subordinate Reactions to Supervisor Sex and Leadership Style

Since there is little support for the existence of real differences in male and female supervisory behavior, the crucial issue appears to lie in how subordinates react to their leaders. Although male and female supervisors appear to behave similarly, reactions of their subordinates to their like behaviors differ.

Studies of the effects of supervisor sex on subordinate reactions have as their basic premise that evaluations of supervisory behavior depend, in large part, on congruence between sex-role norms and the supervisory style exhibited. Thus, since women are supposed to be sympathetic, humanitarian, compassionate (Tyler, 1965), and concerned for the welfare of others (Miner, 1965), male supervisors would be rated higher than their female counterparts when exhibiting initiating and structuring behaviors.

Bartol and Butterfield's study (1976) supported this notion that different standards are used to evaluate male and female supervisors when they use similar styles. Male and female business students were administered one of either a male or female version of a questionnaire containing four stories, each depicting a leadership style based on one of the following leadership dimensions: initiating structure, consideration, production emphasis, and tolerance of freedom. Male managers who exhibited initiating behavior were rated significantly better than female managers who used the same style, regardless of the sex of the evaluator. Also, female managers exhibiting the consideration style were evaluated more highly than male managers using the same style. Rosen and Jerdee's (1973) study of undergraduate students and bank supervisors also found some evidence that the same behavior is evaluated differently when exhibited by hypothetical male and female supervisors. They found that the reward style (that is, advising subordinates that forthcoming recommendations for salary increases would depend on improved performance) was judged as significantly more effective for male supervisors than for female supervisors. There was also a somewhat weaker tendency for the threat style (that is, advising subordinates that they would be discharged unless their work improved significantly) to be seen as more effective for male than for female supervisors.

Aside from affecting evaluations of the supervisor, supervisor sex and supervisory style have also been found to affect the subordinate's general job satisfaction and satisfaction with the supervisor. Once again, there is support for the sex-role congruency notion. Petty and Lee (1975) found that among 165 nonacademic employees at a large university, consideration was significantly more strongly correlated with satisfaction with work for subordinates who had female supervisors than for subordinates with male supervisors. Closer examination of the data showed that this difference was largely due to the fact that low consideration displayed by a female supervisor was associated with much lower job satisfaction in comparison to low consideration exhibited by male supervisors. The sex-role congruence hypothesis for females was also supported by a later study (Petty and Miles, 1976). This study of 51 directors of county-level social service agencies showed that consideration behaviors of female supervisors were more positively related to subordinate satisfaction with the supervisor and more negatively related to subordinate propensity to leave than were male consideration behaviors.

Contradictory results, however, have been found for the sex-role congruence hypothesis for initiation, that is, that male supervisor initiating structure would be more positively related to subordinate satisfaction and motivation than female initiation. The hypothesis was not supported by Petty and Lee's (1975) study, but it found support in the later Petty and Miles (1976) study. More studies on the effects of supervisor initiation are needed to trace out specific conditions under which certain relationships occur.

Sex of Subordinate

Studies looking into the influence of the sex of the subordinate on evaluations of leadership style are fewer and much more equivocal than the studies on effects of supervisor sex. Two general competing hypotheses are considered in these studies. The first suggests that differences exist in the eye of the male or female beholder; thus, male and female evaluators, or subordinates, will differ in their evaluations of the same supervisory style. The second hypothesis suggests that, given the pervasiveness of sex-role influences, male and female evaluators will have similar reactions to perceived supervisory behaviors.

Most of the evidence appears to support the second hypothesis. Rosen and Jerdee (1973), for example, showed similar male and female evaluation of the effectiveness of several supervisory styles in hypothetical situations. Hansen (1974) found no significant sex differences in the relationships between job satisfaction and supervisor facilitation and supervisor support. Likewise, Drexler and Beehr (1977), in an analysis of national probability sample data collected in 1973, found no differences between men and women in the relationships between their satisfaction on a number of work facets and supervisor behaviors — that is, supervisor support, team building, goal emphasis, and work facilitation.

Supervisor and Subordinate Sex

Recent research has gone beyond investigating the independent effects of supervisor sex or subordinate sex. The notion of supervision being an interactive process has led to questions about joint effects of supervisor and subordinate sex. It might be suggested, for example, that a male subordinate of a female supervisor, rarely as such cases occur, would react differently to his supervisor than would a female subordinate of the same supervisor. Studies of this nature are still very few and results are still only suggestive.

One study (Rosen and Jerdee, 1973) examined the way sex-role stereotypes influence evaluations of male and female supervisory behavior when the supervisor and the subordinate are of different sexes. Undergraduates and bank supervisors read one of six versions of a supervisory problem and evaluated the effectiveness of four supervisory styles — threat, reward, helping, and friendly-dependent style. The results show interaction effects for the friendly-dependent style: both males and females reacted more favorably to a friendly and dependent approach when their supervisors were of the other sex. Results along the same lines were found in Petty and Lee's (1975) later field study. They found that the relationships between supervisor consideration and subordinate job satisfaction were higher when supervisors and subordinates were of different sexes.

An interesting finding that has started to emerge in these studies is that the sex of subordinates affects only male reactions to female supervisors. Male subordinates with female supervisors tend to be much less satisfied with work and with their supervisors than subordinates of either sex under male supervisors or female subordinates under female supervisors (Petty and Lee, 1975). These dissatisfied male subordinates perceived their female supervisors as lower in consideration — usually associated with positive feelings — and higher in initiation than did subordinates in the other three groups.

High initiation by female supervisors, whether real or imagined, clashes with sex-role expectations. While both males and females who are supervised by a high initiation female may be uncomfortable with this incongruency, male subordinates have to cope with the additional burden of status inconsistency by virtue of being a male dominated by a female. Thus it is understandable that initiating structure by female supervisors was negatively related to satisfaction for male subordinates but was positively or not related to satisfaction for female subordinates (Petty and Lee, 1975; Petty and Miles, 1976). It should be noted, however, that while female subordinates reacted relatively well to initiation on the part of female supervisors, they reacted significantly more positively to initiation by male supervisors.

WOMEN AND LEADERSHIP AS POWER

Most of the literature on leadership focuses on the relationships between leaders and their subordinates, treating these groups as isolated organizational units (Salancik et al., 1975). An alternative and more realistic perspective on leadership views leaders as occupying a position in a social network that includes individuals other than their subordinates. This larger network may include the leaders' own supervisors, managers of other work groups who control relevant information or other resources, or attendant publics. Thus, instead of employing only what can be called an inward-looking perspective, one can also regard leadership with an upward and outward view, shifting concern to the leaders' relationships with those above and parallel to them in the system. Leadership, according to this viewpoint, is a boundary function (Rice, 1963), and the focus shifts from the leaders' treatment of their subordinates to their handling of their external environment. Thus, the primary variable moves from behavioral styles to the leaders' possession and effective use of influence or power vis-á-vis the larger system.

Power, as used here, is defined in terms of the ability to mobilize resources in order to achieve desired ends. It is "the ability to get for the group, for subordinates or followers, a favorable share of resources, opportunities and rewards possible through the organization" (Kanter, 1977a & b, p. 168). This definition of leader power, emphasizing the concepts of mastery and autonomy within a larger system, is related to Levine's (1977) entrepreneurial perspective on leadership. Levine represents the effective leaders as capable of building broad domains of activities, within the constraints posed by the system, by mustering powers and resources not readily available.

Interestingly, the definition of leadership as power or influence has not received sufficient research attention thus far (Farris, 1974), although it is implicit in many formal definitions of leadership (for example, Katz and Kahn, 1978; Cartwright and Zander, 1968). The limited research available, however, shows that power outside one's work group is as important to subordinates as leader style. In an early industrial study, Pelz (1952) showed that supportiveness in a supervisor was not sufficient to obtain high morale in the work group; it was also necessary that the supervisor have sufficient influence over higher-level people regarding how decisions were made in the department as a whole. Similarly, Kanter (1977) found that credibility upward with one's superiors was a prerequisite to credibility downward with one's subordinates. People with upward credibility can obtain more resources for their subordinates, not the least of which is the transmission of power itself to them. Leaders who are perceived as being more powerful are therefore more effective at getting people to do things and to feel more satisfied about it.

Few studies have looked at male and female leaders from the power perspective. Hansen's (1974) analysis of a national sample survey, one of the few empirical pieces that compares female and male leaders on any dimension of power (that is, autonomy), reports that female supervisors have significantly less autonomy on the job than their male counterparts. Support of this self-report of low autonomy is provided by another finding in Hansen's study: the behavior of female supervisors appears to have smaller impact on the satisfaction of their subordinates than the behavior of male supervisors has on their subordinates' satisfaction. When viewed from the power perspective, this finding is not surprising. If the female supervisors have relatively little leeway to exercise their supervisory prerogatives, it follows that the little they are able to do can have only very limited effects on their subordinates.

The low level of autonomy enjoyed by female supervisors may account, in large part, for the lower levels of satisfaction found in female-led groups in comparison to male-led groups (Hansen, 1974; Roussell, 1974). If the female supervisors do not themselves possess real power within the organization, this puts a severe limitation on the extent to which they can mediate for their subordinates. In fact, this argument of limited powers is also congruent with the Goetz and Herman (1976) explanation for their finding that groups with female supervisors are less satisfied with pay and promotions than those with male supervisors. These authors suggest that employee dissatisfaction with promotions and pay may reflect the degree to which female, as compared to male, supervisors have influence on their own superiors.

The power perspective on leadership may provide an important key to understanding why, presented with similar leader behaviors, subordinates react differently to male and female leaders. Subordinates may be responding, not so much to the leader's sex as such, but to differences in real power within the larger system held by male and female leaders. This is not to discount completely the validity of sex-role incongruency as one source of subordinate responses to leaders of each sex. It is likely that both power and sex-role expectations affect subordinate responses to their leaders. Greater understanding of the effects of leader sex on subordinate effectiveness and satisfaction would be achieved, therefore, by separating the responses due to the leaders' position on the power structure from the responses due to sex-role expectations. This separation, in turn, will be possible only with further investigation of the ways in which power differences are exhibited in the system and how these differences relate to the men and women who occupy positions of leadership.

SUMMARY

The study of leadership is only beginning to include a concern for women leaders. As in other rapidly evolving situations, realities change almost as soon as they are studied, making stable conclusions difficult to draw. At this point, however, it seems that a few general statements can be made about women and leadership.

First, there continue to be strong beliefs, which are not supported by research data, about differences in personality traits and leadership styles between female leaders and their male counterparts. Thus, contrary to popular beliefs, female leaders are not more emotional and suggestible, or less decisive, aggressive, and objective than male leaders. Also contrary to notions about sex specialization in leadership styles, women leaders appear to behave in similar fashion to their male colleagues.

Second, although there have been no consistent sex differences found among leaders, there are large differences in subordinate reactions to similar behaviors when exhibited by male and female leaders. Male and female behaviors that are in line with sex-role expectations are evaluated positively. Thus, considerate female behavior is valued more than considerate male behavior, and male initiating behavior is assessed more positively than female initiation.

Third, awareness of the complexities of leader-subordinate interactions has led to examination of the effects of different sex combinations of leaders and followers. Results of these studies are still inconclusive, although, as one might expect, the most negative reactions appear to occur among male subordinates of female supervisors.

Finally, an insufficiently explored perspective — leadership as power — may provide an important explanation of the generally negative reactions to females in leadership positions. Leader power, more than style or personality, may be the critical determinant of subordinate response. Without real influence, women who hold formal titles of leadership cannot function as effectively as they are expected, and their lack of effectiveness spills over to the subordinates who report to them.

8
VIEW OF WOMEN'S ACHIEVEMENT

The previous discussions of women's entry into and socialization, evaluation, and leadership positions within the work organization have shown how the present structures create obstacles for women with aspirations outside of the traditional female service roles. These limits particular to the occupational structures, however, do not totally account for women's lack of achievement in many fields. In some ways a woman is often viewed as her own worst enemy. The effects of external barriers are compounded by a number of closely related factors involving women's achievement motivation, which is viewed as being substantially different from men's. The belief that the achievement motive operates differently in men and women arose from several systematic programs of research on achievement motivation showing that women consistently responded differently than men in laboratory studies.

The intense interest of psychologists in achievement motivation developed out of the assumption that the motive, need for achievement, underlies an individual's attempt to achieve, accomplish, perform, and succeed. In fact, McClelland (1961) marshalled evidence to support his hypothesis "that the achievement motive is the mainspring of entrepreneurial activity fostering the economic development of society" (Atkinson and Feather, 1966, p. 3). An understanding of achievement motivation might suggest ways to develop the motive in underachievers or, at the very least, differentiate those with high need for achievement from those with little need for achievement in order to place the high need-achievement individuals in situations where their motivation can blossom unrestrained. A society that produces people in entrepreneurial positions with high need for achievement and then rewards that achievement should show economic development and progress.

The need for achievement developed as an active field in psychology almost 30 years ago (see McClelland et al., 1953). Research on need for achievement progressed quickly in well-structured programs of research conducted by McClelland, Atkinson, Weiner, and Feather among others. McClelland established the projective Thematic Apperception Test as the way to elicit social motives including achievement, and Atkinson (1957) proposed a clear and concise model of achievement motivation that, in its initial and modified states, guided much of the research produced by Atkinson and his prolific and enthusiastic colleagues and students for a dozen years or more (see Atkinson and Feather, 1966).

One of the most puzzling but persistent findings was that female subjects did not respond the same as male subjects. The Atkinson model of achievement motivation worked much better for males than females, when the TAT was used to measure achievement motivation (see Weiner, 1972, pp. 225-226).

The search to understand the origins of sex differences in achievement behavior led to a variety of hypotheses and a wealth of empirical data. Most popular was Horner's (1968) concept of fear of success, which has been popularized as a trait women possess that hampers their achievement. More generally, women have been viewed as achieving in social, affiliative situations rather than in academic or occupational situations. That is, achievement itself has been viewed as sex-typed. A preference for vicarious achievement rather than direct achievement has also been suggested as an explanation for sex differences in achievement studies. Finally, women have been viewed as having low self-confidence. Lack of self-confidence weakens the expectation that efforts will lead to desired outcomes, thus undermining the motive to achieve.

In this chapter we discuss four topics: fear of success, sex-typed achievement, vicarious achievement, and low self-confidence. We also propose that differences in men's and women's behavior in achievement settings are due more to external factors than personality dynamics of women.

FEAR OF SUCCESS

Atkinson's model of achievement motivation postulated the existence of a motive to succeed and a motive to avoid failure. Horner, a student of Atkinson's, suggested that a third tendency, the motive to avoid success, exists in women. The proposed motive to avoid success was one attempt to explain confusing and contradictory findings obtained with female subjects (see Alper, 1974; O'Leary, 1974). With the publication of Horner's (1968) concept of "fear of success," a major impetus was given to research on women and achievement. According to Horner, females have anxieties concerning success, because success is seen as leading to negative outcomes, particularly loss of femininity and social rejection. Bardwick (1971) pointed to the same phenomenon, saying that women are torn by their pull toward achievement and affiliation with the opposite sex. Women, she said, see these two orientations as incompatible and mutually exclusive; success in one area is perceived as excluding the possibility of success in the other.

The "fear of success" idea was embraced enthusiastically by people across a wide ideological range. Feminists were attracted to the idea because it did not assert that women were incapable of doing well, but suggested instead that the fear of doing well prevented them from working to full capacity; on the other hand, antifemininists liked the notion becaue it served the traditional assumptions that women do not want success or do not have the capacities (other than ability) to achieve (Epstein, 1976).

The "fear of success" notion spawned a vast literature, both methodological and substantive. Most studies follow Horner's lead, assessing fear of success by responses to a verbal cue about a man's or woman's success in a stated field, for example: "After first term finals, Anne/John finds herself/himself at the top of her/his medical school class." Subjects are asked to describe what happens to Anne/John after this success. Reviews on this research are available (compare Tresemer, 1976; Zuckerman and Wheeler, 1975). Therefore, this discussion will not replicate those efforts but will present general trends.

Results of recent work challenge Horner's view of fear of success as a stable, intrapsychic trait or motive in females. Instead, it is suggested that the so-called motive is a reflection of cultural stereotype that females embarking on traditionally male enterprises experience all sorts of external and internal difficulties (compare Jellison et al., 1975; Lockheed, 1975; Spence, 1974). Thus, Peplau (1976), for example, suggested that females are not anxious about achievement per se, but they are anxious about achievement in areas that represent violation of sex-role norms. Likewise, Lockheed (1975) argued that the "motive to avoid success" is more appropriately conceived of as a normative response to social deviancy, rather than as a deep-seated generalized psychological barrier. In support of this position, she showed that no sex differences in the reported "motive to avoid success" were found when subjects reacted to activities described as typical in both sexes. In addition, more negative consequences for female success were found (particularly among males) when the stimulus activity was presented as deviant for women. Bremer and Wittig (1980) found similar results using adults aged 30-60, rather than the usual college student subjects. They found more fear of success in response to situations of deviance than nondeviant situations. They also found more fear of success in response to situations of role overload than to situations of no role overload. In their study, role overload was operationalized as having three children and doing extensive volunteer work: "She is an elder in the church, is active in P.T.A., and also acts as a bookkeeper for her husband's business" (p. 30).

Support for a cultural, rather than an intrapsychic, explanation of fear of success effects was also obtained by Monahan, Kuhn, and Shaver (1974). Their study showed that both sexes gave more negative response to the Anne cue than to the John cue. Interestingly, the males showed more negative responses to the female cue than did the females, a result that was also obtained by other studies. Further support for the social deviancy explanation is provided by Argote, et al. (1976). They showed that both males and females refrain from achievement striving when it is made clear that negative consequences (in this case, social disapproval) would accompany success, while no such avoidance occurs when positive consequences (social approval) are perceived as accompanying success. An optimistic projection from these results is that when negative valences are no longer attached to female success in a variety of fields, the anxieties in relation to achievement situations may be reduced.

Thinking of the fear of success response as a response to deviance suggests that effects would be stronger among women with traditional sex-role orientations (or more rigidly defined notions about sex-role appropriate and inappropriate success) than those with less traditional orientations. O'Leary and Hammack (1975) found support for this expectation. Peplau (1976) proposed that generalized attitudes toward sex roles are more useful in explaining women's performance than the fear of success concept. Her study found the effects of fear of success to be elusive, and sex-role attitudes emerged as a more substantial and consistent determinant of women's performance. Fear of success seemed to affect only women who held traditional beliefs about the feminine role.

SEX-TYPED ACHIEVEMENT

If women have not been prominent in many fields — art, architecture, science — to a large extent, it is because these fields have not been defined as appropriate to them. The primary arena in which most females are expected to excel is that of social and interpersonal skills (Stein and Bailey, 1973). From early childhood, girls are taught the importance of getting along with and pleasing others. Stein and Bailey (1973) suggested that what has traditionally been considered as affiliative motives in females are actually a form of achievement striving. It is interesting to note that, in support of this idea, females who write fear of success stories tend to focus on the theme of affiliation loss resulting from success (Romer, 1975; Hoffman, 1974b), whereas males focus on other themes, such as questioning the value of success itself.

Other findings support the idea of sex-typed achievement. Various studies, for example, show that women set high attainment value and high performance standards in female sex-role-appropriate tasks (Battle, 1965; Stein, Pohly, and Mueller, 1975). Breedlove and Cicirelli (1974) also showed that fear of success occurred with greater frequency in response to medicine, an area not traditionally considered feminine, compared to elementary education, one of the fields seen as appropriate to women. Bremer and Wittig (1980) found similar results comparing success in engineering and nursing. Their most negative findings were when the stimulus cue was at the top of the engineering class *and* she had extensive family responsibilities. Presumably, she must be neglecting these valued feminine tasks – P.T.A., elder in her church, and bookkeeper for her husband's business. Finally, studies in which the importance of social skill was emphasized have shown increased achievement imagery among women (French and Lesser, 1964).

VICARIOUS ACHIEVEMENT

A variation on the theme of affiliation as achievement is the vicarious achievement orientation, differentiated from direct achievement patterns (Lipman-Blumen, 1973b; Lipman-Blumen and Leavitt, 1976). In general, vicarious achievement involves "finding personal involvement through a relationship with another, through the achievements and qualities of another individual with whom the vicarious achiever, to some degree, identifies" (Lipman-Blumen and Leavitt, 1976, p. 26).

Vicarious achievement roles are enabling, facilitating, and back-up roles. The vicarious achievement orientation can take several forms. In its altruistic form, the vicarious achiever basks in the reflected glory of the individual with whom she identifies. She derives great pleasure in the other's qualities and accomplishments as though they were one's own. One prototype is the self-effacing wife, whose role is simply to nurture her achieving husband. Vicarious achievement could also take the contributing form, in which the person takes pleasure in the belief that she has contributed to the success of the direct achiever. Many a graduate student and political wife would be counted here, as would wives in the two-person career (Papanek, 1973). As Epstein (1976) pointed out, the contributions to the direct achiever frequently meet the person's needs to help and to be helped. Finally, vicarous achievement can take the instrumental form, in which the person uses a relationship in order to achieve other ends – status, money, security – which she may feel unsuited to accomplish alone. The man who marries the boss' daughter represents this type.

Lipman-Blumen and Leavitt (1976) state that males typically are socialized for direct independent achievement, whereas females are reinforced for indirect, vicarious behavior. Whereas boys are pressured into individual effectance and direct environmental mastery, girls are socialized to seek help from others in mastering their surroundings. Affiliation and dependency, therefore, become tools for mastery and support the tendency for vicarious rather than direct achievement.

Lipman-Blumen (1973b) has found that the vicarious achievement orientation is linked to traditional sex-role ideology (that is, women being in the home, taking care of children and other domestic responsibilities, while men could provide economically for their wives and children). In a sample of 634 married female college graduates, she found that 60 percent of the women who report completely vicarious achievement modes endorsed the traditional sex-role ideology, compared to 24 percent of the completely direct achievers who ascribed to this traditional ideology. On the other hand, 47 percent of the women who were completely direct achievers expressed contemporary sex-role ideology (that is, men and women may share role tasks both within and outside the home, with a more egalitarian relationship between the sexes), and only 13 percent of the vicarious achievers endorsed this contemporary ideology. Similar results are reported by Tangri (1972) in her study of traditional and role-innovating women — the traditional woman expects to live through and for others, whereas the role innovator expects to make life for herself through her own efforts. Compared to the traditional, the innovator is also much less traditional in her concerns about family and career.

As adults, women have traditionally entered vicarious achievement from both within the family and within the world of work. The proud mother who lives through "my son [not my daughter] the doctor" is a familiar vicarious achiever. In the employment world, most of the occupations considered traditionally feminine (for example, nurse, secretary) are avenues for vicarious achievement. The vicarious achievement ethic can be very detrimental to women, particularly in a society that rewards and values direct confrontation and achievement, and in a time when increasing numbers of women face economic needs to support themselves and their families.

SELF-CONFIDENCE

Low self-confidence is another internal obstacle that could hamper the achievement of many women. Low self-confidence is a somewhat different factor than fear of success, sex-typed achievement, or vicarious achievement. Low self-confidence may depress women's achievement motivation leading to less achievement behavior but it does not assume that achievement motivation is necessarily different in women and men.

A review of 58 studies on achievement motivation conducted by Maccoby and Jacklin (1974) concluded that women, starting in their college years, have lower levels of self-confidence than men do. They generally expect to do less well than their male counterparts and give lower estimates of their abilities than the men. Even after actual performance, they give lower self-evaluations of their performance than males under the same circumstances (compare Deaux, 1976a; Deaux and Farris, 1977; Deaux, 1979). These results were consistently found in a wide range of situations. For example, female college students expect to do less well than their male peers in manual dexterity tasks (Rychlak and Ecker, 1962) or at anagrams (Feather and Simon, 1973; House and Perney, 1974). In an experiment conducted by Julian, Regula, and Hollander (1968), female subjects, asked to judge which of a panel of lights went off first, were less confident than the male subjects, more often felt they had been wrong, and felt less satisfied with their performance. Feldman-Summers and Kiesler (1974) found that women also expected to be less successful than their male peers in seven anticipated professions. Crandall (1969) reported a series of studies showing that females had lower expectancies of success than males across many achievement areas even when their performance is superior. She found no evidence that various possibilities tested, that is, differences in past success, parental differences in expectations and standards, difference in immediate assimilating of positive and aversive consequences in achievement situations — accounted for the expectancy differences.

Such low expectancies for success are likely to have debilitating effects on women's capacities to achieve. Along these lines, Feather (1966) showed that individuals who approach tasks with low expectancies of success actually perform less well than those with high expectancies. The same results are also found when expectancies are experimentally induced (for example, Diggory, 1966).

Other related findings support the idea of sex differences in self-confidence. In addition to differences in level of expectancy — what persons believe they will be able to do — there are also sex differences in level of aspiration — the level of difficulty the individual chooses to attempt. Veroff (1969), using a variety of tasks, found that boys chose difficult tasks more often than girls, although similar proportions of boys and girls chose tasks of intermediate difficulty — the most adaptive choice for success. The difference occurs among children who set less adaptive goals — girls erred in the direction of overcautiousness by choosing easy tasks, while boys erred in the direction of undercautiousness by choosing difficult tasks.

Canter (1979) showed that expectations about achievement influence women's occupational aspirations. Using 200 upper-level undergraduate women as subjects, she found that own expectation of success, female peer expectations for success, and expected positive and negative consequences of success all influenced achievement-related aspirations.

An additional factor affecting self-confidence and achievement is the way people assign causality to explain success and failure.* Women tend to rely upon external explanation for their successes and failures. A number of studies (for example, Bar-Tal and Frieze, 1977; Feather, 1969; Halperin and Abrams, 1978; McMahon, 1973; Simon and Feather, 1973) showed that women typically use luck as a causal explanation for their performance and are less likely to attribute successful events to their own abilities than men (McMahon, 1973; Frieze, 1973). Nicholls (1975) also showed a self-derogatory bias among girls and not boys, and Deaux and Farris' (1977) findings suggest the self-derogatory bias is especially strong for women in response to failure. Low expectancies, low aspirations, high anxiety, and self-derogatory attributions add up to lowered confidence, an effective mechanism of self-discouragement and low achievement. A study

---

*See discussion of general attribution model in Chapter 6.

involving two samples of male and female first-line managers found similar results (Deaux, 1979). Male managers were more likely than female managers to see their success as due to ability.

Recent work (for example, Lenny, 1977; Frieze et al., 1975), however, suggests that women's low self-confidence is not universal across all achievement situations. Several types of situational variables may influence women's self-confidence relative to men's. Lenny (1977), Deaux and Farris (1977) and Frieze et al. (1975) suggest that sex-linkage of the task is an important factor in determining one's expectancies for success. In general, both men and women appear to have higher expectancies for success in tasks that are presented as sex-appropriate. Various studies (Stein, Pohly, and Mueller, 1975; Montemayor, 1972; Deaux and Emswiller, 1974) show that males expect more success than females in "masculine" tasks whereas the opposite would be true in "feminine" tasks.

Another factor that affects women's self-confidence level, Lenny suggested, is the availability of clear and nonambiguous information about their abilities on specific tasks.* Women tend to underestimate their abilities when no clear information is given them regarding their abilities, before an unfamiliar task (for example, Feather and Simon, 1973; Rychlak and Ecker, 1962), as well as after performance on a task (for example, Julian, Regula, and Hollander, 1968; Schwartz and Clausen, 1970). In addition, Crandall (1969) suggested that when feedback is contradictory, girls, more than boys, tend to focus on the negative feedback as a basis for forming expectancies for the future. When clear feedback is provided, however, there are no sex differences in reported levels of self-confidence (for example, McMahon, 1973; Simon and Feather, 1973). In fact, House and Perney (1974) showed that women have higher self-confidence than men when performance feedback is provided.

Finally, Lenny (1977) pointed out that women's self-evaluations are affected greatly by the presence or nature of social comparison or social evaluation cues. When women work in situations where their performance is likely to be compared with others, their ability estimates tend to be lower than men's, but there are no sex differences when they work alone or do not expect comparisons of performances. For example, in experiments conducted by Feather (1969) and Feather and Simon (1973), it was announced that subjects were expected to solve five out of ten anagrams in order to pass a test. The women's confidence in passing the test was found to be lower than men's. House and Perney (1974), also using an anagrams task, found that females who worked alone with minimal social cues expected to do as well as their male counterparts, but females who had competitors of either sex had lower expectancies and confidence than the competing males or the females working alone.

---

*Both sex-appropriateness of the task and the need for clear and unambiguous information were previously pointed to as important factors in the evaluation of women's achievement by others. It is not surprising that similar factors are crucial to women's self-evaluations and evaluation by others.

In general, the achievement situations in which women's self-confidence is lower than men's far outnumber the opposite situation. Furthermore, a vicious cycle may be established with low expectancies leading to failure, which leads to attributions of lack of ability and even lower expectations. Dweck and her colleagues have postulated that such a cycle can lead to learned helplessness on the part of women (compare Dweck, 1975; Dweck and Gilliard, 1975; Dweck and Bush, 1976; Dweck, Davidson, Nelson, and Enna, 1978; Dweck, Goetz, and Strauss, 1980). Dweck argued that differing attributions for failure in one situation by the two sexes would result in differential transfer of failure effects to new situations. Boys, who typically attribute failure to external, modifiable factors, show greater resilience than girls in response to failure (Dweck et al., 1980). Girls are more likely to respond to failure by assuming the situation is aversive, stable, and uncontrollable, a classic learned helplessness response. Thus, low confidence can have many consequences: low expectancies, internal attributions for failure, learned helplessness, lowered persistence, avoidance of failure situations. Dweck et al. (1980) contend that such a cycle can even account for women's lower math scores relative to men's. Although Dweck's research largely involves school-age children and therefore may be less valid for employed adults, it is a careful, thorough, comprehensive, and coherent program of research that warrants the attention of researchers concerned with working women.

The research of Dweck and colleagues suggested that the pattern of learned helplessness is modifiable. Lenny's (1977) review also ended optimistically. However, she challenged the notion that women have low self-confidence in all achievement contexts and proposed instead that women's self-evaluations are highly influenced, perhaps even unduly influenced, by situational factors. Her conclusions are stimulating and need testing by studies that directly investigate the influence of situational variable on women's self-confidence.

SUMMARY

In an attempt to reconcile sex differences that occurred in studies of achievement motivation, psychologists have postulated several related conceptions of women's achievement. Female workers have been viewed as having a fear of success that hinders their achievement. When they do strive for "achievement," it is in the affiliative domain rather than in the occupational arena, or they are willing to settle for vicarious achievement rather than direct achievement. They have been further viewed as possessing low self-confidence that depresses achievement behavior. Although these achievement-related factors have been viewed as residing in women, that is, they fear success, have low needs for achievement and high need for affiliation, they also can be, and are viewed as being, externally induced, that is, there are negative consequences of women's success and achieving women are viewed as deviant.

The predominant view of the working woman lacks any connotation of success and achievement. In fact, research on attitudes toward women workers suggests that women are viewed the same in the workplace as they are in general. That is, a woman physician or a woman truck driver is viewed foremost as a woman and secondarily as a physician or a truck driver. In their well-known study of graduate student, male managers, Bass, Krusall, and Alexander (1971) found that beliefs about a variety of perceived attributes of women made them unsuitable for managerial positions. Among them were lack of dependability of women, the belief that employees, especially men, prefer male supervisors, and a sense of male deference for "the weaker sex."

Cecil, Paul, and Olins (1973) found that when subjects were describing a white collar job, they described a managerial position when the stimulus cue was male but a secretary when the stimulus was female. Schein (1973; 1975) and Massengill and DeMarco (1979) found that the characteristics used to describe managers were similar to the characteristics used to describe men but dissimilar to the characteristics used to describe women.

Adams, Lawrence, and Cook (1979) suggested that attitudes toward women in blue collar jobs may be even more damaging than they are for women in professional jobs. Adams et al. (1979) looked at women learning craft jobs in the military and found that 20 percent of the variance in the way women were socialized into their jobs could be attributed to the stereotypes held about women. The most important factor was the belief that women lacked the competence to handle the job. Similar results were obtained by Levinson (1975), who noted that women applying for low-paying traditionally male jobs were often told that they lacked requisite characteristics for the job, even though, in some cases, a male applying for the same job was not warned about needing those traits.

Attitudes toward women workers are modified by a person's personal experience with women on the job. For example, Bass et al. (1971) found that the degree to which women were viewed as inappropriate for managerial positions varied with the position of female colleagues. Men who worked only with women in subordinate positions were least likely to think women could be managers, whereas men who worked with women as peers were most likely to think women have the characteristics appropriate for managerial positions. Kanter (1977a) speculated on the number of women necessary in a position before the woman is no longer viewed as unusual. The Bass et al. (1971) article did not examine the number of women in positions among colleagues. Presumably, that would have been important.

The beliefs that women are less capable than men in some jobs, that people prefer to work for a man than a woman, that women should be "deferred to" are all consistent with a view of women as low in achievement motivation and not particularly successful. These general attitudes about women provide a context for viewing achievement in women as deviant.

While stereotyped attitudes of female workers may contribute to reduced achievement behavior in women, a feminist orientation in the female worker may counteract some external influences.

Canter (1979), for example, found feminist orientation to be a key component in her research linking women's expectations about success with their aspirations for success. Women with a feminist orientation or attitudes are also less likely to show fear of success (see Peplau, 1976). In fact, Juran (1979) claimed that Horner's fear of success cues — Anne or John at the top of their medical school class — reflect stereotypes. Women with feminist attitudes are probably less likely to see achievement as sex-typed or to have low self-confidence (see Flaherty and Dusek, 1980). They do not fit traditional stereotypes of women and may even be less likely to be viewed stereotypically.

Operationalizing sex-role orientation using the Bem Sex Role Inventory (BSRI) (1974) provides additional evidence that lack of traditional sex-role orientation in women is associated with greater psychological adjustment, better self-concept, and higher self-esteem (Flaherty and Dusek, 1980; Bem, 1977; Spence, Helmreich, and Stapp, 1975). A nontraditional sex-role orientation (assessed by the BSRI) was associated with patterns of parental modeling and reinforcement (Orlofsky, 1979), suggesting that feminist attitudes or nontraditional sex-role orientation can be influenced during socialization and presumably later as well.

The "internal" factors that make women their "own worst enemies" in achievement situations are in reality partially or predominantly externally induced. Avoiding success, achieving in the affiliative domain, and achieving vicariously have been reinforced in women. A variety of environmental factors have contributed to women's low self-confidence in achievement settings. Furthermore, the general belief that women lack ability and "drive" serves to depress women's achievement motivation. However, effects of external factors on women's achievement appear to be attenuated by feminist attitudes or nontraditional orientation.

9
ORGANIZATIONAL REWARDS
FOR WOMEN

The workplace offers many types of rewards, ranging from the most apparent, such as financial rewards and promotion, to others that are not so obvious, such as social rewards and opportunities for growth. A number of attempts have been made to specify taxonomies of job rewards, largely in the context of job satisfaction. An early taxonomy was proposed by Herzberg, Mausner, and Snyderman (1959). Their two-factor theory distinguished between intrinsic factors (for example, achievement, recognition, responsibility) considered as motivators, and extrinsic factors (for example, pay, quality of supervision, job security), which were labeled as "hygiene" factors on the job. A later series of studies done at the University of Michigan proposed five different reward factors: job resources, financial rewards, challenge, relations with coworkers, and comfort (Quinn and Cobb, 1971; Quinn and Shepard, 1974). Other reward taxonomies are implicit in the need theories proposed by Maslow (1954), which included a five-step hierarchy starting from the lowest level of physiological needs to the highest, self-actualization, and in Alderfer's (1969, 1972) reformulation of the Maslow hierarchy into three basic needs: existence, relatedness, and growth.

Rewards, particularly those that are directly controllable by the organization, are powerful influences on employee motivation to stay and perform well

An earlier version of this chapter was published as a chapter in B. A. Gutek, ed., *New Directions for Education, Work and Careers: Enhancing Women's Career Development* (San Francisco, Jossey-Bass, 1979).

in the organization. This is generally true, even though there are large individual differences in the extent to which individuals value different rewards. Not surprisingly, a review of the allocation of various organizational rewards — pay, promotion, intrinsic, and social — shows that women do not fare well in comparison to men. The favored recipients of most types of organizational rewards tend to be the men who control their allocation.

PAY

Because of the value placed on pay by most employees and because it is so easily measured, sex disparities in this area have received the most frequent and extensive documentation. For example, the U.S. Bureau of the Census (1980) reports that in 1979, full-time, year-round women workers had a median income of $10,548, about 60 percent of the $17,533 median for men. In the same year, 25 percent of the women who had any income had incomes under $1,000, in comparison to only 9 percent of the men. At the upper end of the scale, only 2.9 percent of the women earned over $20,000, compared with nearly 25 percent of the men. In addition, a comparison of median wage or salary incomes of full-time women and men over time reveals that not only are women's incomes considerably less than men's, but also that the gap is widening. In 1955, women working full time earned $2,734, 64 percent of their male counterparts' median income of $4,241.

Many reasons have been presented to account for the pay disparities between the sexes. One line of reasoning uses the logic of need and interest. Since women are always supported economically by men, so the argument goes, their incomes are not really necessary to maintain adequate standards of living. Women's incomes go to "extras" — the second car, the special vacation — and not to "essentials" — food, housing, medical expenses. Two conclusions are drawn from this set of assessments: that women are less interested in pay than men are, and that consequently they are less willing to do the work required to obtain higher pay.

Part of this argument is supported by data — studies in a variety of contexts converge on the finding that men are more interested in pay than women are (Blum and Ross, 1942; Centers and Bugental, 1966; Gilmer, 1957; Lawler, 1971; Quinn and Shepard, 1972). The assumed link between the degree of interest in pay and the willingness to do work, however, represents a moot point that requires testing. Further, it is necessary to determine the extent to which women's values in this area are influenced by the realities they face. Barthol (1979) has data suggesting that both males and females expect women to make much less than male employees. These realistic expectations may very well explain the sex differences in expressed interest in pay.

The "need" portion of the argument is even more debatable. The number of women who can rest confident of continuous economic support by men is constantly dwindling. Over the past decade, female-headed families have grown almost ten times as fast as two-parent families (Sawhill, 1976). Even in husband-wife families the wife's earnings are often essential to family well-being. Bell (1974), for example, showed that among working wives, 22 percent contributed to over 50 percent of the total family income. Obviously for these growing numbers of women, financial need is just as pressing as it is for men.

Another common justification for the inequality of income between men and women is the claim that women are more likely to be sick, to be absent, and to quit their jobs. The validity of these assertions, however, is open to question. The Bureau of Labor Statistics for 1968 (the last year in which such information was collected by sex) shows that the quit rate in manufacturing was 2.6 percent for women, compared with 2.2 for men. According to the U.S Department of Labor (1975), women in recent years have had relatively stable job tenure, in comparison to previous years. The same study also noted that part of the reason for the difference in quit propensities between the sexes is due to the concentration of women in lower paying jobs.

It has also been suggested that women earn less than men simply because they are found in lower-paying occupations. Our previous chapters have discussed this condition of women at work. Sex stereotyping still seems to restrict or discourage women from entering into many higher paying, tradi-tionally male occupations, and thus the earnings gap is a result, in large part, of the high concentration of women in relatively lower paying occupations and in lower status positions within the higher paid major occupation groups. Whereas about one-fifth of all women workers were in clerical jobs, for example, about 5 percent of the men held such jobs in 1979. In contrast, about 17 percent of the men workers, compared to 1 percent of the women workers, were in craft jobs, and about 11 percent of the men compared to 4 percent of the women held jobs in any managerial or administrative capacity (U.S. Bureau of the Census, 1980).

When the analysis is restricted to broad occupational groupings, however, the status and income differences between the sexes remain substantial. Among professional and technical workers, for example, men earned 56 percent more than women and were likely to be doctors, lawyers, engineers, or architects, while the women were likely to be noncollege teachers, nurses, librarians, or dieticians. Likewise, among sales workers, men earned 92 percent more than women and were likely to be in high paying commissioned, nonretail jobs, while women worked primarily in the retail trade (U.S. Bureau of the Census, 1980). Suter and Miller (1973) had similar findings. In comparing the salaries of men and women 30-44 years of age in 1967, they found that among professional and technical men and women with continuous work histories, the women earned only 66 percent of the male average; among clerical workers, women earned 79 percent as much as men; and among operatives and service workers, the women earned only half as much as the men did.

Sex stratification and segregation of occupations, therefore, accounts for much of the sexual pay disparity. However, it does not provide the total explanation. In white collar jobs, for example, sex and marital status are more important determinants of earnings than the type of job performed (Bridges and Berk, 1974). Sexual pay disparities decrease somewhat with increasing occupational specificity, but they remain substantial, hovering around 20 percent within narrowly defined occupations (Buckley, 1971; McNulty, 1967). A number of studies provide examples of the existing disparities within highly specific occupational groups. For example, a survey taken of women scientists in 1970 by the National Science Foundation showed that they composed 10 percent of the sample, and their median income was $11,600, or 76 percent of the men's $15,200 median. More specifically, a 1974 survey of the American Chemistry Society showed that the average salary of women chemists was $14,000, about 73 percent of the $19,700 average of men. Among engineers, an extremely male-dominated profession (only 1.6 percent were women in 1970), the median salary for women in 1972 was $14,200, 85 percent of the male median of $16,700. In the academic world, the differences appear to be smaller. For lecturers to associate professors in universities, women's median salaries were about 95 percent of men's, decreasing to 91 percent at the professional level (U.S. Department of Labor, 1975). In public junior colleges, women's salaries were about 91 percent of men's in 1973-74.

In addition to occupational status, education is often presented as a rationale for the different levels of earnings for men and women. Education can determine both the type of job as well as the level with an occupation for which a worker can qualify. However, equal education does not appear to provide the magic key to equal pay. In 1974, women with four years of college had lower incomes than men with equivalent education. Women high school graduates earned only 57 percent of what their male counterparts did; they earned less than men who had not completed elementary school. Suter and Miller (1973) show that, in comparison to men, women receive decidedly lower increments for equal step increases in educational level and occupational status. Treiman and Terrell (1975) came to similar conclusions — the payoff for each additional year of schooling for women is two-thirds of what it is for men, controlling number of hours worked. It is clear that education does not produce the same return in investment for men as for women. Instead of formal education, it appears that a more important influence on wage levels is training received on the job. Data presented by Corcoran and Duncan (1979) indicate that men receive much more on-the-job training than women. These differences in job training can explain 11 percent of the wage gap between white men and white women and 8 percent of the gap between white men and black women.

Another reason presented for the earning differential between men and women is the number of years worked by the individual. The number of years a woman works is, on the average, less than that of men, although the gap has been narrowing. In 1900, the work life expectancy of men was 32.1 years compared to 6.3 for women; this has moved to 40.1 years for men in 1970 compared to 22.9 years for women (U.S. Department of Labor, 1975). A recent national survey showed that, compared to white men, the average white woman had five more years out of the labor force and was more likely to have worked part time (Corcoran and Duncan, 1979). The gaps occur all throughout a woman's work history (Corcoran, 1979), largely because of the woman's family and childbearing responsibilities, which produce discontinuity in women's work lives. The gaps result in lower total job experience, job tenure, and seniority than men. Existing evidence, however, suggests that the earning differential between men and women cannot be attributed to differences in the number of years they worked. Suter and Miller (1973), for example, showed large salary discrepancies between men and women with continuous work histories. Among professionals, women earned 66 percent of the male average; among clerical workers, 79 percent; and among operatives and service workers, 50 percent. In addition, they showed that the payoff for each additional year of work experience was higher for white men than for any other groups. Corcoran and Duncan (1979) also indicate that, in general, labor force withdrawals have only very small effects on wages.

Recent studies have recognized the joint effects of different factors and have tried to look at the earnings differential taking them into account. Even when factors are jointly accounted for, however, the sex earnings differential remains. Fuchs (1971), using data from the 1960 Census, found that, on the average, women earned about 60 percent as much as men in hourly earnings. When the data were adjusted for race, schooling, age, city size, marital status, social class, and length of work, the ratio was raised to only 66 percent. Suter and Miller (1973) showed that women earn only 62 percent of the male income after adjusting for education, occupational status, differences in work status during the income year, and in amount of total work participation over the years. Levitin, Quinn, and Staines (1971), studying a 1969 national probability sample of workers 16 years and older, found that the average woman received 58 percent of a man's income with equivalent education, tenure with employer, tenure on specific job, number of hours worked each week, amount of supervisory responsibility, and occupational prestige.

PROMOTIONS

National statistics show that women tend to be concentrated at the bottom of most organizations (U.S. Department of Labor, 1975). These general findings have been shown repeatedly in studies using more limited numbers of organizations. Miner (1974), for example, studied a group of business managers and a group of educational administrators. The women were located at lower levels in the organizations and were older than the men included in the sample. Roussell's (1974) study of high school principals also shows that women do not progress up the hierarchy at a rate comparable to men. The study indicates that female principals remain in their present positions almost twice as many years as males. Similarly, a study by the National Academy of Sciences (1968) found that the rate at which women achieve full professorships is slower than men, with a lag of two to five years in the biological sciences and up to ten years in the social sciences. Many similar studies (for example, Rossi, 1970b), find the same discouraging results.

It is not surprising, therefore, that studies show women to be dissatisfied with their promotion opportunities. A study of men and women in four organizations (Hulin and Smith, 1964) reports that in three of the four plants, women were more dissatisfied with their promotional opportunities than any other factor. Herman and Gyllstrom (1977) also found that among 500 university employers, women were significantly less satisfied with their promotional opportunities than were men.

A number of reasons could be proposed to account for the differences in organizational ranks achieved by men and women. Education levels, for instance, may account for the fact that women tend to cluster at the low end of the organizational ladder. Similarly, women's lack of vertical mobility in the organization may be attributed to discontinuities in their labor force participation. There are only a few studies that attempt to separate these different potential causes. Those that do exist, however, suggest that women's typical location in the lower ranks cannot totally be explained by such "rational" causes. Malkiel and Malkiel (1973), for example, found that only half of the sex differences in job level assignments could be explained by factors such as education and experience. Within academe, Astin and Bayer (1972) conducted a study of 3,438 women and 3,454 men who had regular faculty appointments and who were taken from a nationally representative sample of institutions. Like other studies, they found that men occupied the highest academic ranks; 25 percent of the men, for example, were full professors, compared to 9 percent of the women. In order to assess inequalities due to sex and not to factors such as types of degree held, type of work, and institution, the effects of the four sets of predictors (demographic characteristics, educational background, professional/work activities, and institutional characteristics) on three criteria — academic rank, tenure status, and basic institutional salary — were estimated and controlled. The extent to which sex per se explained the residual variance in the criteria was examined. They found that, after 30 variables (out of 76 that had been entered into a stepwise multiple regression) entered the regression equation significantly explaining 62 percent of the variance in rank, there was still a significant relationship between being female and low rank. Sex was a better independent predictor of rank than other factors such as the number of years since completion of education, number of years employed at present institution, or number of books published.

In addition to the factors studied by Astin and Bayer (1972), women's lack of upward mobility in organizational ranks has been hypothesized to be a result of the relatively less central position occupied by career success in women's than in men's lives (Brayfield, Wells, and Strate, 1957; Kuklen, 1963; Rosenberg,

1957). It is popularly believed that women care less about career-related outcomes such as promotions and professional growth than men do. This belief is justified by other assumptions that women obtain satisfaction in life from a number of areas, whereas men tend to derive their satisfactions solely from their careers. The corollary to this argument is that an individual who is not interested in getting ahead on the job will put forth only the minimal level of effort that is acceptable to his/her employer and therefore will be justifiably confined to lower level jobs.

On the surface, a number of studies appear to support this argument. Crowley, Levitin, and Quinn (1973) found that more women than men in a nationwide survey said they never wanted to be promoted. Manhardt (1972) also found that college women placed less importance on career success than college men. Roussell's (1974) study of department heads showed that 50 percent of the males and only 14 percent of the females expressed a desire for further promotion.

An alternative explanation, however, is equally possible. Crowley et al. (1973) suggested that women may scale down their ambition, in order to approximate reality more closely. If women perceived that their probability of promotion was equal to that of men, there would be no reason to expect that women would not value success and show as much desire to get ahead as men. Crowley et al. tested the validity of this explanation and found support for it. When they controlled for the expectation that one would be promoted, the observed sex difference in desire for promotion evaporated. Hahn (1974) provides additional support for the influence of expectations on women's desires. She found that the desire for promotion was much less dependent on the importance one places on promotion than on the expectation that promotion was likely to occur. Thus, the finding that women were less interested than men in promotions seemed to be largely a result of their resignation to the expectation that they were not going to be promoted.

INTRINSIC REWARDS

In addition to the extrinsic rewards officially allocated by the organization, there are others that are afforded directly by the work itself. Women are generally found at the lower occupational levels where opportunities for challenge and growth tend to be limited (House and Wigdor, 1967; Armstrong, 1971). Their jobs generally provide fewer intrinsic rewards than jobs held by men (Quinn and Shepard, 1974).

As is the case for promotions, the lack of intrinsic rewards in women's jobs is rationalized by the argument that they are not interested in such opportunities. An early review of the importance given by male and female employees to 11 job facets (Herzberg et al., 1957) provides fuel for such a position. It concludes that "in general, intrinsic aspects of the job appear to be more important to men than to women" (p. 72). Herzberg and his colleagues contended that women were motivated more through external hygiene factors than motivators. Thus, women were viewed as valuing clean working conditions and friendly coworkers more than they valued recognition or achievement. A plant on Secretary's Day might be viewed as a more valued outcome than responsible work. Or one might believe that women are willing to work with little responsibility as long as the surroundings are clean and pleasant.

Subsequent investigations have found no support for this assertion. Burke (1966a, 1966b), for example, had male and female college students rank five intrinsic (for example, challenge and autonomy) and five extrinsic (for example, comfortable working conditions, pleasant coworkers) job characteristics in terms of importance. He found that both sexes expressed similar preferences, and both ranked the intrinsic factors as more important than extrinsic ones. Other studies on college populations (Saleh and Lalljee, 1969; Manhardt, 1972) have also found no sex differences in the ranking of intrinsic and extrinsic job factors. Similar results have been obtained in working populations. In a study of a selected cross-section of the working population, Centers and Bugental (1966) found no consistent sex differences in the overall value placed on three intrinsic versus three extrinsic job components. Likewise, Saleh and Lalljee (1969) found no sex differences in orientation toward intrinsic and extrinsic job factors in a sample of public school teachers and clerks and supervisors in a technical division of a large service-oriented organization.

It appears that rather than reflecting real sex differences, the findings reported by Herzberg et al. (1957) are, in reality, reflections of differences in organizational level and/or education. Earlier studies have shown that there is greater importance assigned to intrinsic rather than extrinsic rewards in higher level occupations (Centers, 1948; Gurin, Veroff, and Feld, 1960). In support of this argument, Saleh and Lalljee (1969) found that higher level supervisors were more intrinsically oriented than lower level clerks. In addition, they found that although greater intrinsic orientation was generally found among male than among female employees, such differences disappeared when organizational level was controlled.

SOCIAL REWARDS

Women value social relations on the job more than men do. This is one instance in which there is consistent agreement between stereotypic belief and empirical data. The early Herzberg et al. (1957) conclusions that women attach greater importance to a job's social aspects than men do have been supported in subsequent research. For example, Kilpatrick, Cummings, and Jennings' (1964) national survey showed that more women than men felt that the social aspects of their jobs were important. Likewise, a study based on 692 employed adults by Centers and Bugental (1966) found that women placed a higher value on interpersonal relations than did men. Crowley et al (1973) also found more women than men in their national probability sample of households indicating that it was very important to them that their coworkers be friendly and helpful; and Schuler (1975) found that females valued the opportunity to work with pleasant employees more than males did.

Whether women actually obtain the social benefits they desire, however, is open to question. Little research has been conducted on the social experiences, interaction patterns, and exchanges of social rewards that develop in organizations. One exception is a study conducted by Miller, Labovitz, and Fry (1975) on 178 men and 157 women in five small, highly professionalized organizations — a public school system, two research firms, a food processing concern, and an alcohol rehabilitation agency. They found, using sociometric measures, that more men than women were chosen frequently for friendship as well as for work-related information. In comparison to women, men were four times more likely to be perceived as influential and three times more likely to be named as one whose professional judgment is valued. In addition, men were more able to interact with their friends at work and had greater access to persons in authority. An interesting sidelight of their study shows that parallel to the research in evaluation, the disadvantages that women faced were more pronounced for those who had advanced education, high occupational rank, and authority. These findings tend to support a "vested interest" interpretation, namely, that the organizational structure functions to protect men's vested interests by allowing interpersonal barriers to exist that are not explainable by a rational view of organizational influence. It remains to be seen whether the same pattern of social rewards would be found in other types of jobs or organizations, particularly those that are less professional in orientation. Investigation into the social rewards received by men and women at work also needs to be expanded beyond the sociometric and access measures used in the Miller, Labovitz, and Fry (1975) study, to include measures that parallel value or desirability questions. In order to find out whether women get what they want, in terms of social job aspects, they should be asked whether, indeed, their coworkers were pleasant and friendly, and whether their jobs gave them opportunities for rewarding social interaction.

COMFORT

Another type of reward provided by work organizations to their members is comfort. Originally, comfort and social relations at work were classified together as the "hygiene" aspects of work (Herzberg et al., 1957), which were contrasted with "job motivators." Later work (Quinn and Cobb, 1971; Quinn and Shepard, 1974), however, suggested that the two factors were quite separate. The comfort factor included comfortable surroundings, good hours, and good transportation.

Data from a national sample (Crowley et al., 1973) found support for this stereotype. According to data collected from a national probability sample of households, women did value good hours, ease of travel to and from work, and pleasant physical surroundings more than men did. The sex differences in importance persisted even when controls on the actual conditions present in the workers' jobs were introduced.

The data from this national survey (Quinn and Shepard, 1974) show further that women, on the whole, do have more comfortable jobs than men do. As in the case of intrinsic job factors, it is likely that this statistic speaks more to the segregation of men and women into different types of jobs rather than the existence of differences within similar jobs.

SUMMARY

The data show persisting disadvantages for women in a number of areas. Women's jobs provide fewer opportunities for challenge than men's jobs, which is consistent with their generally lower positions in the occupational hierarchy. Their jobs show slower promotional progress and lower pay levels than those of men, even when the effects of occupation and organization are controlled. They may also be relatively disadvantaged with regard to their social rewards at work, although the evidence is extremely limited in this respect. The one area in which women appear to benefit from the present occupational structure is comfort — women's jobs tend to have better hours and general working conditions than men's jobs.

A factor that complicates the interpretation of the data presented here is that the general tendency is for occupations to be sex-segregated (Oppenheimer, 1968; Schrank and Riley, 1976). Only a small minority of the labor force are in occupations in which the male-female ratio was balanced (50 percent of each sex) or close to balanced. Many of the differences found in the rewards that men and women receive reflect the separate work world that male and female workers occupy. In general, there are not enough data available to compare what men and women want and get within specific occupations.

Across many areas of reward, the rationalization of women's preferences has tended to be used to justify the low reward levels they attain. Women are thought to downplay the importance of pay and promotion, for example, and this is given as the reason for what they receive. A message emerging from this review, however, is that, in many instances, one's realistic expectations shape one's desires and aspirations. What women want from a job tends to be shaped by what they expect to receive, and what they expect tends to be shaped by what they or others like them are receiving or have received in the past. The realities of the present affect aspirations for the future.

In addition to affecting women's aspiration levels, it is also possible that present reward realities affect their efforts to perform to the best of their abilities. Expectancy theories applied to work behavior (Vroom, 1964; Lawler, 1973) suggest, in essence, that effort to perform is a function of three determinants: the expectation that effort will lead to task accomplishment or good performance, the instrumentality of task accomplishment for obtaining certain outcomes (that is, rewards or punishments), and the valence or attractiveness of those outcomes. That is, people will be motivated to the extent that they believe their efforts lead to desired performance *and* that performance leads to valued outcomes.

In Chapter 6 we discussed evidence that women's performance tends to be attributed to external factors, and that high performance does not necessarily lead to valued outcomes such as promotion. This chapter shows that rewards for working women are limited and their allocation based on factors other than commonly accepted legitimate criteria. As previously stated, beliefs about sex differences in the valence of different outcomes are used to rationalize the differential allocation of rewards between men and women. For women, therefore, the performance-reward contingencies presently existing are not at all conducive to eliciting performance up to potential.

10
APPROACHES TO CHANGE

FOUR EXPLANATIONS OF WOMEN'S WORK STATUS

Legislation has opened up many external barriers to women's progress in the workplace. Legal force has been applied to require equal work for equal pay, to set affirmative action goals, and to make previously all-male occupations formally accessible to women. However, legal efforts alone will not redress historical inequity. As Hennig and Jardim (1977) pointed out, it is relatively easy to legislate against segregation, but equity and true integration cannot be achieved by legislation alone.

The goal of achieving greater equity for women who work outside the home can be reached by a number of different, but complementary, avenues. The avenues that one chooses to follow for effecting change depend on one's diagnosis of the causes of the present unsatisfactory situation. Women have not achieved as much as men have, it can be said, because they possess characteristics that block their way to success or, conversely, they do not have certain prerequisites for achievement. Or it can be said that institutional structures have oppressed women and kept them down. Another explanation involves the expectations that society sets up for men and women, roles that define men as achieving in the work world and women as nurturing in the home. Still another might say that, regardless of the specifics considered appropriate for men and women, the basic fact is that men as a group are more powerful than women as a group — automatically, therefore, males and what they do will be valued more than females and what they do.

Four different models are implied in these explanations. The first model can be called the individual deficit model, which views the problem as residing primarily in the women and men as individuals. Women's weaknesses are seen as the causes of their position at work and in the world. Problems emerge from their differences in innate biology or in their early socialization and training, whose results are fairly permanent in adulthood. Women are more emotional, less stable than men. They are not logical and rational like men. Further, they are not motivated by the same things as men are, since they are not really serious about their jobs. They shirk from challenge and only want to feel secure and comfortable on the job.

The individual deficit model suggests that female traits make women unfit for certain functions such as leadership. Investigations of individual motivation and performance show that women "fear success" and that much of what they do can be characterized as indirect or "vicarious" achievement. Thus women's inferior positions have been explained in terms of their deficits in motivation, in personality development, and in necessary traits such as assertiveness and sensitivity to networks and games played in the organization.

The individual model can be applied to individual male coworkers and supervisors as well, although there is considerably less attention on men than on women. When the model is used this way, the focus shifts to male attitudes toward women workers (particularly in higher levels or other positions where their presence would be more unusual), or to their perceptions and beliefs about women. In addition, a focus on individual male workers may also suggest that women's problems in the workplace lie in male insecurities about their own masculinity, which is threatened by competition with supposedly inferior females.

When applied to women, the individual model takes the character of other cases of "blaming the victim" (see Ryan, 1971). The individual level of explanation, which tends to be favored by much of the psychological literature, only partially explains the realities of women's condition, even when both men and women are considered. Further, it tends to ignore the external influences that create these individual characteristics.

A second perspective that usefully supplements the individual model is the structural-institutional model, which focuses on the impact that work organizations have on the people in them, and on the ways in which the people eventually reflect their situations in their behavior (see Kanter, 1977a). This viewpoint sees women's personalities and motivations more as the consequences of work structures rather than as their causes. Explanatory factors are sought that explain women's situations as well as the situations of others who occupy similar positions.

The structural model suggests that women's expectations and aspirations are often low because their work structure provides little real opportunity — thus low aspirations are primarily adaptive adjustments to reality. Their difficulties in integrating into previously all-male situations frequently result from their token positions in the organization, which make them extremely visible — thus susceptible to pressure — and isolated from the informal network of information and alliances. In addition, women's problems while in supervisory or leadership positions appear to be less the result of absent leadership traits or inappropriate leadership styles, but more of the type of powerless and dead-end positions they tend to occupy.

Examined in structural-institutional terms, the limitations faced by women workers are shared by other groups who do not control the operations of the work organizations. Women's problems, therefore, are the problems of all new-comers who do not constitute the majority of the work force and for whom there remain basic questions of legitimacy and entitlement. Problem analysis in structural-institutional terms threatens established systems in ways that individually based analyses do not. Using this framework, the aspects of scrutiny and potential target for change efforts are the organizational structures themselves.

Yet a third perspective weaving through our examination of women's work is the sex-role model, which is tied to societal definitions of sex-appropriate behaviors and attitudes. This model focuses on general societal definitions of male and female roles that include, but are not limited to, work-related aspects of life. This model owes much to Talcott Parsons' theory on the necessary division of labor between the "instrumental" husband and the "expressive" wife, differentiations that have been applied to the other roles of men and women.

The focus of the third model is the degree of congruence between a woman's exhibited behaviors or attitudes and those prescribed by general sex-role ideals, or those appropriate to specific female roles such as wife, mother, and sex object. The model suggests that sex-role prescriptions provide direction to a wide range of work-related behaviors. Thus women "choose" traditionally female fields, even if they are typically crowded and low paying, because they conform to society's views of appropriate activities for women. Women grow up believing that "success" is defined by marriage, in their roles as wife and mother. Contrary to actual statistics, many women believe that if they do get employed, their foray into the employment world will be brief, or merely supplementary, temporary, and therefore relatively unimportant.

According to the sex-role model, many of the problems of the woman worker stem from the inappropriate spill over of her other roles into the workplace. Role spill over on the job tends to push women into performing functions similar to those they perform in their other roles. In many female jobs (for example, nurse or secretary) the work role conforms completely to sex role.

Simply by virtue of her gender, expectations derived from the traditional definition of female roles such as nurturers and supporters (rather than achievers) are set for the woman worker, even though these expectations are irrelevant or even damaging to the performance of her work role. Because she is a woman, an employee may automatically be considered incapable of a wide range of activities, and she is told that her primary role in the workplace is to support and often train the men who will then supervise her. Her functions are typically auxiliary and her satisfactions vicarious. She is made to feel that certain behaviors linked to advancement on the job are appropriate only for her male colleagues, thus leaving her with the choice of stagnation or deviance, with its accompanying penalties.

For women workers who are also wives and mothers, the role conflicts tend to be most severe. Even though employment is becoming increasingly important in women's lives, and both male and female attitudes on work issues are rapidly changing, by and large women are still expected to accommodate their work lives to the demands of home and hearth. Interrupted patterns and part-time employment still characterize the labor force activity of many women who adopt such employment behaviors in order to design their work around their family lives. Needless to say, the same adjustments are not made by their husbands, who are expected to adjust their family responsibilities to suit their work demands.

The sex-role model points to the problems resulting from violations of traditional sex-role prescriptions. Entry and acceptance are difficult in areas traditionally reserved for men. If a woman defies the limits that her sex role imposes on her, she is punished externally by hostility, ostracism, or harassment. Internally she has to cope with strains resulting from role conflicts, and with the uncertainty and self-doubt resulting from a nonsupportive environment.

Like the structural model, the sex-role-status model focuses on the effects of context on male and female work-related behaviors and interactions. However, it goes beyond the structures of particular work organizations to the larger social differentiations between the sexes and the sex-linked assignment of responsibilities for work and family.

A fourth model can be characterized as the intergroup model, focusing on the relationships between males and females as groups. Its basic premise states that, simply by virtue of group membership, male and female interactions tend to be characterized by factors that typically develop in relationships between groups. When groups are formed on the basis of a dominant characteristic, differences between them are emphasized, while in-group similarities are underlined. Thus, "all men are highly motivated and career-committed" while "all women are not interested in achievement and only want undemanding, intermittent work." Stereotypes result from these tendencies to exaggerate within-group similarities and between-group differences.

In addition, intergroup relationships tend to create hierarchical relationships between the groups. Not only are the groups different, but one is clearly superior to the other. Although lip service is paid to the separate but equal and complementary nature of the two sexes, literature showing that males are viewed as superior is extensive. In the workplace, men clearly belong to the "in-group" and women to the "out-group." Male characteristics, therefore, set the norms for "goodness," from which deviance becomes defined as deficit. Thus many of the "deficits" discussed by the first model research are based on assumptions that, where differences between men and women are found, the male characteristics are automatically considered better. In addition to the assumed superiority of male traits is the assumption that male activities are superior to female activities. In fact, simply changing the composition of an occupation from male to female has been shown to lower the desirability and prestige of that occupation (Touhey, 1974).

Membership in two different groups affects the interaction between any two individuals who belong to the groups. Further, there is evidence suggesting that the more salient membership is to the individuals, the greater its effects are on the interaction. Ickes and Barnes (1978) showed that individuals with stereotyped sex roles talked, looked, and gestured to each other less than individuals who were more androgynous. Apparently, the more stereotyped the individuals the more stress is evoked when they are put into an interactive situation, since the stereotyped sex roles generate incompatible sets of behavior. Such stress would serve to heighten the distance between the groups and to support the stereotyped characterization of group members.

The intergroup model shows that treatment of an individual depends critically on group membership. Membership conveys notions of status, so that knowing what an actor is enables one to know what to expect of the individual. In the work setting, such memberships are critical, because they are obvious in many situations where other characteristics may not be immediately evident. In such cases, where the only information available concerns a person's sex or race, expectations on performance level, power, and prestige are aroused, even if an individual's sex or race bears no relationship to the task at hand (Berger, Cohen, and Zelditch, 1972).

The "woman status" is a dominant one that tends to eclipse other characteristics more relevant to work at hand (for example, position and education) and to create perceptions of inferiority detrimental to women's position in the workplace. In task groups, differentiation in observable influence, acceptability, and prestige often result from expectations generalized from the status difference (Freese and Cohen, 1973). High-status individuals (that is, males) expect to be more competent, initiate more interactions, and become more influential. Low-status individuals (that is, females), in contrast, expect less, initiate less, overevaluate high-status people, and underevaluate themselves. Like other irrelevant but dominant statuses, such as age and race, the burden of proof is on showing that inferences drawn from the status characteristics are *not* relevant.

A similar way of viewing the intergroup relationships between women and men is the power perspective. Hacker (1951) suggested that women can be viewed as a caste or minority group, which has clearly subordinate status in general society. According to her, women and blacks exhibit similar characteristics due to their low caste status. They are confined to limited jobs appropriate to their "place" in society and they are socially and professionally segregated.

Women often exhibit psychological characteristics typical of lower caste members — for example, denigration of other members of their own group, accepting the dominant group's definitions of them, and preferring to work and to be identified with members of the top group. Ironically, they are regarded by the dominant male group as inferior beings, yet the kinds of barriers set up against them suggest that their competition is feared greatly.

The subordinate status of women is associated with the control that each sex has over the resources valued by society. Men control a wide array of resources — power, money, land, political influence, legal power, intellectual and occupational resources; women control a greatly limited set — sexuality, youth, beauty, and the promise of paternity for their male partners (Lipman-Blumen, 1976). The dominance pattern is historical, traceable to the resource-acquiring and resource-protecting roles that males had, while women were limited by relative size and childbearing.

Blumberg (1979) suggests that the central variable that appears to account for status differences between men and women in many societies is each sex's relative economic power. When women lose control of the means and fruits of productive activity, their general status declines. Hartmann (1976) further suggests that when women's work becomes private and family centered rather than social, as with the Industrial Revolution, their public stature is diminished even more.

Central to the power perspective is the idea of protection of the established system of reward allocation and resource control by the dominant male group. Women belong to the out-group, and their entry into the largely male occupational world and particularly their vertical mobility after entry are controlled by the established order. Rationalizations for preserving the status quo are borrowed from individual deficit portrayals of females, from expositions on the naturally separate spheres of men and women, and from prediction of catastrophes when the "natural order" is violated.

IMPLICATIONS FOR CHANGE

Individual Model

It is clear that the model that one adopts to explain women's work situation dictates one's prescriptions for change. If one holds the belief that the factors causing current inequities lie in individuals, one would look to ways to address their deficits. Thus, the focus would be on self-improvement and training programs, teaching women how to remedy their deficiencies.

One such program, for example, may focus on deficits in information. Women would be provided accurate information on the kinds of occupational and career options that may be available to facilitate early and later career choices. Another may focus on the "rules of the game" in a work environment that is largely alien to women's experience and early socialization (for example, Harragan, 1977). Other programs address a variety of issues with a more behavioral orientation. Some provide necessary skill training in areas previously closed to women. Others provide help on questions such as "How does one assess one's assets?" "How does one plan, set goals, and implement them?" "How does one communicate clearly without being offensive?" "How does one project the image of self-confidence?"

In addition to programs addressing women's deficiencies at the workplace, other programs focus on career planning, for the woman starting or restarting a career. Such programs provide information on the range of occupational options available, her own self-identity, and the match between the self and the occupation (Hall, 1976). An important aspect of these career counseling programs is targeting them to the career stages of their participants.

Interventions aimed at remediation of women's shortcomings vary in what in women they attempt to modify and how they produce the modifications. They are labelled variously consciousness-raising, management training, or career planning sessions. Whatever their label, they share the basic philosophy of providing women with personal ammunition to overcome their barriers to entry and mobility at work.

A variant of the self-improvement programs targeted at women are those designed for their male coworkers and supervisors. Such programs aim at confronting men with their own prejudices and may provide data to dispel popular myths about female capabilities and motivations for working. Education for male workers on the limitations imposed on women by traditional protective behaviors would facilitate women's functioning as "full workers."

The training approach is popular, particularly among psychologists, educators, and personnel trainers. Clearly individual improvement programs provide useful services. Many women benefit from the boost in self-confidence produced by these sessions. The roadmaps to a work world with unfamiliar rules provided by trainers ease a difficult entry period for many. Insight into the interpersonal dynamics at work and practice in new behavioral skills enable women to control their environment to some extent. Further, these sessions provide the women with a support group of others facing similar circumstances, which counteracts the isolation that many encounter in the workplace. Consciousness-raising for men also has its value, particularly where problems are the result of ignorance and not of lack of good will.

Yet as Kanter (1977a) suggests, the individual training approach alone is severely limited. It allows the status quo to continue unchallenged. The work establishment can be magnanimous in its support of seminars aimed at helping women overcome their deficiencies, since by so doing, the system itself remains unexamined and therefore unchanged.

Structural Models

Adopting the structural mode of explanation would clearly lead one to different foci on change. If the problem is in the structure of the work organization, then the solution lies therein as well. The assumption is that structural changes will be more likely to change individual behavior than vice-versa. Thus the focus would be on altering institutional operations to foster greater equity between the sexes.

One way of achieving structural change would be to alter the opportunity and reward structures within work organizations. Jobs traditionally assigned to either sex, for example, would be opened up, so that relevant ability rather than sex becomes the most salient selection criterion. Blockages to vertical mobility could be minimized by examining artificial limits to job ladders and by making it easier to move across different job categories if there are linkages in the types of skills required. Many of the changes in opportunity structures would depend on a thorough reassessment of the true requirements of jobs. It will not be sufficient to say "male wanted," if what is truly required is a "person able to sell $5,000 worth of insurance a month." The recent legislation on equal opportunity is a step in the right direction in the movement toward ability-based job assignment. Clearly such legislation will have to be supplemented by greater analyses of what jobs entail in order to reduce the artificial truncation and immobility that presently characterize many job ladders.

Another related type of opportunity-based structural intervention focuses on the investments organizations make in their women workers. Traditionally women have received minimal levels of on-the-job training (Corcoran and Duncan, 1979). They tend to enter work organizations with the necessary training for a specific job, and since job ladders for women are usually artificially truncated, there is no incremental training provided them. The lack of investment in women workers is justified by expectations of short and undependable tenures.

Attempts to increase the possibility of mobility between levels and across types of jobs should be accompanied by active efforts to increase the number of women in areas previously closed to them. Affirmative action programs belong to this category of numbers-increasing interventions. Increasing the numbers of women outside of their traditional realm is extremely important. Research has shown that "solos" can be expected to have problems attributable to their rarity. The issue of number, however, is not straightforward. It is desirable that women are not scattered individually throughout work organizations, because they become excessively visible and isolated. However, it is also important that women do not get grouped into yet other "pink ghettos" such as a women's career specialist division, with little power and advancement possibilities, isolated from the mainstream of organizational life. Also, while solo women have many difficulties, sudden increases in numbers may also be the occasion for backlash from the threatened majority that small numbers do not generate. As Hall (1976) points out, small numbers of "new types" can be assimilated relatively easily, but large numbers will require major accommodation by the organization. Sudden increases will be likely to engender hostility in members of the "old type" group that would be crowded out in the distribution of scarce rewards. An additional complication in efforts to increase women's numbers is that an incremental approach, that is, increasing the number of females in a few occupations or positions, may result in their redefinition as "women's jobs," which are then downgraded. The mere increase of women in certain prestigious occupations has been shown experimentally to result in a loss of prestige for those occupations. The classic historic example is the prestige loss suffered by the bank teller job when it shifted from being a male to a female job. Thus, creating more equitable access to both sexes may be only a partial answer. If changes in access to male-dominated positions occur incrementally over a period of time, there is a danger that these newly opened jobs become redefined as low-status dead-end positions.

Another kind of change would alter the present inequitable reward system without necessarily altering the segregated occupational structures. Such changes would aim, not at equal pay for equal work, but equal pay for "work of equal value." Thus it would examine the reasons for the lower reward structure in the traditionally female nursing profession, for example, in comparison to the traditionally male occupation of garbage collector. It is obvious that the assessment of "work of equal value" is not a simple question, but it can be helped by better comprehension of the true demands, in terms of dimensions typically considered as indicators of "worth" of work, for example, demands for skills, strength, training, and intelligence. An example of "comparable worth" investigations was one conducted by the State of Washington (U.S. Department of Labor, 1978). The study of 121 Washington State jobs found that no woman's job was paid as much as the poorest paid male job of equivalent worth, when worth was defined by job requirements for knowledge and skill, mental demands, accountability, and labor conditions. In the end, such analysis will still require a value judgment on the relative worth of diverse characteristics such as strength versus training, but even having such assumptions clearly stated and universally applied would help move toward a system that pays equally for "work of equal value."

Still another type of structural intervention would focus on organizational policies and practices that recognize employees' competing concerns outside of work. Both women and men would benefit from greater flexibility in work schedules and location. Many experiments have already been proven beneficial in the area of flexible work hours (for example, Wade, 1973). Related to the idea of flexible work hours is increased legitimacy for part-time work. Not only have such jobs typically been confined to jobs with low skill requirements and little potential for upward mobility, they have also been limited in the accrual of benefits (for example, vacation and retirement) that are provided to full-time employees. Greater legitimacy of part-time work would benefit the large number of women who choose this mode in order to simultaneously fulfill their family responsibilities. Greater flexibility in the locales where job tasks are performed — for example, word processing, data processing, or stuffing envelopes — would also help many women and men. It would ease many difficulties resulting from overly segmented work and home lives.

Structural intervention could also center on the work-benefit packages provided to employees. Already companies have assumed responsibilities for workers' health care. Companies could extend this interest in their employees by institutional benefits such as child daycare. Such innovations would be especially beneficial to single parents, for whom childcare problems pose important barriers to work responsibilities. They would also result in positive consequences for the organization such as decreased absenteeism and tardiness.

Structural change efforts, like individually oriented improvement programs, are limited solutions to the problems of women and work. One limiting factor lies in general resistance to any type of organizational change (compare Barnes, 1967; Bennis, Benne, and Chin, 1969), particularly those that may operate to the detriment of some men, at least in the short run. Given typical situations of finite resources, structural change efforts aimed at equalizing opportunities for men and women would elicit the greatest amount of resistance from the less able men who would be most negatively affected by the removal of barriers that had served to protect them in the past.

Resistance from such less able men is supported by the larger social structure, which defines the work world as male domain. These men would lose some of their privileges in the workplace, without recompense in satisfactions from other life domains. It would be necessary, therefore, particularly for such men, to develop other sources of security and fulfillment outside of the world of work.

Sex-Role Model

Clearly a potential arena for expanding male fulfillment would be in the private family sphere. Traditionally, sex-role definitions have assigned the family sphere to women and the work sphere to men. However, this sex-linked role assignment will be modified as a result of women's increased participation in the work world. Thus changes suggested by the institutional and structural perspective must be complemented by further changes in the sex-role domain.

Effecting change in sex-role assignments and definitions necessitates basic redefinitions in male responsibilities and rewards in the family arena, just as women expand their responsibilities and rewards in the work world. Men, therefore, must take on a larger share of the care and joys associated with the two major areas in the family realm — homemaking and childcare and -rearing — that presently take insignificant amounts of their time and energy. Thus there would be greater role overlap between male and female roles, as each role expands to include elements that were previously found exclusively in the other role. As yet, no great attention has been focused on increasing men's homemaking role. In contrast, discussion of fathering is becoming fashionable, and conventional wisdoms that have guided father-child relationships to date have been found lacking (Fein, 1978). The emergent perspective on fathering suggests that men are not only psychologically able to engage in a full range of parenting behaviors, but also that it may be good for both parents and children if men take active roles in childcare and childrearing.

Changes in the sex appropriateness of work and family roles imply changes in the definitions of desirable behaviors and attitudes to accompany the shifts in functional responsibility. For men this suggests a movement from "traditional masculinity," which emphasizes physicality, suppression of tenderness, and a purely functional relationship between the sexes, toward "modern masculinity," in which interpersonal skills are more important and heterosexual tenderness allowed (see Pleck, 1976). Recent findings (O'Leary and Donoghue, 1978) show that there may be increasing latitude allowed in the definition of the masculine sex role, in contrast to earlier findings that showed that sex-role deviance was severely punished for males (for example, Costrich et al., 1975; Seyfried and Hendrick, 1973). O'Leary and Donoghue suggest that once a young man has established a masculine identity, he may be free to elaborate at the periphery of the masculine core to adopt some traits traditionally viewed as feminine. For women, a broadening of behaviors considered acceptable means that they incorporate such traditionally male characteristics as assertiveness and competitiveness into the definition of femininity.

Both sexes would benefit from a move toward greater latitude in sex role definitions, toward the idea of androgyny or the combination of femininity and masculinity (Bem, 1974, 1975). A similar idea wherein individuals can adapt appropriately to situations without adherence to rigid sex-role prescriptions has been labeled sex-role transcendence (Rebecca, Hefner, and Oleshansky, 1976). With the loosening of sex-role restraints, each sex would have a wider repertoire of behaviors to apply to particular contexts. The "bitter fruits of extreme sex role specialization" (Bernard, 1976) — for example, pathogenic mothers, empty-shell marriages, repressed and constricted men — would be ameliorated. Further, sex-role expansion would mean that sex norms would reflect more accurately the large overlap that actually exists in the attitudes, abilities, and behaviors the females and males exhibit. Block (1973) suggests that the integration of masculine and feminine traits and values represents the highest level of ego functioning. Even so, it is clear that there is strong resistance from various quarters against the beginning trends toward increasing role overlap between men and women.

Still another change area implied by a redefinition of sex roles is the fundamental structure of the life stages of men and women, particularly concerning the linkages between work and careers, on the one hand, and marriage, childbearing, and childrearing, on the other. Career stages and family stages will have to be integrated, not only for each individual, but for couples as equal partners. Individuals and couples will need to develop greater understanding of the extent and timing of the demands made by the work and family spheres, in order to create mechanisms that allow maximum satisfaction in and minimum conflict between both spheres, for all the relevant parties. When and how much to push the career, when or whether to have children, what kind of support to expect or develop on the home and work fronts — these are becoming increasingly inter-dependent decisions. In the past, achieving women tended to have children early, waiting for their children to be well on their way before they felt free to focus on their own work objectives. Although that pattern still exists, increasingly early babies are being seen as interfering with the total investment of energy required by many careers (Bird, 1979).

Sex-role redefinitions are highly dependent on structural shifts. When jobs that had been defined as male become open to females, then the behavior defined as appropriate to them becomes more accessible for incorporation into the female role. As opportunities for women open in the work world, the boundaries of the female role expand to add long-term meaningful work to its traditional repertoire.

Structural shifts are important for sex-role shifts in another way. As long as women earn significantly less and have less responsibilities than men do as a result of occupational segregation and blocked opportunity channels, it will be difficult for men to assume home-related responsibilities. If a child is sick, or if a broken appliance needs repair, it is likely that it will be the woman who will attend to such duties, particularly if it means losing a day's pay.

Interventions along the sex-role model may differ in terms of time per-spective. Changes based on long-run perspective would focus on early sex-role socialization, with the hope for change deferred to future generations. Short-run interventions would be based, in contrast, on a model of on-going development, and would work for more immediate changes in adult environ-ments. Whether the perspective taken is short or long run, sex-role redefinition can be facilitated by differentiating more clearly the functions that exist within each general role. Lipman-Blumen (1973a) suggests that such component analysis makes it easier to examine the qualifications necessary to perform specific functions instead of assigning clusters of functions to types of individuals.

Long-term interventions directly focused on expanding sex-role definitions would focus on issues such as channeling of motivation into specific arenas, deemphasis on the sex-appropriateness of sex-typed behaviors and tastes (for example, in toys and games) and in the inclusion of a wide range of occupations for active consideration. Laws (1979) suggests that exposure to androgynous models would enhance the development of an androgynous self-concept. Potential target groups for such interventions would consist of the early social-izers of sex and occupational roles. Among others, school textbooks, vocational and guidance counselors, and the media have been noted by researchers as potentially powerful agents for change or support of the status quo.

An immediate avenue of change is the definition of desirable behaviors at the workplace. It has been stated earlier that traditionally male values set the standard by which worker behavior is judged. Although this may be attributable, to a large extent, to the generally superior position that men hold vis-á-vis women, it may also be the result, at least in part, of the fit of those characteristics to the demands of the days of early industrialism (Bernard, 1975). The complexities of the modern work organization, however, seem to be moving in directions away from the rugged individual. Increasingly work has to be accomplished by teamwork rather than by individuals working alone. In addition, occupations that call for the qualities in which women have traditionally excelled – for example, service and people orientation – are on the increase relative to male-dominated heavy industry. Also, there is a relatively new emphasis on introducing supportive elements into the workplace, with the push toward improvements in the quality of working life, job satisfaction, and social gratification from work (see Davis and Cherns, 1975). Thus certain attributes of the hard-boiled he-man may be increasingly dysfunctional in the newly evolving forms of organizational work life.

A totally different change approach would focus on freeing the woman worker from behavioral prescriptions that are carried over from her other female roles and that are detrimental to her worker role. Such spill over affects the way women workers are treated and evaluated on the job, since male norms tend to govern the workplace (for example, independence, aggressiveness, and dominance) and often contradict valued female behaviors.

One move that would benefit women workers (as well as their male colleagues) would be to make work-related expectations and norms as clear and as behaviorally focused as possible, so that attention is directed toward work-relevant factors rather than to irrelevant norms drawn from sex-role ideals. Such a move would also make it less necessary to make inferences about nonobservable aspects such as worker traits and motivations, which are much more vulnerable to bias. Various tools (for example, behaviorally based rating scales) exist that can help maintain focus on job-relevant behavior.

Explicit statement of work-related expectations benefits women in an important way other than facilitating fair evaluations. A problem for many is confusion on how to behave when sex-role and work norms are in conflict. Since either set of norms may be invoked, and the application of each may occur in erratic ways, women suffer from ambiguity and not knowing how to shape their actions in order to obtain desired rewards. Explicit and public work objectives, therefore, would provide an antidote to uncertainty, although they may not necessarily posit prescriptions that are agreeable to the women worker.

There are obvious limitations, however, to prescriptions on explicit statements of work objectives. One is the difficulty, particularly for complex and nonroutinized jobs, in defining completely what the work role demands. For such jobs, there may be real limits to the extent that it is even desirable to introduce the inevitable rigidity accompanying detailed behavioral specifications.

Another problem with the segmentation approach is that both men and women carry with them all the roles they occupy, even if only one should be primary at any particular point in time. The lines separating various roles tend to blur, particularly for male and female sexual roles, since they do not require other parties (for example, children and spouse) outside the work situation to be brought into the picture, and since many men and women view the workplace as an appropriate place to meet members of the other sex.

Intergroup Model

Conditions defined by the intergroup model may be the most fundamental and thus the least amenable to change. Even if both men's and women's roles change substantially, so that there is greater recognition given to the similarities and overlap between the groups, it is unlikely and perhaps even undesirable that all distinctions disappear. Therefore it does not seem real to suggest that one homogenized group should be an objective for change.

What may be more realistic, however, are efforts to minimize the negative consequences of intersex-group relationships. One such negative outcome is the exaggeration of within-group similarities and of between-group differences. Polarization creates stereotypes that are strongly held, despite the fact that they contradict many findings that intragroup differences are often larger than intergroup differences (Bernard, 1975). Further, polarization tends to be accompanied by hierarchy, and male stereotypes are automatically defined as superior to female stereotypes. The intergroup model suggests that people are not treated as individuals, but are members of a superior and inferior group.

As noted earlier, polarization between the sexes and assumptions of intrasex homogeneity may be loosened if sex-role prescriptions and structural boundaries segregating the sexes are altered. Greater behavioral latitude allowed each sex will expand the range within each as well as ensure more observable similarities between them. Further, if structural alterations on the job do, in fact, bring men and women into closer contact performing similar functions, it is likely that unreal stereotypes will dissipate. In support of this hypothesis, Durning (1978) found that male plebes at the newly integrated Naval Academy became more egalitarian over the course of the academic year. Stereotypes can also be addressed cognitively via information-provision sessions, if one believes assumptions of the first model that such stereotypes result at least partly from ignorance about reality.

Given that women as a group will continue, for somewhat longer, to be characterized by stereotyped portrayals, individual women should take measures to avoid suffering from unwarranted application of general unfavorable stereotypes to themselves. In Chapter 6, it was suggested that providing additional information relevant to the task at hand would minimize the inappropriate application of stereotypes. Information minimizes the necessity to resort to inferences based on general stereotypes. Women should make special efforts to ensure that accurate information about their work reaches their evaluators. Such information should be made available to all relevant parties, since without doing so, both men and women would retain the tendency to underrate women's performance relative to men's. The expectations of *both* sexes, therefore, must be specifically modified to attain "equal status interaction" in situations where both would be expected to work together.

However, generalizations and stereotypes will continue to follow individual women as long as the traditional power and hierarchic relationships between the sexes remain as they are. In the long run, necessary shifts in sex-related perceptions and expectations, which so strongly influence the treatment and behavior of women at work, can take place only with changes in the power structure of the larger society. All the recommendations for change previously discussed have implications for the distribution of power between the sexes. For example, altering definitions of work and family responsibilities and changing sex-role prescriptions for attitudes and behaviors means that differences between male roles and female roles, and between male traits and female traits, will be minimized. Therefore status distinctions attached to sex-role differentiations will be weakened as well. Opening up the institutional structures of reward and opportunity will have similar effects. In effect, power now attached to the male status will be shared to a greater extent with females by blurring the distinctions separating the two groups.

Another indirect way in which the power structure may be redefined could be in the drift of society at large to increased appreciation of values that have been defined traditionally as female. Interdependence is a characteristic that is beginning to typify more and more areas of life, and it is becoming increasingly difficult to operate as an individualistic independent. Perhaps women's traditional roles, which have emphasized nurturance, interpersonal sensitivity, and supportiveness, will have prepared them well for a shift in general societal requirements.

It is unrealistic, however, to expect that power will be relinquished easily. One factor that will help is increased appreciation of the alternate gains to which males could have access outside of the structure as presently defined. There is increasing evidence that the attraction of alternate gains is growing. Definitions of "success" are changing for men — they are putting less emphasis on external factors such as salary and position level, and more emphasis on self-fulfillment and happiness (Yankelovich, 1974). They are deriving greater satisfactions from their families, hobbies, recreation, and religion.

Nevertheless, alteration of the present power balance will require the application of power-oriented strategies. Power comes from the acquisition of control over important societal resources such as education, money, occupational prestige, and political organization. Legislation has been an important first step to the acquisition of additional resources, and increasingly it is being reinforced by the development of political consciousness among women as a group. Women have become newly aware of the power that they can wield by pooling their individually gained resources. By developing economic, political, occupational, and legal networks, women can use each other for mutual benefit, particularly to exert pressure in various areas to achieve changes toward greater equity.

The acquisition of resources and power feeds on itself. Acquiring one form allows access to others. Possession of education and financial assets, for example, can be negotiated into political power. In addition, as women achieve greater control over resources, their relationships among themselves and with men will change. The need for vicarious achievement through men will be minimized as direct modes become available. Further, the increased benefits in interacting with other women who also possess significant resources will provide incentive for the development of closer links among women, in the same way that male-held resources encouraged the development of a homosocial male world (Lipman-Blumen, 1976).

The development and use of female networks and power bases has already begun, with institutions such as the National Organization of Women (NOW), the National Political Women's Caucus, and the Women's Equity Action League (WEAL). It is clear that to some men and to some women the prospect of women with power is frightening, conjuring up the image of the castrating female. It is also clear that the implications of female power are not yet well understood. As with the previous three avenues for change, a change in the power relationship between the sexes implies fundamental changes in multiple areas, areas relevant to the way each sex functions individually and in relation to each other, at work, and at home.

SELECTING A STRATEGY FOR ACTION

The discussion of the four models and their implications for change makes it clear that no single model presents an adequate analysis of or change strategy for women's current situation in the world of work. The relative importance of factors attended to by each model is debatable, and factors that are viewed as causes of some phenomena by one model are examined as consequences of other occurences by another. Thus, for example, personality factors that are used as explainers of differences in male and female statuses are themselves regarded as outcomes of organizational and societal structures. Changes in both occupational and family systems are necessary in order for both sexes to achieve equal status where roles are not assigned on the sole basis of gender (Safilios-Rothschild, 1976). Attributions of causalility to any one factor, therefore, are impossible given the interdependence and mutual influence among them.

Action, however, demands a selection or at least an ordering of models and strategies. Ultimately, such a ranking requires a value judgment regarding the relative efficacy of using any particular model as a guide to initiating action, while continuing to recognize the effects that such a starting point will have on other parts of the system. A number of considerations are relevant to such a choice.

A necessary assessment involves the ease or difficulty with which an intervention effort can be launched and maintained. This assessment must then be balanced with another judgment on the long- and short-run impact of such an effort. Change strategies implied by the four models receive contradictory evaluations when these criteria are applied.

Of the four models discussed it is clear that interventions aimed at remediation of individual deficits are the most feasible and attainable. Long traditions of individualism and self-help make such interventions ideologically appealing. In addition, the fields of education and training have established technologies that can be applied to bolster women's work-related shortcomings, and psychology supplies useful technologies such as behavior modification and role playing. Even more important to feasibility is the fact that programs aimed at individual change are usually acceptable to organizational management, who do not feel threatened by short-term workshops attended at infrequent intervals by limited groups of individuals. To them, the costs of supporting such programs are relatively minor.

Although feasibility is high, however, benefits obtainable from individual remediation efforts alone are fairly limited. Unless the individuals involved occupy strategic positions in their work organizations, any benefits obtained from the training sessions tend to be confined to the specific individuals and dissemination to others can be expected to be slow.

Evidence from related fields, such as T-groups and laboratory training, provides other insights into the basic limitations of individual change approaches in the work context. Studies have shown that gains from individual training sessions have short after-lives if the organizational structures into which the individuals return remain unchanged (for example, Dunnette and Campbell, 1970; Bass, 1967; Campbell and Dunnette, 1968). Further, newly acquired behaviors often encounter resistance because of their lack of fit with established interaction patterns in place at the actual work situation.

In comparison to individual change programs, structural intervention efforts are considerably more complex. Feasibility assessments, therefore, vary greatly depending on the particular structural features defined as the targets for change. To the extent that certain changes can be defined in terms that conform to generally accepted tenets of work design and organization, such changes will be viewed as acceptable, legitimate, and therefore highly feasible. Thus attempts to introduce greater rationality into the workplace (for example, improvement of selection mechanisms and performance evaluation technology) would have high probabilities of obtaining organizational acceptance. Such efforts do not challenge existing values of work organizations. Therefore, the feasibility question is reduced to one of technology viability. Here, too, the assessment of feasibility is positive, given the extensive work done by industrial psychologists and management experts on administrative and personnel problems.

In contrast, efforts designed to alter the sexual composition of the work force have already elicited various strong opposing voices. Affirmative action efforts are viewed by some as contradicting strongly held ideologies regarding individual merit and seniority as the basis for reward, particularly where there is the appearance of reverse discrimination. Number-altering interventions clearly threaten individuals already included within the system and would not be feasible at all without strong support from the legal system and from the organizational hierarchy. In addition, altering the sexual composition of work organizations poses many new technical difficulties, even for those who are ideologically committed to increasing sexual equity at work via structural change. Organizational specialists still have to learn how to improve opportunities for one group without diminishing opportunities for other groups. New definitions such as "work of equal value" and "equitable opportunity structures" must be developed as basic tools toward implementing such concepts in organizational structures. These problems are so thorny that some people (for example, Agassi, 1979) believe that efforts to eliminate sex-typing are so slow that some of the sex-typed occupations will disappear as a result of unconnected external factors, such as technological change, before some improvement occurs.

The relative difficulty involved in implementing the more threatening structural interventions would be offset by the amount of change they would effect. Behavioral changes that would result from structural shifts would be likely to be maintained if the structures support them. Although individuals will always retain some latitude in deciding how to act, social structures heavily shape the options and tools available to them (Kanter, 1977a). Individual behaviors adapt to their environment.

Changes in sex roles necessitate fundamental changes that would have wide-ranging effects in many basic areas — definitions of appropriate behaviors for men and women, allocation of tasks between the sexes and the extent to which tasks are allocated on the basis of sex, and the nature of the linkages existing between the worlds of work and family for each sex at any one point in time and over the life cycle. By their very nature, the changes are societal in nature and are not limited to individuals or specific institutions.

The basic issue here is not one of amount or magnitude of impact. Rather it is the meaning and desirability of these changes. Resistance is already evident from a variety of sources, to changing "natural law." There are wide-ranging and deeply held viewpoints regarding the desirability of loosening up sex-role differentiations. Objections that exist are tied in to self-images and basic identities and thus are extremely difficult to address. Many of these objections come from sectors of the population that perceive benefits from the present structure, including men who are able to achieve power and prestige by having a wife dedicated completely to supporting their needs, affluent women who enjoy their "leisure" and do not feel restricted by the status quo, and housewives who define themselves primarily in the context of their family responsibilities.

Changes in sex-role definitions have already started. Thus to some extent the feasibility of initiating change is no longer a question. Guiding and directing these changes, however, are still at issue, since the process of change is incremental and amorphous. Many of these changes become manifest in scattered experimentation in new life styles and new family structures that allow greater sex-role overlap in private and intimate settings. Much remains to be understood regarding what changes, both public and private, are already underway in the sex-role area and why they are occurring.

A bit better understood are the processes of early sex-role formation. Consequently, the existing technologies for sex-role change focus on alterations in early childhood socialization (for example, changes in school books and child-rearing practices). Changes resulting from these efforts, however, will not be immediate and will likely be seen only in forthcoming generations.

Like the sex-role model, the intergroup or power model also refers to the society as a whole. The changes it calls for similarly imply a major reconstruction of society. These changes, like the sex-role changes, are feared because they threaten basic self-definitions and relationships. Also, parallel to the sex-role model, the ultimate effects of a radical shift in the power balance between the sexes are unknown.

Women have begun to learn how to obtain and wield power as a group. Women have begun to organize networks and political lobbies that make their presence noticed in various areas — for example, sports, work, media, and education. Lipman-Blumen and Bernard (1979), however, caution that the achievement of a widespread "sisterhood" is more difficult than it first appears. Historically, women have been separated from each other by class, race, ethnicity, generation, and religion. In addition, family and spouse allegiancies have made it traditionally difficult for women to band together to speak for themselves.

Perhaps the most difficult task is to create solidarity among women without separating from men. Baude (1979) and Safilios-Rothschild (1979) have noted that the involvement and collaboration of high-level male political leaders in the sex-role debate helped raise the issue of equality between the sexes to one of national importance in countries like Sweden and Israel. Complete separatism is not likely to work as a power strategy for women.

CONCLUDING REMARKS

It is clear from this discussion that increasing equity for women at work is a many-headed effort. Forces that support the present unequal system and those that can serve as avenues for change occur at all levels — the individual, the organizational, and the societal. Their relationships are so entangled that alterations in any one sphere are bound to have repercussions in others. Thus one of the classic questions in the area of planned change — "Does one begin to change attitudes, behavior, institutions, or societal norms?" — has no clear-cut answers, and the ultimate goal is to achieve changes in each area that support changes made in others.

The processes of change in many of the areas discussed have already begun. The mere numbers of women entering the labor force make change in many basic social forms inevitable. Not only are more women seeking employment, more women are taking on uninterrupted work patterns, and increasingly women are committed to seek success, promotions, and responsibility. Bernard (1976) suggests a J-curve model of change that can be applied to changes among working women and the institutions they affect. Based on Allport's (1934, 1939) J-curve of conformity to norms, the model describes the acceptance of innovation over time, dividing the population into innovators, early acceptors, an early majority, a late majority, and laggards (Rogers, 1962). Already many so-called innovators of a few years back — for example, women entering into traditionally male occupations for the first time, and women in high-level positions — have become acceptable to at least an "early majority." Such increased legitimacy is shown in diverse contexts, including increased marketing and advertising targeted at women professionals and media shows depicting the new breed of woman as normal individuals.

Innovations in different areas differ in their positions on this curve. For example, the idea of equal pay for equal work has been accepted by almost everyone, at least in theory, whereas the idea of role-sharing and power-equalization across the sexes are probably accepted by only a small group of "innovators." The position of various changes on the diffusion curve is determined partly by the content of the change, its distance from commonly accepted practice, and the balance between those who would benefit and those who would stand to lose from the change. Our review has shown, for example, that discrimination has greatest negative impact on competent and higher-level women — clearly, they would derive the greatest personal benefit from greater work equity while at the same time providing benefits to society at large by better utilization of their talents. On the other hand, men who would not be able to handle increased competition can be expected to lose their previous advantages. Changes in the work-family role allocations would benefit men and women who feel constrained by the present role specialization and would threaten those whose identities are tied to the existing system. Thus predictions regarding the acceptability of any particular change would require analysis of those who would gain or lose by its diffusion.

The acceptability of change is also affected by its context. Lipman-Blumen (1973a) suggests that changes are hastened by crisis situations in which the resources and mechanisms usually allocated to a problem become inadequate. In stable periods, certain resources can be repressed and society can afford to allocate tasks according to a stratification system that focuses on the identity and status of individuals rather than their performance. In crisis periods, however, the importance of goal achievement makes maximal utilization of resources necessary; therefore, roles may be reallocated with greater weight to adequacy of performance and may include those held in reserve or repressed. It may be that the no-growth economic conditions of late, coupled with the still rising expectations of most people with regard to their standards of living, and with current dissatisfactions about the structure of work and family life, are sufficient to define the crisis that may facilitate the changes discussed here.

What would a sex-equitable work world look like? While it would be impossible to present a complete picture of such a work utopia, we suggest a number of criteria. Within a work institution Schein's (1971) conceptualization of an individual's career in an organization may provide one picture of equity. Schein sees individuals moving along three dimensions: the vertical corresponds to the notion that rank and level in the organization levels are separated by hierarchic boundaries; the radical corresponds to the notion of one's centrality in the organization, the degrees of being more or less "on the inside"; and the circumferential corresponds to the notion of divisions or functions within the organization.

The measures of true sex equality in an organization would be even distribution of men and women along all three dimensions. More important than the circumferential or functional dimension are the opportunities for vertical or hierarchic mobility, as well as for radial mobility, from the outer spheres to the inner core of the organization. When women are able to negotiate these changing boundaries successfully on the same basis that men can, then it can be said that the truly open and sex-integrated organization has arrived.

Other criteria for a sex-equitable work world can be proposed outside of particular institutional contexts. A work world that was characterized by equity for women and men would provide for women a proportional share of pay, social benefits, professional opportunity status, and power (Agassi, 1979), based on the same allocation system as that applied to men. Options and opportunities would be based on talent, not sex. Not only should exceptional women have the same opportunities as exceptional men, but working women who are mediocre should also be treated similarly to their male counterparts. Clearly equity would not necessarily mean that the sex composition must be perfectly balanced within each sphere of activity. Equity, not uniformity, is the criterion. Bernard (1976) suggests that neither the present state of sex specialization nor a 50-50 sex composition is likely to be the result of a move toward greater equity. Some occupations would still have a preponderance of either men or women, but for many occupations, a rough equality would be expected. The linkage between work and family suggests parallel effects — a small proportion of men and women may choose to perform sex-specialized domestic and provider roles, and perhaps some of them may cross over traditional role assignments, but the larger proportion would tend to share both functions.

Rossi (1969) suggests three potential models of sex equality: the pluralist model, in which marked differences are retained and valued for their diversity; the assimilation model, in which the subordinate group gets absorbed into the dominant group and loses its distinguishing characteristics; and the hybrid model, in which there are changes in both dominant and subordinate groups. Of the three, the hybrid model corresponds to the complementary alterations in several spheres that we have suggested are necessary to achieve equity for women at work. As Rossi (1969) pointed out, it is dubious whether a truly pluralist society, one in which all groups have equal status, power, or rewards, has ever existed. We have also argued that the maintenance of strict sex differences, which is implied by the pluralist approach, is a large barrier to occupational equity. The present system enables men to work at high levels of efficiency by having wives and families who act as their shock absorbers and nurturers. The assimilationist model is an operational model for many at present. It implies that women will have increased access to existing occupational opportunities while basic work and family structures remain unchanged. While this may be a necessary transition stage, already it is obvious that the model results in overburdened women who have dual responsibilities for career achievement and family maintenance. Also in accepting the status quo, it rejects the potential contribution that alternative values and structures can bring for all individuals, male and females, who work. The assimilationist model cannot be the goal of sexual equity at work. Virtually every institution in society must change to achieve equity at work.

REFERENCES

Abramowitz, S. I., Weitz, L. J., Schwartz, J. M., Amira, S., Gomes, B., & Abramowitz, C. V. Comparative counselor inferences toward women with medical school aspirations. *Journal of College Student Personnel*, 1975, *16*(2), 128-130.

Abramson, P. E., Goldberg, P. A., Greenberg, J. H., & Abramson, L. M. The talking platypus phenomenon: Competency ratings as a function of sex and professional status. *Psychology of Women Quarterly*, 1977, *2*, 114-124.

Adams, J. R., Lawrence, F. P., & Cook, S. J. Analyzing stereotypes of women in the work force. *Sex Roles*, 1979, *5*(5), 581-594.

Agassi, J. Beyond equality. In J. Lipman-Blumen and J. Bernard (Eds.), *Sex Roles and Social Policy*. London: Sage Publications, 1979.

Ahlum, C. Kalamazoo: A model for change. *Inequality in Education*, No. 18, Cambridge, Mass.: Center for Law and Education, Harvard University, 1974, 47-52.

Albrecht, S. L. Social class and sex stereotyping of occupations. *Journal of Vocational Behavior*, 1976, *9*, 321-328.

Alderfer, C. P. An empirical test of a new series of human needs. *Organizational Behavior and Human Performance*, 1969, *4*, 142-175.

Alderfer, C. P. Existence, relatedness and growth. *Human needs in organizational settings*. New York: The Free Press, 1972.

Allgeier, E. R. Beyond sowing and growing: The relationship of sex-typing to socialization, family plans and future orientation. *Journal of Applied Social Psychology*, 1975, *5*, 217-226.

Allport, F. R. The J-curve hypothesis of conforming behavior. *Journal of Social Psychology*, 1934, *5*, 141-183.

Allport, F. R. Rule and custom as individual variations of behavior distributed upon a continuum of conformity. *American Journal of Sociology*, 1939, *44*, 897-921.

Almquist, E. M., & Angrist, S. S. Career salience and atypicality of occupational choice among college women. *Journal of Marriage and the Family*, 1970, *32*, 242-249.

Almquist, E. M., & Angrist, S. S. Role model influences on college women's career aspirations. *Merrill-Palmer Quarterly*, 1971, *17*, 263-279.

Alper, T. G. Achievement motivation in college women: A now you see it, now you don't phenomena. *American Psychologist*, 1974, *29*, 194-203.

Altman, S. L., & Grossman, F. K. Women's career plans and maternal employment. *Psychology of Women Quarterly*, 1977, *1*, 365-376.

Andrisani, P. J., & Shapiro, M. B. Women's attitudes towards their jobs: Some longitudinal data on a national sample. *Personnel Psychology*, 1978, *31*, 15-33.

Angrist, S. S., & Almquist, E. M. *Career and contingencies.* New York: Dunellen, 1975.

Argote, L. M., Fisher, J. E., McDonald, P. J., & O'Neal, E. C. Competitiveness in males and in females: Situational determinates of fear of success behavior. *Sex Roles*, 1976, *2*.

Aries, E. Interaction patterns and themes of male, female and mixed groups. *Small Group Behavior*, 1976, *7*, 7-18.

Arkin, W., & Dobrofsky, L. R. Job sharing. In R. Rapoport & R. Rapoport (Eds.), *Working couples.* New York: Harper, 1978.

Armstrong, T. B. Job content and context factors related to satisfaction for different occupational levels. *Journal of Applied Psychology*, 1971, *55*, 57-65.

Aronoff, J., & Crano, W. D. A re-examination of task segregation and sex-role differential in the family. *American Sociological Review*, 1975, *40*, 12-20.

Aronson, W., Willerman, B., & Floyd, J. The effect of a pratfall on increasing interpersonal attractiveness. *Psychonomic Science*, 1966, *4*, 227-228.

Astin, H. Factors associated with the participation of the woman doctorate in the labor force. *Personnel Guidance Journal*, 1967, *45*, 240-246.

Astin, H. S. Career development of girls during the high school years. *Journal of Counseling Psychology*, 1968, *15*(6), 536-540.

Astin, H. *Women and achievement: Occupational entry and persistence.* Invited paper presented at the Eastern Psychological Association meeting, 1978.

Astin, H. S. Patterns of women's occupations. In J. Sherman and F. Denmark (Eds.), *The psychology of women: Future directions on research*. New York: Psychological Dimensions, 1979.

Astin, H., and Bayer, A. Sex discrimination in academe. *Educational Record*, 1972, *54*, 101-118.

Atkinson, J. W. Motivational determinants of risk-taking behavior. *Psychological Review*, 1957, *64*, 359-372.

Atkinson, J. W., & Feather, N. T. (Eds.). *A theory of achievement motivation*. New York: Wiley, 1966.

Bailyn, L. Mass media and children: A study of exposure habits and cognitive habits. *Psychological Monographs*, 1959, *73*, (no. 471).

Bailyn, L. Notes on the role of choice in the psychology of professional women. *Daedalus*, 1964, *93*, 700-710.

Bailyn, L. Accommodation of work to family. In R. Rapoport & R. Rapoport (Eds.), *Working couples*. New York: Harper, 1978.

Baker, E. F. *Technology and women's work*. New York: Columbia University Press, 1964.

Bales, R. *Interaction process analysis: A method for the study of small groups*. Cambridge, Mass.: Addison Wesley, 1950.

Bales, R., & Slater, P. Role differentiation in small decision-making groups. In T. Parsons & R. F. Bales (Eds.), *Family, socialization and interaction process*. Glencoe, Ill.: The Free Press, 1955.

Bardwick, J. M. *Psychology of women: A study of bio-cultural conflict*. Evanston, Ill.: Harper & Row, 1971.

Bardwick, J. M., & Douvan, E. Ambivalence: The socialization of women. In J. M. Bardwick (Ed.), *Readings on the psychology of women*. New York: Harper & Row, 1972.

Barnes, L. B. Organizational change and field experiment methods. In V. R. Vroom (Ed.), *Methods of organizational research*. Pittsburgh: University of Pittsburgh Press, 1967.

Barnes, W. F., & Jones, E. B. Women's increasing unemployment: A cyclical interpretation. *The Quarterly Review of Economics and Business*, 1975, *15*, 61-69.

Barnett, R. C. Personality correlates of vocational planning. *Genetic Psychology Monographs*, 1971, *83*, 349-356.

Barnett, R. C. Sex differences and age trends in occupational preference and occupational prestige. *Journal of Counseling Psychology*, 1975, *22*(1), 35-38.

Barnett, R. C., & Baruch, G. Career competence and well-being of adult women. In B. Gutek (Ed.), *New directions for education, work and careers: Enhancing women's career development.* San Francisco: Jossey-Bass, 1979.

Barrett, N. S. Women in the job market: Occupations, earnings, and career opportunities. In R. E. Smith (Ed.), *The subtle revolution.* Washington, D.C.: The Urban Institute, 1979.

Barrett, N. S., & Morgenstern, R. D. Why do blacks and women have high unemployment rates? *Journal of Human Resources*, 1974, *9*, 452-464.

Bar-Tal, D., & Frieze, I. Attributions of success and failure for actors and observers. *Journal of Research and Personality*, 1976, *10*, 256-265.

Bar-Tal, D., & Frieze, I. H. Achievement motivation for males and females as a determinant of attributions for success and failure. *Sex Roles*, 1977, *3*, 301-314.

Barthol, R. Personal communication, 1979.

Bartol, K. M. *Male and female leaders of small groups.* East Lansing: Michigan State University, Bureau of Economic and Business Research, 1973.

Bartol, K. M., & Butterfield, D. A. Sex effects in evaluating leaders. *Journal of Applied Psychology*, 1976, *61*(4), 446-545.

Bartol, K. M., & Wortman, M. S. Male versus female leaders: Effects on perceived leader behavior and satisfaction in a hospital. *Personnel Psychology*, 1975, *28*, 533-547.

Baruch, G. K. Maternal influences upon college women's attitudes toward women and work. *Developmental Psychology*, 1972, *6*(1), 32-37.

Baruch, R. The achievement motivation in women: Implications for career development. *Journal of Personality and Social Psychology*, 1967, *5*, 260-267.

Bass, B. M. *Leadership psychology and organizational behavior.* New York: Harper & Row, 1960.

Bass, B. M. *Organizational psychology.* Boston: Allyn and Bacon, 1965.

Bass, B. M. The anarchist movement and the T-groups. *Journal of Applied Behavioral Science*, 1967, *3*, 211-226.

Bass, B., Krusall, J., & Alexander, R. A. Male managers' attitudes toward working women. *American Behavioral Scientist*, 1971, *15*(2), 221-236.

Battle, E. S. Motivational determinants of academic task persistence. *Journal of Personality and Social Psychology*, 1965, *2*, 209-218.

Baude, A. Public policy and changing family patterns in Sweden 1930-1977. In J. Lipman-Blumen and J. Bernard (Eds.), *Sex roles and social policy*. London: Sage Publications, 1979.

Becker, H. S., & Strauss, A. L. Careers, personality and adult socialization. *American Journal of Sociology*, 1956, *62*(3), 253-263.

Bell, C. S. Unemployed women: Do they matter? *Wall Street Journal*, March 15, 1972, p. 18.

Bell, D. Why participation rates of black and white wives differ. *Journal of Human Resources*, 1974, *9*, 465-479.

Bem, S. L. The measurement of psychological androgyny. *Journal of Consulting and Clinical Psychology*, 1974, *42*, 155-162.

Bem, S. Sex role adaptability: One consequence of psychological androgyny. *Journal of Personality and Social Psychology*, 1975, *21*, 634-643.

Bem, S. L. On the utility of alternative procedures for assessing psychological androgyny. *Journal of Consulting and Clinical Psychology*, 1977, *45*, 196-205.

Bem, S. Gender schema theory: A cognitive account of sex typing. *Psychological Review*, 1980, in press.

Bennis, W. G., Benne, K. D., & Chin, R. (Eds.) *The planning of change*. New York: Holt, Rinehart & Winston, 1969.

Benson, D. J., & Thomson, G. *Sexual harassment on a university campus: The confluence of authority relations, sexual interest, and gender stratification.* Paper presented at the American Sociological Association meeting, New York City, 1980.

Berger, J., Cohen, B. P., & Zelditch, M., Jr. Status characteristics and social interaction. *American Sociological Review*, 1972, *37*, 241-515.

Berger, M., Foster, M., & Wallston, B. S. Finding two jobs. In R. Rapoport & R. Rapoport (Eds.), *Working couples*. New York: Harper, 1978.

Berk, R. A., & Berk, S. F. *Labor and leisure at home: Content and organization of the household day*. Beverly Hills: Sage, 1979.

Bernard, J. *Academic women.* University Park: Pennsylvania State University Press, 1964.

Bernard, J. *Women and the public interest. An essay on policy and protest.* Chicago: Aldine, 1971a.

Bernard, J. The paradox of the happy housewife. In V. Gornick and B. K. Moran (Eds.), *51 Percent.* New York: Basic Books, 1971b.

Bernard, J. *The future of marriage.* New York: World Books, 1972.

Bernard, J. *Women, wives and mothers: Values and options.* Chicago: Aldine, 1975.

Bernard, J. Change and stability in sex-role norms and behavior. *Journal of Social Issues*, 1976, *32*, 207-223.

Bernstein, J. The elementary school: Training ground for sex-role stereotypes. *Personnel and Guidance Journal*, 1972, *51*(2), 97-101.

Bigoness, W. Effect of applicant's sex, race and performance on employers' performance ratings: Some additional findings. *Journal of Applied Psychology*, 1976, *61*, 80-84.

Bingham, W. C., & House, E. W. Counselors' attitudes toward women and work. *Vocational Guidance Quarterly*, 1973, *22*, 16-23.

Bird, C. *The two paycheck marriage: How women at work are changing life in America.* New York: Rawson, Wade, 1979.

Blauner, R. *Alienation and freedom: The factory worker and his industry.* Chicago: University of Chicago Press, 1964.

Block, J. H. Conceptions of sex role. *American Psychologist*, 1973, *28*, 512-552.

Blood, R. O. Long-range causes and consequences of the employment of married women. *Journal of Marriage and the Family*, 1965, *27*, 43-47.

Blood, R. O., & Wolfe, D. M. *Husbands and wives: The dynamics of married living.* Glencoe, Ill.: The Free Press, 1960.

Blum, M. L., and Ross, J. J. A study of employee attitudes toward various incentives. *Personnel Psychology*, 1942, *19*, 438-444.

Blumberg, R. L. A paradigm for predicting the positions of women: Policy, implications and problems. In J. Lipman-Blumen and J. Bernard (Eds.), *Sex roles and social policy.* London: Sage Publications, 1979.

Bonacich, P., & Lewis, G. H. Function specialization and sociometric judgement. *Sociometry*, 1973, *36*, 31-41.

Borah, L. A. Effects of threat in bargaining: Critical and experimental analysis. *Journal of Abnormal and Social Psychology*, 1963, *66*, 37-44.

Boulding, E. Familial constraints on women's work roles. In M. Blaxall and B. Reagan (Eds.), *Women and the workplace*. Chicago: University of Chicago Press, 1976.

Bowman, G. W., Worthy, N. B., & Greyser, S. A. Are women executives people? *Harvard Business Review*, 1965, *43*, 14-17.

Brayfield, A. H., Wells, R. V., & Strate, R. W. Interrelationships among measures of job satisfaction and general satisfaction. *Journal of Applied Psychology*, 1957, *41*, 201-205.

Breedlove, C. J., & Cicirelli, V. G. Women's fear of success in relation to personal characteristics and type of occupation. *Journal of Psychology*, 1974, *86*, 181-190.

Bremer, T. H., & Wittig, M. A. Fear of success: A personality trait or a response to occupational deviance and role overload? *Sex Roles*, 1980, *6*(1), 27-46.

Bridges, W. P., & Berk, R. A. Determinants of white collar income: An evaluation of equal pay for equal work. *Social Science Research*, 1974, *3*, 211-233.

Brief, A. P., VanSell, M., & Aldag, R. J. Vocational decision making among women: Implications for organizational behavior. *Academy of Management Review*, 1979, *4*(4), 521-530.

Brim, O. G. Socialization through the life cycle. In O. G. Brim and S. Wheeler (Eds.), *Socialization after childhood*. New York: John Wiley, 1966.

Broverman, I. K., Broverman, D. M., Clarkson, F. E., Rosenkrantz, P. S., & Vogel, S. R. Sex-role stereotypes and clinical judgements of mental health. *Journal of Counseling and Clinical Psychology*, 1970, *34*(1), 1-7.

Broverman, I. K., Vogel, S. R., Broverman, D. M., Clarkson, F. E., & Rosenkrantz, P. S. Sex-role stereotypes: A current appraisal. *Journal of Social Issues*, 1972, *28*(2), 59-78.

Bryson, J. B., & Bryson, R. B. (Eds.). Dual career couples. *Special Issue of Psychology of Women Quarterly*, 1978, *3*, 5-120.

Bryson, R., Bryson, J., & Johnson, M. F. Family size, satisfaction and productivity in dual career couples. *Psychology of Women Quarterly*, 1978, *3*(1), 67-77.

Bryson, R., Bryson, J., Licht, M., & Licht, B. The professional pair: Husband and wife psychologists. *American Psychologist*, 1976, *31*, 10-16.

Buckley, J. Pay differences between men and women in the same jobs. *Monthly Labor Review*, 1971, *94*, 36-39.

Bumpass, L., & Westoff, C. F. *The later years of childbearing.* Princeton, N. J.: Princeton University Press, 1970.

Burke, R. Differences in perception of desired job characteristics of the opposite sex. *Journal of Genetic Psychology*, 1966a, *109*, 27-37.

Burke, R. Differences in perception of desired job characteristics of the same sex and the opposite sex. *Journal of Genetic Psychology*, 1966b, *109*, 37-46.

Byrne, D. *The attraction paradigm.* New York: Academic Press, 1971.

Byrne, D., & Griffitt, W. Similarity and awareness of similarity of personality characteristics as determinants of attraction. *Journal of Experimental Research in Personality*, 1969, *3*, 177-186.

Campbell, A., Converse, P. E., & Rodgers, W. L. *The quality of American life.* New York: Russell Sage Foundation, 1976.

Campbell, J. P., & Dunnette, M. D. Effectiveness of T-group experiences in managerial training and development. *Psychological Bulletin*, 1968, *70*, 73-104.

Canter, R. Achievement-related expectations and aspirations in college women. *Sex Roles*, 1979, *5*(4), 453-470.

Caplow, T. *The sociology of work.* New York: McGraw-Hill, 1964.

Cartwright, D., & Zander, A. (Eds.). *Group dynamics.* New York: Harper & Row, 1968.

Cash, T. F., Gillen, B., & Burns, D. S. Sexism and "beautyism" in personnel consultant decision-making. *Journal of Applied Psychology*, 1977, *62*, 301-310.

Cattell, R. B. *Personality and mood by questionnaire.* San Francisco: Jossey Bass, 1973.

Cecil, E. A., Paul, R. J., & Olins, R. A. Perceived importance of selected variables used to evaluate male and female job applicants. *Personnel Psychology*, 1973, *26*, 397-404.

Centers, R. Motivational aspects of occupational stratification. *Journal of Social Psychology*, 1948, *28*, 187-217.

Centers, R., & Bugental, D. Intrinsic and extrinsic job motivations among different segments of the working population. *Journal of Applied Psychology*, 1966, *50*, 193-197.

Clark, E. T. Influence of sex and social class on occupational preference and perception. *Personnel and Guidance Journal*, 1967, *45*, 440-441.

Cochran, M. M., & Bronfenbrenner, U. Child rearing, parenthood, and the world of work. In C. Kerr and J. Rosow (Eds.), *Work in America: The decade ahead*. New York: Van Nostrand Reinhold, 1979.

Cohen, M. Sex differences in compensations. *Journal of Human Resources*, 1971, *6*, 432-447.

Cohen, S. L. & Bunker, K. A. Subtle effects of sex role stereotype and recruiters hiring decision. *Journal of Applied Psychology*, 1975, *60*, 566-572.

Collver, A. O. Women's work participation and fertility in metropolitan areas. *Demography*, 1968, *5*(1), 55-60.

Cook, T. D., Bean, J. R., Calder, B. J., Frey, R., Krovetz, M. L., & Reisman, S. R. Demand characteristics and three conceptions of the frequently deceived subject. *Journal of Personality and Social Psychology*, 1970, *14*, 185-194.

Cooper, S. Career patterns of women. *Vocational Rehabilitation and Education Quarterly*, 1963, 13-14; 21-28.

Coopers & Lybrand, Office of the Future Amalgamates People, Equipment Systems, Coopers and Lybrand Newsletter, 1979, *21*(10), October, 4-5.

Corcoran, M. The economic consequences of marital dissolution for women in the middle years. *Sex Roles*, 1979, *5*(3), 343-354.

Corcoran, M., & Duncan, G. J. Work history, labor force attachment and earnings: Differences between races and sexes. *Journal of Human Resources*, 1979, *14*, 3-20.

Costrich, N., Feinstein, J., Kidder, L., Maracek, J., & Pascale, L. When stereotypes hurt: Studies of penalties for role reversals. *Journal of Experimental Social Psychology*, 1975, *11*, 520-530.

Crandall, V. C. Sex differences in expectancy of intellectual and academic reinforcement. In C. P. Smith (Ed.), *Achievement-related motives in children*. New York: Russell Sage Foundation, 1969.

Crowley, J., Levitin, T. E., & Quinn, R. P. Seven deadly half-truths about women. In C. Tavris (Ed.), *The female experience*. Del Mar, Calif.: CRM, 1973.

Cuca, J. Women psychologists and marriage: A bad match? *American Psychological Association Monitor*, 1976.

Davis, L. E., & Cherns, A. B. (Eds.). *The quality of working life*. New York: The Free Press, 1975.

Day, D. R., & Stogdill, R. M. Leader behavior of male and female supervisor: A comparative study. *Personnel Psychology*, 1972, *25*, 353-360.

Deaux, K. *The behavior of women and men*. Monterey, Calif.: Brooks/Cole, 1976a.

Deaux, K. Sex: A perspective on the attribution process. In J. Harvey, W. Ickes, & R. Kidd (Eds.), *New directions in attribution research*. Hillsdale: Erlbaum Associates, 1976b.

Deaux, K. Self-evaluations of male and female managers. *Sex Roles*, 1979, *5*(5), 571-580.

Deaux, K., & Emswiller, T. Explanations of successful performance on sex-linked tasks: What is skill for the male is luck for the female. *Journal of Personality and Social Psychology*, 1974, *29*, 80-85.

Deaux, K., & Farris, E. Attributing causes for one's own performance: The effects of sex, norms and outcome. *Journal of Research in Personality*, 1977, *11*, 59-72.

Deaux, K., & Taynor, J. Evaluation of male and female ability: Bias works two ways. *Psychology Reports*, 1973, *31*, 20-31.

deBoer, C. The polls: Women at work. *Public Opinion Quarterly*, 1977, *41*, 268-277.

Dickerson, K. G. Are female college students influenced by the expectations they perceive their faculty and administration have for them? *Journal of National Association of Women Deans and Counselors*, 1974, *37*(4), 167-172.

Dickinson, J. Labor supply of family members. In *Five thousand American families-patterns of economics progress* (Vol. 1). Ann Arbor: University of Michigan, Institute for Social Research, 1974, pp. 177-250.

Diggory, J. Self-evaluation. *Concepts and studies*. New York: John Wiley, 1966.

Dipboye, R. L., Arvey, R. B., & Terpstra, D. E. Sex and physical attractiveness of raters and applicants as determinants of resume evaluations. *Journal of Applied Psychology*, 1977, *62*, 288-294.

Dipboye, R. L., Fromkin, H. L., & Wiback, J. K. Relative importance of appli-cant sex, attractiveness, and scholastic standing in evaluation of job applicant resources. *Journal of Applied Psychology*, 1975, *60*, 39-43.

Dipboye, R. L., & Wiley, J. W. Reactions of college recruiters as a function of interviews sex and self-presentation style. *Journal of Vocational Behavior*, 1977, *10*, 1-12.

Douvan, E., & Pleck, J. Separation as support. In R. Rapoport & R. Rapoport (Eds.), *Working couples*. New York: Harper, 1978.

Drexler, J. A., & Beehr, T. A. Behaviors as predictors of satisfaction for men and women, 1977, unpublished manuscript.

Duncan, O. D., & Duncan, B. A methodological analysis of segregation indexes. *American Sociological Review*, 1955, *29*, 210-217.

Dunnette, M. D., & Campbell, J. P. Laboratory education: Impact on people and organizations. In G. W. Dalton, P. R. Lawrence, & L. E. Greinal (Eds.), *Organizational change and development*. Homewood, Ill.: Irwin Dorsey, 1970.

Durning, K. P. *Women at the naval academy: The first year of integration.* NPRDC TR 78-12, Navy Personnel Research and Development Center, 1978.

Dweck, C. S. The role of expectations and attributions in the alleviation of learned helplessness. *Journal of Personality and Social Psychology*, 1975, *31*, 674-685.

Dweck, C. S., & Bush, E. S. Sex differences in learned helplessness: I. Differ-ential debilitation with peer and adult evaluators. *Developmental Psychol-ogy*, 1976, *12*, 147-156.

Dweck, C. S., Davidson, W., Nelson, S., & Enna, B. Sex differences in learned helplessness: II. The contingencies of evaluative feedback in the classroom; and III. An experimental analysis. *Developmental Psychology*, 1978, *14*, 268-276.

Dweck, C. S., & Gilliard, D. Expectancy statements and determinants of reactions to failure: Sex differences in persistence and expectancy change. *Journal of Personality and Social Psychology*, 1975, *32*, 1077-1084.

Dweck, C. S., Goetz, T. E., & Strauss, N. L. Sex differences in learned helpless-ness: IV. An experimental and naturalistic study of failure generalization and its mediators. *Journal of Personality and Social Psychology*, 1980, *38*, 441-452.

Elder, G. H., & Rockwell, R. C. Marital timing in women's life patterns. *Journal of Family History*, 1976, *1*(1), 34-53.

Entwistle, D. R., & Greenberger, E. Adolescents' views of women's work role. *American Journal of Orthopsychiatry*, 1972, *42*(4), 648-656.

Epstein, C. F. Women and professional careers: The case of the woman lawyer. Ph.D. dissertation, Columbia University, 1968.

Epstein, C. Encountering the male establishment: Sex-status limits on women's careers in the professions. *American Journal of Sociology*, 1970a, *75*(6), 965-982.

Epstein, C. *Woman's place: Options and limits in professional careers*. Berkeley: University of California Press, 1970b.

Epstein, C. F. Current and emerging occupation-centered feminine life-career positions and trends. *Annals of the New York Academy of Science*, 1970c, *175*, 898-909.

Epstein, C. F. Law partners and marital partners: Strains and solutions in the dual-career family enterprise. *Human Relations*, 1971, *24*, 549-564.

Epstein, C. F. Sex role stereotyping, occupations and social exchange. *Women's Studies*, 1976, *3*, 185-194.

Equal Employment Opportunity Commission. Sixth Annual Report. Washington, D. C.: USGPO, 1972.

Etaugh, C. Effects of maternal employment on children: A review of recent research. *Merrill-Palmer Quarterly*, 1974, *20*, 71-98.

Etaugh, C., & Brown, B. Perceiving the causes of success and failure of male and female performers. *Developmental Psychology*, 1975, *11*, 103.

Farkas, G. Education, wage rates and the division of labor between husband and wife. *Journal of Marriage and the Family*, 1976, *38*, 473-483.

Farley, L. *Sexual shakedown: The sexual harassment of women on the job*. New York: McGraw-Hill, 1978.

Farmer, H. S., & Bohn, M. J. Home-career conflict reduction and the level of career interest in women. *Journal of Counseling Psychology*, 1970, *17*, 228-232.

Farris, A. Commuting. In R. Rapoport & R. Rapoport (Eds.), *Working couples*. New York: Harper, 1978.

Farris, G. F. Leadership and supervision in the informal organization. In J. G. Hunt & L. L. Larson (Eds.), *Contingency approaches to leadership*. Carbondale: University of Illinois Press, 1974.

Feather, N. T. Effects of prior success and failure on expectations of success and failure. *Journal of Personality and Social Psychology*, 1966, *3*, 287-298.

Feather, N. T. Attribution of responsibility and valence of success and failure in relation to initial confidence and task performance. *Journal of Personality and Social Psychology*, 1969, *13*, 129-144.

Feather, N. T. Positive and negative reactions to male and female success and failure in reaction to sex-typed appropriateness of occupations. *Journal of Personality and Social Psychology*, 1975, *31*, 536-548.

Feather, N. T., & Simon, J. G. Fear of success and causal attribution of outcomes. *Journal of Personality*, 1973, *41*, 525-542.

Feather, N. T., & Simon, J. G. Reactions to male and female success and failure in sex-linked occupations: Impressions of personality, causal attribution, and perceived likelihood of difference consequences. *Journal of Personality and Social Psychology*, 1975, *31*, 20-31.

Fein, R. A. Research on fathering: Social policy and an emergent perspective. *Journal of Social Issues*, 1978, *34*, 122-135.

Feldman, S. D. *Escape from the doll's house: Women in graduate and professional school education*. A report prepared for the Carnegie Commission on Higher Education. New York: McGraw-Hill, 1974, 208 pp.

Feldman-Summers, S., & Kiesler, S. B. Those who are number two try harder: The effect of sex on attributions of causality. *Journal of Personality and Social Psychology*, 1974, *30*, 846-855.

Ferber, M. A., & Lowry, H. M. Women: The new reserve army of the underemployed. In M. Blaxall & B. Reagan (Eds.), *Women and the workplace: Implications of occupational segregation*. Chicago: University of Chicago Press, 1976.

Feshbach, N. D. A primer for non-sexism in schools. Draft for *Educational Horizons*, 1975, 16 pp.

Festinger, L. A theory of social comparison processes. *Human Relations*, 1952, *5*, 327-346.

Fidell, L. S. Empirical verification of sex discrimination in hiring practice in psychology. *American Psychologist*, 1970, *25*, 1094-1098.

Fine, S. A. *Three kinds of skills: An approach to understanding the nature of human performance.* Proceedings of the 75th Annual Convention of the APA, 1967, 365.

Finegan, T. A. Participation of married women in the labor force. In C. B. Lloyd (Ed.), *Sex, discrimination and the division of labor.* New York: Columbia University Press, 1975.

Flaherty, J. F., & Dusek, J. B. An investigation of the relationship between psychological androgyny and components of self-concept. *Journal of Personality and Social Psychology*, 1980, *38*(6), 984-992.

Flaim, P. O., & Fullerton, H. N. Labor force projections to 1990: Three possible paths. *Monthly Labor Review*, 1978(Dec.), 25-35.

Fleishman, E. A. A leader behavior description for industry. In R. M. Stogdill and A. E. Coons (Eds.), *Leader behavior: Its description and measurement.* Columbus: Ohio State University, Bureau of Business Research, Monograph No. 88, 1957, 103-119.

Fogarty, M., Allen, A. J., Allen, I., & Walters, P. *Women in top jobs: Four studies in achievement.* London: Allen and Unwin, 1971.

Fogarty, M. P., Rapoport, R., & Rapoport, R. N. *Career, sex and family.* London: Allen and Unwin, 1971.

Folger, J. K., Astin, H. S., & Bayer, A. E. *Human resources and higher education.* New York: Russell Sage, 1970.

Foster, M. A., Wallston, B. S., & Berger, M. Feminist orientation and job-seeking behavior among dual-career couples. *Sex Roles*, 1980, *6*(1), 59-66.

Frank, F. D., & Drucker, J. The influence of evaluatee's sex on evaluations of a response on a managerial selection instrument. *Sex Roles*, 1977, *3*, 59-64.

Freese, L., & Cohen, B. P. Eliminating status generalization. *Sociometry*, 1973, *36*, 177-193.

French, E. G., & Lesser, G. S. Some characteristics of the achievement motive in women. *Journal of Abnormal and Social Psychology*, 1964, *68*(2), 119-128.

Frieze, I. Studies of information processing and the attributional process. Ph.D. dissertation, UCLA, 1973.

Frieze, I. H. The role of information processing in making causal attributions for success and failure. In J. S. Carroll & J. W. Payne (Eds.), *Cognition and social behavior.* Hillsdale, N.J.: Erlbaum Associates, 1976.

Frieze, I. H., McHugh, M. C., Fisher, J., & Valle, V. A. *Attributing the causes of success and failure: Internal and external barriers to achievement in women.* Paper presented at the APA-NIMH Conference on New Directions for Research on Women, Madison, 1975.

Fuchs, S. V. Differences in hourly earnings between men and women. *Monthly Labor Review*, 1971, *94*, 9-15.

Geiken, K. F. Expectation concerning husband-wife responsibilities in the home. *Journal of Marriage and the Family*, 1964, *26*(3), 349-352.

Gergen, K. J. Social psychology as history. *Journal of Personality and Social Psychology*, 1973, *26*, 309-320.

Gibb, C. A. Leadership. In G. Lindzey & E. Aronson (Eds.), *Handbook of social psychology*. Reading, Mass.: Addison-Wesley, 1969, *4*, 205-282.

Giele, J. *Women and the future.* New York: The Free Press, 1978.

Gilmer, B. *Industrial psychology.* New York: McGraw-Hill, 1957.

Gilmer, B. *Industrial psychology.* New York: McGraw-Hill, 1961.

Goetz, T. E., & Herman, J. B. *Effects of supervisors' and subordinates' sex on productivity and morale.* Paper presented at the American Psychological Association 84th annual convention, Washington, D.C., September 1976.

Goldberg, P. Are women prejudiced against women? *Trans-Action*, 1968, *5*, 28-30.

Gordon, F., & Strober, M. (Eds.). *Bringing women into management.* New York: McGraw-Hill, 1975.

Gramm, W. L. Household utility maximization and the working wife. *The American Economic Review*, 1975, *65*, 90-100.

Green, L. B., & Parker, H. J. Parental influence upon adolescents' occupational choice: A test of Roe's theory. *Journal of Counseling Psychology*, 1965, *12*, 379-385.

Grigg, A. E. Childhood experience with parental attitudes: A test of Roe's hypothesis. *Journal of Counseling Psychology*, 1959, *6*, 153-156.

Gronseth, E. Work sharing: A Norwegian example. In R. Rapoport & R. Rapoport (Eds.), *Working couples.* New York: Harper, 1978.

Grossman, A. S. Women in the labor force: The early years. *Monthly Labor Review*, 1975, *98*, 3-9.

Guion, R. M. *Personnel testing.* New York: McGraw-Hill, 1965.

Gurin, G., Veroff, J., & Feld, S. *Americans view their mental health.* New York: Basic Books, 1960.

Gutek, B. A., & Hotchkiss, H. *Effects of family responsibilities of women on their reactions to their jobs.* Paper presented at the annual convention of the Western Psychological Association, San Francisco, April 1978.

Gutek, B. A., & Nakamura, C. Y. Sexuality, sex roles and work behavior. In E. R. Allgeier & N. B. McCormick (Eds.), *The changing boundaries: Gender roles and sexual behavior.* New York: Mayfield, in press (1981).

Gutek, B. A., Nakamura, C. Y., Gahart, M., Handschumacher, I., & Russell, D. Sexuality and the workplace. *Basic and Applied Social Psychology,* 1980, *1,* 3 (Oct.).

Gutek, B. A., Nakamura, C. Y., & Nieva, V. F. The interdependence of work and family roles. *Journal of Occupational Behavior,* 1980, *1.*

Gutek, B. A., & Stevens, D. A. Effect of sex of subject, sex of stimulus cue and androgyny level on evaluation in work situations which evoke sex role stereotypes. *Journal of Vocational Behavior,* 1979, *14,* 12-32.

Haavio-Mannila, E. Sex-role attitudes in Finland, 1960-1970. *Journal of Social Issues,* 1972, *28*(2), 93-110.

Hacker, H. M. Women as a minority group. *Social Forces,* 1951, *30,* 60-69.

Haefner, J. E. Race, age, sex and competence as factors in employed selection of the disadvantaged. *Journal of Applied Psychology,* 1977a, *62,* 199-202.

Haefner, J. E. Sources of discrimination among employees: A survey investigation. *Journal of Applied Psychology,* 1977b, *62,* 265-270.

Hagen, R. L., & Kahn, A. Discrimination against competent women. *Journal of Applied Social Psychology,* 1975, *5,* 362-376.

Hahn, D. L. The importance of pay. In R. P. Quinn and others (Eds.), *The 1972-73 quality of employment survey: Continuing chronicles of an unfinished enterprise.* Ann Arbor, Mich.: Survey Research Center, 1974.

Hall, D. T. A model of coping with role conflict: The role behavior of college educated women. *Administrative Science Quarterly,* 1972, *17,* 471-486.

Hall, D. T. *Careers in organizations.* Pacific Palisades, Calif.: Goodyear Publications, 1976.

Hall, D. T., & Gordon, F. E. Career choices of married women: Effects on conflict, role behavior and satisfaction. *Journal of Applied Psychology*, 1973, *58*(1), 42-48.

Hall, F. S., & Hall, D. T. Effects of job incumbents' race and sex on evaluation of managerial performance. *Academy of Management Journal*, 1976, *14*(3), 476-481.

Hall, F. S., & Hall, D. T. Dual careers — how do couples and companies cope with the problems? *Organizational Dynamics*, 1978 (Spring), 57-77.

Haller, M., & Rosenmayr, L. The pluridimensionality of work commitment. *Human Relations*, 1971, *24*(6), 501-518.

Halperin, M. S., & Abrams, D. L. Sex differences in predicting final examination grades: The influence of past performance, attributions and achievement motivation. *Journal of Educational Psychology*, 1978, *70*, 763-771.

Halpin, A. W., & Winer, B. J. A factorial study of the leader behavior descriptions. In R. M. Stogdill & A. E. Coons (Eds.), *Leader behavior: Its description and measurement*. Columbus: Ohio State University, Bureau of Business Research Monograph No. 88, 1957, 39-51.

Hamilton, D. A. Cognitive biases in the perception of social groups. In J. E. Carrol & J. W. Payne (Eds.), *Cognition and social behavior*. Hillsdale, N.J.: Erlbaum, 1976, pp. 81-93.

Hamner, W. C., Kim, J. S., Baird, L., & Bigoness, W. Race and sex as determinants of ratings by potential employers in a simulated work-sampling task. *Journal of Applied Psychology*, 1974, *59*, 705-711.

Hansen, D. *Sex differences and supervision*. Paper presented at 82nd annual meeting of the American Psychological Association, New Orleans, 1974.

Harmon, L. Anatomy of career commitment in women. *Journal of Counseling Psychology*, 1970, *17*, 77-80.

Harmon, L. W. The childhood and adolescent career plans of college women. *Journal of Vocational Behavior*, 1971, *1*(1), 45-56.

Harragan, B. L. *Games mother never taught you*. New York: Warner Books, 1977.

Hartmann, H. Capitalism, patriarchy and job segregation by sex. In M. Blaxall & B. Reagan (Eds.), *Women and the workplace*. Chicago: University of Chicago Press, 1976.

Havens, E. M., & Gibbs, J. P. The relations between female labor force partici- pation and fertility. *Sociological Methods and Research*, 1975, *3*, 258-290.

Hawley, P. What women think men think: Does it affect their career choice? *Journal of Counseling Psychology*, 1971, *18*(3), 193-199.

Hedges, J. N., & Barnett, J. K. Working women and the division of household tasks. *Monthly Labor Review*, 1972 (April), 9-14.

Heer, D. M. Dominance and the working wife. *Social Forces*, 1958, *26*, 341-347.

Heider, F. *The psychology of interpersonal relations.* New York: John Wiley, 1958.

Heilbrun, A. B., Jr. Parental identification and the patterning of vocational inter- ests in college males and females. *Journal of Counseling Psychology*, 1969, *16*(4), 342-347.

Helmreich, R., Aronson, E., & LeFan, J. To err is humanizing-sometimes: Effects of self-esteem, competence and a pratfall on interpersonal attraction. *Journal of Personality and Social Psychology*, 1970, *16*, 259-264.

Heneman, H. G. Impact of test information and applicant sex on applicant evaluations in a selection simulation. *Journal of Applied Psychology*, 1977, *62*, 524-526.

Hennig, M., & Jardim, A. *The managerial women.* New York: Anchor Press/ Doubleday, 1977.

Herman, J. B., & Gyllstrom, K. K. Working men and women: Inter- and intra- role conflict. *Psychology of Women Quarterly*, 1977, *1*, 319-333.

Herzberg, F., Mausner, B., Peterson, R. O., & Capwell, D. F. *Job attitudes: Review of research and opinion.* Pittsburgh: Psychological Services of Pittsburgh, 1957.

Herzberg, F., Mausner, B., & Snyderman, B. *The motivation to work.* New York: John Wiley, 1959.

Hofferth, S. L., & Moore, K. A. Women's employment and marriage. In R. E. Smith (Ed.), *The subtle revolution.* Washington, D.C.: The Urban Institute, 1979.

Hoffman, L. W. Effects of maternal employment on the child — A review of the research. *Developmental Psychology*, 1974a, *10*(2), 204-228.

Hoffman, L. W. Fear of success in males and females: 1965 and 1971. *Journal of Consulting and Clinical Psychology*, 1974b, *42*(3), 353-358.

Hoffman, L. W. Psychological factors. In L. W. Hoffman and F. I. Nye (Eds.), *Working mothers.* San Francisco: Jossey-Bass, 1974c.

Hoffman, L. W. Employment of women and fertility. In L. W. Hoffman and F. I. Nye (Eds.), *Working mothers.* San Francisco: Jossey-Bass, 1974d.

Hoffman, L. W. Maternal employment: 1979. *American Psychologist,* 1979, *34*, 859-865.

Hoffman, L. W., & Maier, N. R. F. Social factors influencing problem solving in women. *Journal of Personality and Social Psychology,* 1966, *4*(4), 382-390.

Hoffman, L. W., & Nye, F. I. (Eds.). *Working mothers.* San Francisco: Jossey-Bass, 1974.

Holland, J. I. *Making vocational choices: A theory of careers.* Englewood Cliffs, N.J.: Prentice-Hall, 1973.

Hollander, E. P. Conformity, status and idiosyncracy credit. *Psychological Review,* 1958, *65*, 117-127.

Hollander, E. P., Julian, J. W., & Haaland, G. A. Conformity process and prior group support. *Journal of Personality and Social Psychology,* 1965, *2*, 852-858.

Holter, H. Sex roles and social change. *Acta Sociologica,* 1971, *14*, 2-12.

Horner, M. Sex differences in achievement motivation and performance in competitive and non-competitive situations. Ph.D. dissertation, University of Michigan, 1968.

House, R. J., & Wigdor, L. A. Herzberg's dual factor theory of job satisfaction and motivation: A review of criticism and evidence. *Personnel Psychology,* 1967, *20*, 369-389.

House, W. C., & Perney, V. Valence of expected and unexpected outcomes as a function of locus of control and type of expectancy. *Journal of Personality and Social Psychology,* 1974, *29*, 454-563.

Hoyt, D. P., & Kennedy, C. E. Interest and personality correlates of career-motivated and homemaking-motivated college women. *Journal of Counseling Psychology,* 1958, *5*(1), 44-49.

Hughes, E. Dilemmas and contradictions of status. *American Journal of Sociology,* 1944, *50*, 353-359.

Hulin, C. L., & Smith, P. C. Sex differences in job satisfaction. *Journal of Applied Psychology,* 1964, *48*, 88-92.

Ickes, W., & Barnes, R. D. Boys and girls together and alienated: On enacting stereotyped sex roles in mixed-sex dyads. *Journal of Personality and Social Psychology*, 1978, *36*, 669-681.

Iglitzen, L. B. A child's eye view of sex roles. *Today's Education*, 1972, *61*, 20-31.

Inderlied, S. Goal setting and career development of women. In B. Gutek (Ed.), *New directions for education, work and careers: Enhancing women's career development*. San Francisco: Jossey-Bass, 1979.

Iris, B., & Barrett, G. V. Some relations between job and life satisfaction and job importance. *Journal of Applied Psychology*, 1972, *56*, 301-304.

Jacobson, M. B., & Effertz, J. Sex roles and leadership perceptions of the leaders and the led. *Organizational Behavior and Human Performance*, 1974, *12*, 383-397.

Jellison, J. M., Jackson-White, R., Bruder, K. A., & Martyna, W. Achievement behavior: A situational interpretation. *Sex Roles*, 1975, *1*(4), 369-384.

Julian, J. W., Regula, C. R., & Hollander, E. P. Effects of prior agreement by others on task confidence and conformity. *Journal of Personality and Social Psychology*, 1968, *9*, 171-178.

Juran, S. A measure of stereotyping in fear-of-success cues. *Sex Roles*, 1979, *5*(3), 287-298.

Kahn, A., Hottes, J., & Davis, W. L. Cooperation and optimal responding in the prisoner's dilemma game. *Journal of Personality and Social Psychology*, 1971, *17*, 267-279.

Kane, J. S., & Lawler, E. E., III. Performance appraisal effectiveness: Its assessment and determinants. In B. Staw (Ed.), *Research on organizational behavior* (Vol. 1). Greenwich, Conn.: JAI Press, 1979.

Kanter, R. M. *Men and women of the corporation*. New York: Basic Books, 1977a.

Kanter, R. M. Some effects of proportions on group life: Skewed sex ratios and responses to taken women. *American Journal of Sociology*, 1977b, *82*(5), 965-990.

Kanter, R. M. *Work and family in the United States: A clinical review and agenda for research*. New York: Russell Sage, 1977c.

Katz, D., & Kahn, R. L. *The social psychology of organizations* (2d ed). New York: John Wiley, 1978.

Kessler-Harris, A. Women, work and social change. In B. Carroll (Ed.), *Liberating women's history*. Urbana, Ill.: University of Illinois Press, 1976.

Kiesler, S. B. Actuarial prejudice toward women and its implications. *Journal of Applied Social Psychology*, 1975, *5*, 201-216.

Kilpatrick, F., Cummings, M., & Jenning, M. *Source book of a study of occupational values and the image of the federal service*. Washington, D.C.: The Brookings Institution, 1964.

Kirchner, E. P., & Vondracek, S. I. *What do you want to be when you grow up? Vocational choice in children aged three to six*. Paper presented at biennial meeting of the Society for Research in Child Development. Philadelphia, March 1973.

Klein, D. P. Women in the labor force: The middle years. *Monthly Labor Review*, 1975 (November), *98*, 10-16.

Komorita, S. S., & Mechling, J. Betrayal and reconciliation in a two-person game. *Journal of Personality and Social Psychology*, 1967, *6*, 349-353.

Kriger, S. F. nAch and perceived parental child-rearing: Attitudes of career women and homemakers. *Journal of Vocational Behavior*, 1972, *2*, 419-432.

Kristal, J., Sanders, B., Spence, J. T., & Helmreich, R. Inferences about the femininity of competent women and their implications for like-ability. *Sex Roles*, 1975, *1*, 33-40.

Kuklen, R. G. Needs, perceived need satisfaction opportunities, and satisfaction with occupation. *Journal of Applied Psychology*, 1963, *47*, 56-64.

Lao, R. C., Upchurch, W. H., Corwin, B. J., & Crossnickle, W. F. Biased attitudes toward females as indicated by ratings of intelligence and likeability. *Psychology Reports*, 1975, *37*, 1315-1320.

Lawler, E. E., III. *Pay and organizational effectiveness: A psychological view*. New York: McGraw-Hill, 1971.

Lawler, E. E., III. *Motivation in work organizations*. Monterey, Calif.: Brooks/ Cole, 1973.

Laws, J. L. A feminist review of marital adjustment literature: The rape of the locke. *Journal of Marriage and the Family*, 1971, *33*, 483-516.

Laws, J. L. The psychology of tokenism: An analysis. *Sex Roles*, 1975, *1*, 51-67.

Laws, J. L. *The second X: Sex role and social role*. New York: Elsevier, 1979.

Lehman, H. C., & Wittig, P. A. Some factors which influence the child's choice of occupations. *Elementary School Journal*, 1963, *31*, 285-291.

Leik, R. L. Instrumentality and emotionality in family interaction. *Sociometry*, 1963, *26*, 131-145.

Lenny, E. Women's self-confidence in achievement settings. *Psychological Bulletin*, 1977, *84*, 1-13.

Leventhal, G. S., & Michaels, J. W. Locus of cause and equity motivation as determinants of reward allocation. *Journal of Personality and Social Psychology*, 1971, *17*, 229-235.

Levine, C. Comments on Osborn & Hunt's paper. In J. G. Hunt & L. L. Larson (Eds.), *Leadership frontiers*. Kent, Ohio: Kent State University Press, 1977.

Levinson, R. M. Sex discrimination and employment practices. *Social Problems*, 1975, *22*(4), 533-543.

Levitin, T., Quinn, R. L., & Staines, G. Sex discrimination against the American working woman. *American Behavioral Scientist*, 1971, *15*, 237-254.

Levitt, E. A. Vocational development of professional women. A review. *Journal of Vocational Behavior*, 1972, *2*, 375-385.

Lewis, E. C. *Developing women's potential*. Ames: Iowa State University Press, 1968.

Lewis, G. H. Role differentiation. *American Sociological Review*, 1972, *37*, 424-434.

Lipman-Blumen, J. How ideology shapes women's lives. *Scientific American*, 1972, *226*, 34-42.

Lipman-Blumen, J. Role de-differentiation as a system response to crisis: Occupational and political roles of women. *Sociological Inquiry*, 1973a, *13*, 105-129.

Lipman-Blumen, J. *The vicarious achievement ethic and non-traditional roles for women*. Presented at the annual meeting of the Eastern Sociological Society, New York, 1973b.

Lipman-Blumen, J. Toward a homosocial theory of sex-roles: An explanation of the sex segregation of social interaction. In M. Blaxall & B. Reagan (Eds.), *Women and the workplace*. Chicago: University of Chicago Press, 1976.

Lipman-Blumen, J., and Bernard, J. (Eds.). *Sex roles and social policy*. London: Sage Publications, 1979.

Lipman-Blumen, J., & Bernard, J. The policy promissory note: Time to deliver. In J. Lipman-Blumen and J. Bernard (Eds.), *Sex roles and social policy*. London: Sage Publications, 1979.

Lipman-Blumen, J., & Leavitt, H. J. Vicarious and direct achievement patterns in adulthood. *The Counseling Psychologist*, 1976, *6*, 26-31.

Lockheed, M. E. Female motive to avoid success psychological barrier or response to deviancy? *Sex Roles*, 1975, *1*, 41-50.

Long, L. Women's labor force participation and the residential mobility of families. *Social Forces*, 1974 (March), *52*, 342-348.

Looft, W. R. Sex differences in the expression of vocational aspirations by elementary school children. *Developmental Psychology*, 1971a, *5*(2), 366-372.

Looft, W. R. Vocational aspirations of second-grade girls. *Psychological Reports*, 1971b, *28*, 241-242.

Lorber, J. *Trust, loyalty and the place of women in the informal organization of work*. Paper presented at the annual meeting of the American Sociological Association, 1975.

Lunneborg, P. Sex and decision-making styles. *Journal of Counseling Psychology*. 1978, *25*, 299-305.

Lyle, J. R., & Ross, J. L. *Women in industry*. Lexington, Mass.: D. C. Heath, 1973.

Maccoby, E. and Jacklin, C. *The psychology of sex differences*. Stanford, Calif.: Stanford University Press, 1974.

MacKinnon, C. A. *Sexual harassment of working women*. New Haven, Conn.: Yale University Press, 1979.

Mahoney, T. A. Factors determining the labor-force participation of married women. *Industrial and Labor Relations Review*, 1961, *14*, 563-577.

Majchrzak, A., & Gutek, B. A. *Satisfactions and dissatisfactions of secretaries*. Paper presented at the open symposium on women, sponsored by Division 35, APA, San Francisco, August 29, 1977.

Malkiel, B. G., & Malkiel, J. A. Male-female pay differentials in professional employment. *American Economic Review*, 1973, *63*, 693-704.

Manhardt, P. J. Job orientation of male and female college graduates in business. *Personnel Psychology*, 1972, *25*, 361-368.

Mann, R. D. A review of the relationships between personality and performance in small groups. *Psychological Bulletin*, 1959, *56*, 241-270.

Maslow, A. *Motivation and personality*. New York: Harper & Row, 1954.

Massengill, D., & DiMarco, N. Sex-role stereotypes and requisite management characteristics: A current replication. *Sex Roles*, 1979, *5*, 561-570.

McClelland, P. C., Atkinson, J. W., Clark, R. A., & Lowell, E. L. *The achievement motive*. New York: Appleton-Century-Crofts, 1953.

McClelland, P. C. *The achieving society*. Princeton, N.J.: Van Nostrand, 1961.

McGregor, D. *The professional manager*. New York: McGraw-Hill, 1967.

McMahon, F. D. Relationships between causal attributions and expectancy of success. *Journal of Personality and Social Psychology*, 1973, *28*, 108-114.

McNulty, D. Pay differences between men and women workers. *Monthly Labor Review*, 1967, *90*, 40-43.

Mead, M. A proposal: We need sexual taboos at work. *Redbook*, April, 1978.

Medvene, A. M., & Collins, A. Occupational prestige and its relationship to traditional and non-traditional view of women's roles. *Journal of Counseling Psychology*, 1974, *21*(2), 139-143.

Merton, R. K. *Social theory and social structure*. Glencoe, Ill.: The Free Press, 1957.

Miller, J., Labovitz, S., & Fry, L. Inequities in the organizational experiences of women and men. *Social Forces*, 1975, *54*, 365-381.

Miller, R. R. No play: A means of conflict resolution. *Journal of Personality and Social Psychology*, 1967, *6*, 150-156.

Miner, J. B. *Studies in management education*. New York: Springer, 1965.

Miner, J. B. Motivation to manage among women: Studies of business managers and educational administrators. *Journal of Vocational Behavior*, 1974, *5*, 197-208.

Moen, P. Family impact of the 1975 recession: Duration of unemployment. *Journal of Marriage and the Family*, 1979, *41*, 561-572.

Molm, L. D. Sex role attitudes and the employment of married women: The direction of causality. *The Sociological Quarterly*, 1978, *19*, 522-533.

Monahan, L., Kuhn, D., & Shaver, P. Intra-psychic vs. cultural explanations of the "Fear of Success" motive. *Journal of Personality and Social Psychology*, 1974, *29*(1), pp. 60-64.

Montemeyor, R. *Children's performance on and attraction to an activity as a function of masculine, feminine on neutral labels and sex-role preference.* Paper presented at EPA, April 1972.

Morgan, M. A. (Ed.). *Managing career development.* New York: Van Nostrand, 1980.

Morrison, R. F., & Sebald, M. L. Personal characteristics differentiating female executive from female non-executive personnel. *Journal of Applied Psychology*, 1974, *59*(5), 656-659.

Munley, P. H. Interests of career and homemaking oriented women. *Journal of Vocational Behavior*, 1974, *4*, 43-48.

National Academy of Sciences. *Careers of Ph.D.'s* Washington: National Academy of Sciences – National Research Council, 1968.

Nelson, R. C. Knowledge and interests concerning sixteen occupations among elementary and secondary school students. *Educational and Psychological Measurement*, 1963, *23*(4), 741-754.

Newman, B. Beyond the total woman: Creative life planning to meet women's needs. *Personnel and Guidance Journal*, 1979 (March), 359-361.

Nicholls, J. G. Causal attribution and other achievement-related cognitions: Effects of task outcome, attainment value, and sex. *Journal of Personality and Social Psychology*, 1975, *31*, 379-389.

Niemi, B. The male-female differentials in unemployment rates. *Industrial and Labor Relations Review*, 1974, *27*, 331-350.

Niemi, B. Geographic immobility and labor force mobility: A study of female unemployment. In C. B. Lloyd (Ed.), *Sex, discrimination and the division of labor*. New York: Columbia University Press, 1975.

Nieva, V. Supervisor-subordinate similarity. A determinant of subordinate ratings and rewards. Doctoral dissertation, University of Michigan, 1976.

Nilson, L. B. The occupational and sex-related components of social standing. *Sociology and Social Research*, 1976, *60*, 328-336.

Nisbett, R. E., & Gordon, A. Self-esteem and susceptibility to social influence. *Journal of Personality and Social Psychology*, 1967, *5*, 268-276.

Nord, W. R. Social exchange theory: An integrative approach to social conformity. *Psychological Bulletin*, 1969, *71*, 174-208.

Nye, F. I., & Hoffman, L. *The employed mother in America*. Chicago: Rand-McNally, 1963.

O'Hara, R. P. The roots of careers. *Elementary School Journal*, 1962, *62*, 277-280.

O'Leary, V. E. Some attitudinal barriers to occupational aspirations in women. *Psychological Bulletin*, 1974, *81*, 809-826.

O'Leary, V. E., & Donoghue, J. M. Latitudes of masculinity: Reactions to sex role deviance in men. *Journal of Social Issues*, 1978, *34*, 17-28.

O'Leary, V. E., & Hammack, B. Sex-role orientation and achievement context as determinants of the motive to avoid success. *Sex Roles*, 1975, *1*, 225-234.

Oliver, L. W. The relationship of parental attitudes and parent identification to career and homemaking orientation in college women. *Journal of Vocational Behavior*, 1975, *7*, 1-12.

Oppenheimer, V. The sex-labeling of jobs. *Industrial Relations*, 1968, *7*, 219-234.

Oppenheimer, V. Demographic influence on female employment and the status of women. *American Journal of Sociology*, 1973, *79*, 946-961.

Orlofsky, J. L. Parental antecedents of sex-role orientation in college men and women. *Sex Roles*, 1979, *5*, 495-512.

Osipow, S. *Emerging woman: career analysis and outlook*. New York: Merrill, 1975.

O'Toole, J. The reserve army of the underemployed. *Change*, 1975 (May), *63*, 26-33.

Papanek, H. Men, women and work: Reflections on the two person career. *American Journal of Sociology*, 1973, *78*, 852-870.

Parnes, H. S., Jusenius, C. L., Blau, F., Nestel, G. Shortlidge, R., Jr., & Sandell, S. *Dual careers: A longitudinal analysis of the labor market experience of women*. Columbus, Ohio: Center for Human Resource Research, December, 1975.

Parsons, T., & Bales, R. F. (Eds.). *Family socialization and interaction process*. New York: Free Press of Glencoe, 1955.

Pelz, D. C. Influence: A key to effective leadership in the first line supervisor. *Personnel*, 1952, *29*, 2-11.

Peplau, L. A. Impact of fear of success and sex-role attitudes on women's competitive achievement. *Journal of Personality and Social Psychology*, 1976, *34*(4), 561-568.

Perucci, C. C., Potter, H. R., & Rhoads, D. L. Determinants of male family-role performance. *Psychology of Women Quarterly*, 1978, *3*(1), 53-66.

Petty, M. M., & Lee, G. K. Moderating effects of sex of supervisor and subordinate on relationships between supervisory behavior and subordinate satisfaction. *Journal of Personality and Social Psychology*, 1975, *60*(5), 624-628.

Petty, M. M., & Miles, R. H. Leader sex-role stereotyping in social service organizations. In R. L. Taylor, M. J. O'Connel, R. A. Zawacki, & D. D. Warrich (Eds.), *Proceedings of the annual meeting of the Academy of Management*. Kansas City, Mo.: Academy of Management, 1976.

Pheterson, G. T., Kiesler, S. B., & Goldberg, P. A. Evaluation of the performance of women as a function of their sex, achievement and personal history. *Journal of Personality and Social Psychology*, 1971, *19*, 110-114.

Pifer, A. Women working toward a new society. *The Urban and Social Change Review*, 1978, *11*, 3-11.

Piore, M. The dual labor market: Theory and implications. Reprinted from M. J. Piore, Jobs and training, in Beer and Barringer (Eds.), *The state and the poor*. New York: Winthrop, 1970.

Pleck, J. H. The male sex role: Definitions, problems and sources of change. *Journal of Social Issues*, 1976, *32*, 155-164.

Pleck, J. H. The work-family role system. *Social Problems*, 1977, *24*, 417-427.

Pleck, J. H. *Conflicts between work and the family lines of men and women*. In V. F. Nieva (chair), Work and other life spheres of men and women. Paper presented at the annual convention of the APA, New York, September 1979.

Polachek, S. W. Discontinuous labor force participation and its effect on women's market earnings. In C. B. Lloyd (Ed.), *Sex discrimination and the division of labor*. New York: Columbia University Press, 1975.

Porter, L. W., Lawler, E. E., & Hackman, J. R. *Behavior in organizations*. New York: McGraw-Hill, 1975.

Power, M. Women's work is never done — by men: A socioeconomic model of sex-typing in occupations. *Journal of Industrial Relations*, 1975, *17*, 225-240.

Pressley, B. O. Survey of guidance and counseling divisions of State Departments of education. *The Commission for Women 1973-1974 Report Summary*. Washington, D.C.: American Personnel and Guidance Association, 1974, p. 3.

Quinn, R. Coping with cupid: The formation, impact and management of romantic relationships in organizations. *Administrative Science Quarterly*, 1977, *22*, 30-45.

Quinn, R., & Cobb, W. *What workers want: Factor analysis of importance ratings of job facets*. Ann Arbor, Mich.: Institute of Social Research, 1971.

Quinn, R. L., & Shepard, L. *The 1972-73 quality of employment survey*. Ann Arbor, Mich.: Survey Research Center, 1974.

Rand, L. Masculinity or femininity? Differentiating career-oriented and home-making-oriented college freshman women. *Journal of Counseling Psychology*, 1968, *15*(5), 444-450.

Rapoport, R., & Rapoport, R. N. The dual career family: A variant pattern and social change. *Human Relations*, 1969, *22*(1), 3-30.

Rapoport, R., & Rapoport, R. (Eds.). *Working couples*. New York: Harper, 1978.

Rebecca, M. *Voluntary childlessness as a conflict-reducing mechanism*. Paper presented at the Association of Women in Psychology annual meeting, Pittsburgh, 1978.

Rebecca, M., Hefner, R., & Oleshansky, B. A model of sex role transcendence. *Journal of Social Issues*, 1976, *32*, 197-206.

Reeves, T. Z. The EEOC cracks down on sexual harassment with tougher guidelines for employers. Unpublished manuscript, California State University, Dominguez Hills, 1980.

Rezler, A. G. Characteristics of high school girls choosing traditional or pioneer vocations. *Personnel and Guidance Journal*, 1967, *45*, 659-665.

Rice, A. K. *The enterprise and its environment*. London: Tavistock Publications, 1963.

Rich, A. Privilege, power and tokenism. *Ms.*, 1979 (September), 42-44.

Richardson, M. S. The dimensions of career and work orientation in college women. *Journal of Vocational Behavior*, 1974, *5*, 161-172.

Richardson, M. S. Self-concepts and role concepts in the career orientation of college women. *Journal of Counseling Psychology*, 1975, *22*(2), 122-126.

Robinson, J. P., & Converse, P. E. *Summary of U.S. Time-Use Survey*. Ann Arbor, Mich.: Survey Research Center Monograph, 1966.

Roe, A. Early determinants of vocational choice. *Journal of Counseling Psychology*, 1957, *4*, 212-217.

Roe, A., & Siegelman, M. *Origin of interests. APGA inquiry studies – No. 1*. Washington, D.C.: American Personnel and Guidance Association, 1964.

Roethlisberger, F. J., & Dickson, W. J. *Management and the worker*. Cambridge, Mass.: Harvard University Press, 1939.

Rogers, E. M. *Diffusion of innovation*. New York: The Free Press, 1962.

Romer, H. The motive to avoid success and its effect on performance in school-age males and females. *Developmental Psychology*, 1975, *2*(6), 689-699.

Rosen, B., & Jerdee, T. H. The influence of sex-role stereotypes on evaluations of male and female supervisory behavior. *Journal of Applied Psychology*, 1973, *57*(1), 44-48.

Rosen, B., & Jerdee, T. H. Influence of sex role stereotypes on personnel decisions. *Journal of Applied Psychology*, 1974, *59*, 9-14.

Rosen, B., Jerdee, T. A., & Prestwich, T. L. Dual-career marital adjustments: Potential effects of discriminating managerial attitudes. *Journal of Marriage and the Family*, 1975, *37*, 565-572.

Rosenberg, M. *Occupations and values*. Glencoe, Ill.: The Free Press, 1957.

Rosenthal, R., & Jacobson, L. R. Teacher expectations for the disadvantaged. *Scientific American*, 1968, *218*, 19-23.

Ross, H. L., & Sawhill, I. V. *Time of transition*. Washington, D.C.: Urban Institute, 1975.

Rossi, A. S. Barriers to the career choice of engineering, medicine or science among American women. In J. A. Mattfield & C. G. VanAken (Eds.), *Women and the scientific professions*. Cambridge, Mass.: MIT Press, 1965a.

Rossi, A. S. Women in science, why so few? *Science*, 1965b, *148* (May 28), 1196-1202.

Rossi, A. S. Sex equality: The beginnings of ideology. *The Humanist*, 1969 (September-October), 3-6.

Rossi, A. S. Discrimination and demography restrict opportunities for academic women. *College & University Business*, 1970a (February), 1-4.

Rossi, A. S. Job discrimination and what women can do about it. *Atlantic*, 1970b, *225*, 99-103.

Rousseau, D. The relationship of work to non-work. *Journal of Applied Psychology*, 1978, *63*, 513-517.

Roussell, C. Relationship of sex of department head to department climate. *Administrative Science Quarterly*, 1974, *19*(2), 211-220.

Ryan, W. *Blaming the victims*. New York: Random House, 1971.

Rychlak, B., & Ecker, J. N. The effects of anxiety, delay and reinforcement on generalized expectancies. *Journal of Personality and Social Psychology*, 1962, *30*, 123-134.

Ryder, N. B., & Westoff, C. F. *Reproduction in the United States 1965*. Princeton, N.J.: Princeton University Press, 1971.

Saario, T. N., Jacklin, C. N., & Tittle, C. K. Sex role stereotyping in the public schools. *Harvard Educational Review*, 1973, *43*(3), 386-416.

Safilios-Rothschild, C. Dual linkages between the occupational and family systems: A macro-sociological analysis. In M. Blaxall & B. Reagan (Eds.), *Women in the workplace*. Chicago: University of Chicago Press, 1976.

Safilios-Rothschild, C. Women as change agents: Toward a conflict model of sex role change. In J. Lipman-Blumen and J. Bernard (Eds.), *Sex roles and social policy*. London: Sage Publications, 1979.

Safilios-Rothschild, C., & Dijkers, M. Handling unconventional asymmetries. In R. Rapoport and R. Rapoport (Eds.), *Working couples*. New York: Harper, 1978.

Salancik, G. R., Calder, B. J., Rowland, K. M., Leblebici, H., & Conway, M. Leadership as an outcome of social structure and process: A multidimensional approach. In J. G. Hunt & L. L. Larson (Eds.), *Leadership frontiers*. Kent, Ohio: Kent State University Press, 1975.

Saleh, S., & Lalljee, M. Sex and job orientation. *Personnel Psychology*, 1969, *22*, 465-471.

Sawhill, I. Discrimination and poverty among women who head families. In M. Blaxall & B. Reagan (Eds.), *Women and the workplace*. Chicago: University of Chicago Press, 1976.

Schein, E. H. Organizational socialization and the profession of management. *Industrial Management Review*, 1968, *9*, 1-16.

Schein, E. H. The individual, the organization and the career: A conceptual scheme. *Journal of Applied Behavioral Science*, 1971, *7*, 401-426.

Schein, E. H. *Career dynamics: Matching individual and organizational needs.* Reading, Mass.: Addison-Wesley, 1978.

Schein, V. E. The relationship between sex-role stereotypes and requisite management characteristics. *Journal of Applied Psychology*, 1973, *57*(2), 95-100.

Schein, V. E. Relationship between sex-role stereotypes and requisite management characteristics among female managers. *Journal of Applied Psychology*, 1975, *60*, 240-344.

Scherrei, R. A. Changes in career aspirations of women entering college. In B. A. Gutek (Ed.), *New directions for education, work and careers: Enhancing women's career development.* San Francisco: Jossey-Bass, 1979.

Schlossberg, N. K., & Goodman, J. A. A woman's place: Children's sex stereotyping of occupation. *Vocational Guidance Quarterly*, 1972, *20*, 266-270.

Schmidt, F. L., & Johnson, R. H. The effect of race on peer ratings in an industrial situation. *Journal of Applied Psychology*, 1973, *57*, 237-241.

Schrank, T. H., & Riley, J. W. Women in work organizations. In J. M. Kreps (Ed.), *Women and the American economy.* Englewood Cliffs, N.J.: Prentice-Hall, 1976.

Schreiber, C. T. *Changing places: Men and women in traditional occupations.* Cambridge, Mass.: MIT Press, 1979.

Schriesheim, C. Personal communication. January, 1980.

Schuler, R. S. Sex, organizational level and outcome importance: Where the differences are. *Personnel Psychology*, 1975, *28*, 365-376.

Schwartz, S. H., & Clausen, G. T. Responsibility norms and helping in an emergency. *Journal of Personality and Social Psychology*, 1970, *16*, 299-316.

Schweitzer, S. O., & Smith, R. E. The persistence of the discouraged worker effect. *Industrial and Labor Relations Review*, 1974, *27*(2), 249-260.

Sedney, M. A., & Turner, B. F. A test of causal sequences in two models for development of career-orientation in women. *Journal of Vocational Behavior*, 1975, *6*, 281-291.

Seyfried, B. A., & Hendrick, C. When do opposites attract? When they are opposite in sex and sex role attitudes. *Journal of Personality and Social Psychology*, 1973, *25*, 15-20.

Shaffer, D. R., & Wegley, C. Success-orientation and sex-role congruence as determinants of the attractiveness of competent women. *Journal of Personality and Social Psychology*, 1974, *29*, 586-600.

Shaw, E. A. Differential impact of negative stereotypes in employee selection. *Personnel Psychology*, 1972, *25*, 333-358.

Shea, R. J. et al. *Dual careers: A longitudinal study of labor market experience of women* (Vol. 1). Columbus: Center for Human Resources Research, Ohio State University, 1970, p. 171.

Shepard, W. O., & Hess, D. T. Attitudes in four age groups toward sex role division in adult occupations and activities. *Journal of Vocational Behavior*, 1975, *6*, 27-39.

Shepela, S. T. Affirmative-action backlash. *AWP Newsletter*, June-July, 1977.

Shinar, E. H. Sexual stereotypes of occupations. *Journal of Vocational Behavior*, 1975, *7*, 99-111.

Shomer, R. W., Davis, A. H., & Kelley, H. Threats and development of coordination: Further studies of the Deutsch and Krauss trucking game. *Journal of Personality and Social Psychology*, 1966, *4*, 119-126.

Shuval, J. T. Occupational interests and sex-role congruence. *Human Relations*, 1963, *16*, 171-182.

Siegel, A. E., & Curtis, E. A. Familial correlates of orientation toward future employment among college women. *Journal of Educational Psychology*, 1963, *44*, 33-37.

Siegel, A. E., & Haas, M. B. The working mother: a review of research. *Child Development*, 1963, *34*, 513-542.

Siegel, C. Sex differences in the occupational choices of second graders. *Journal of Vocational Behavior*, 1973, *3*, 15-19.

Simon, J. G., & Feather, N. T. Causal attributions for success and failure at university examinations. *Journal of Personality and Social Psychology*, 1973, *16*, 299-310.

Slocum, W. L. *Occupational careers*. Chicago: Aldine, 1966.

Slocum, W. L., & Bowles, R. T. Attractiveness of occupations to high school students. *Personnel and Guidance Journal*, 1968, *46*(8), 754-761.

Smith, R. E. (Ed.). *The subtle revolution*. Washington, D.C.: Urban Institute, 1979.

Smith-Lovin, L., & Tickamyer, A. R. Nonrecursive models of labor force participation, fertility behavior and sex role attitude. *American Sociological Review*, 1978, *43*, 541-557.

Sobol, M. G. Commitment to work. In F. I. Nye and L. W. Hoffman (Eds.), *The employed mother in America*. Chicago: Rand-McNally, 1963.

Sobol, M. G. A dynamic analysis of labor force participation of married women of child bearing age. *The Journal of Human Resource*, 1973 (Fall), *8*, 497-505.

Speer, D. C. Marital dysfunctionality and two person non-zero sum game behavior. *Journal of Personality and Social Psychology*, 1972, *21*, 18-24.

Spence, J. T. The TAT and attitude toward achievement in women: A new look at the motive to avoid success and a new method of measurement. *Journal of Consulting and Clinical Psychology*, 1974, *42*(3), 427-437.

Spence, J. T., & Helmreich, R. The attitude toward women scale: An objective instrument to measure attitudes toward the rights and roles of women in contemporary society. *(JSAS) Catalog of Selected Documents in Psychology*, 1972a, *2*, 66.

Spence, J. T., & Helmreich, R. Who likes competent women? Competence, sex role, congruence of interests and subjects attitudes toward woman as determinant of interpersonal attraction. *Journal of Applied Social Psychology*, 1972b, *2*, 197-213.

Spence, J. T., Helmreich, R., & Stapp, J. Likeability, sex-role congruence of interest and competence: It all depends on how you ask. *Journal of Applied Social Psychology*, 1975, *5*, 93-109.

Staines, G. L. Spillover vs. compensation: A review of the literature between work and non-work. *Human Relations*, 1980, *33*, 111-129.

Staines, G., Gutek, B., Pleck, J., Shepard, L., O'Connor, P., & Allen, H. *A study of occupational sex typing*. Final report to Department of Labor, Grant No. 91-26-76-51, 1979.

Staines, G. L., Pleck, J. H., Shepard, L. J., & O'Connor, P. Wives' employment status and marital adjustment: Yet another look. *Psychology of Women Quarterly*, 1978, *3*(1), 90-120.

Staines, G., Tavris, C., & Jayaratne, T. E. The queen bee syndrome. In C. Tavris (Ed.), *The female experience*. Del Mar: Communications Research, 1973.

Standley, K., & Soule, B. Women in male-dominated professions: Contrasts in their personal and vocational histories. *Journal of Vocational Behavior*, 1974, *4*, 245-258.

Stein, A. H., & Bailey, M. M. The socialization of achievement motivation in females. *Psychological Bulletin*, 1973, *80*, 345-366.

Stein, A. H., Pohly, S. R., & Mueller, E. The influence of masculine, feminine and neutral tasks on children's achievement behavior, expectances of success and attainment values. *Child Development*, 1975, *42*, 195-207.

Stogdill, R. M., Goode, O. S., & Day, D. R. New leader behavior description subscales. *Journal of Psychology*, 1962, *54*, 259-569.

Stolzenberg, R. M., & Waite, L. J. Fertility expectations and employment plans. *American Sociological Review*, 1977, *42*(5), 769-783.

Strache, K. *Personality characteristics of men and women administrators.* Paper presented at the annual APA convention, Washington, D.C., 1976.

Strauss, A. Some neglected properties of status passage. In H. D. Becker, B. Geer, D. Reisma, & R. S. Weiss (Eds.), *Institutions and the person*. Chicago: Aldine, 1968.

Suchner, R. W., & More, D. M. Stereotypes of males and females in two occupations. *Journal of Vocational Behavior*, 1975, *6*, 1-8.

Super, D. *The psychology of careers*. New York: Harper & Row, 1957.

Super, D., Crites, J., Hummel, R., Moser, H., Overstreet, P., & Warnath, D. *Vocational development: A framework for research.* New York: Teachers College Press, 1957.

Surette, R. F. Career versus homemaking: perspectives and proposals. *Vocational Guidance Quarterly*, 1967 (Dec.), 82-86.

Suter, L. E., & Miller, H. P. Income differences between men and career women. *American Journal of Sociology*, 1973, *78*, 962-974.

Tangri, S. Determinants of occupational role innovation among college women. *Journal of Social Issues*, 1972, *28*, 177-199.

Taylor, S. E., Fiske, S. T., Etcoff, N. L., & Ruderman, A. J. Categorical and contextual basis of person memory and stereotyping. *Journal of Personality and Social Psychology*, 1978, *36*, 778-793.

Taynor, J., & Deaux, K. When women are more deserving then men: Equity, attribution and perceived sex differences. *Journal of Personality and Social Psychology*, 1973, *28*, 360-367.

Taynor, J., & Deaux, K. Equity and perceived sex differences: Role behavior as defined by the task, the mode and the action. *Journal of Personality and Social Psychology*, 1975, *32*, 381-390.

Terborg, J. Women in management: A research review. *Journal of Applied Psychology*, 1977, *62*, 647-664.

Terborg, J. R., & Ilgen, D. R. A theoretical approach to sex discrimination in traditionally masculine occupations. *Organizational Behavior and Human Performance*, 1975, *13*, 352-376.

Terman, L. M., & Oden, M. H. *Genetic studies of genius. V. The gifted group at mid-life: Thirty-five years' follow-up of the superior child.* Stanford, Calif.: Stanford University Press, 1959.

Terry, R. The white male club: Biology and power. *Civil Rights Digest*, 1974 (Spring), 66-77.

Thomas, A. H., & Stewart, N. R. Counselor response to female clients with deviate and conforming career goals. *Journal of Counseling Psychology*, 1971, *18*(4), 352-357.

Tiger, L. *Men in groups.* New York: Random House, 1972.

Tipton, R. M. Attitudes toward women's roles in society and vocational interests. *Journal of Vocational Behavior*, 1976, *8*, 155-165.

Touhey, J. C. Effects of additional women professionals on ratings of occupational prestige and desirability. *Journal of Personality and Social Psychology*. 1974, *29*(1), 86-89.

Treiman, D. J., & Terrell, K. Sex and the process of status attainment. *American Sociological Review*, 1975, *40*, 174-200.

Tresemer, D. The cumulative record of research on fear of success. *Sex Roles*, 1976, *2*, 217-236.

Trigg, L., & Perlman, D. Social influences on women's pursuit of a nontraditional career. *Psychology of Women Quarterly*, 1976, *1*(2), 180-189.

Turner, B. F., & McCaffrey, J. H. Socialization and career orientation among black and white college women. *Journal of Vocational Behavior*, 1974, *55*, 307-319.

Turner, R. H. Some aspects of women's ambition. *American Journal of Sociology*, 1964, *70*, 271-285.

Tyler, L. *The Psychology of Human Differences* (2nd Ed.). New York: Appleton-Century-Crofts, 1965.

U.S. Bureau of the Census. *Data User News, 15*(5). Washington, D.C.: Bureau of the Census, 1978.

U.S. Bureau of the Census. Current Population Reports Series P-60, No. 125. Money and persons in the United States: 1979 (advance report). Washington, D.C.: USGPO, 1980.

U.S. Department of Labor, Bureau of Labor Statistics, *Employment and Earnings*, 1978, *25* (January).

U.S. Department of Labor, Bureau of Labor Statistics, *Employment and Earnings*, 1979, *26* (January).

Utton, A. C. Recalled parent-child relations as determinants of career choice. *Journal of Counseling Psychology*, 1962, *9*, 49-53.

Veroff, J. Social comparison and the development of achievement motivation. In C. P. Smith (Ed.), *Achievement related motives in children*. New York: Russell Sage, 1969.

Vetter, L. Career counseling for women. *The Counseling Psychologist*, 1973, *4*(1), 54-66.

Vetter, L., & Lewis, E. C. Some correlates of homemaking vs. career preference among college home economics students. *Personnel and Guidance Journal*, 1964, *42* (Feb.), 593-598.

Vetter, L., Stockburger, S. W., & Brose, C. *Career guidance materials: Implications for woman's career development*. Columbus: Center for Vocational Education, Ohio State University, 1974.

Vinacke, W. Sex roles in a three person game. *Sociometry*, 1959, *22*, 343-359.

Vogel, S. R., Broverman, I. K., Broverman, D. M., Clarkson, F. E., & Rosenkrantz, P. S. Maternal employment and perception of sex roles among college students. *Developmental Psychology*, 1970, *3*(3), 384-391.

Vroom, V. H. *Work and Motivation*. New York: John Wiley, 1964.

Vroom, V. H. Leadership. In M. D. Dunnette (Ed.), *Handbook in industrial and organizational psychology*. Chicago: Rand-McNally, 1976.

Wade, M. *Flexible working hours in public*. New York: John Wiley, 1973.

Wagman, M. Interests and values of career and homemaking oriented women. *Personnel and Guidance Journal*, 1966, *44*, 794-801.

Wahrman, R., & Pugh, M. D. Competence and conformity: Another look at Hollander's study. *Sociometry*, 1972, *35*, 376-386.

Wahrman, R., & Pugh, M. D. Sex, nonconformity and influence. *Sociometry*, 1974, *37*(1), 137-147.

Waite, L. J. Working wives: 1940-1960. *American Sociological Review*, 1976, *41*, 65-80.

Waite, L. J., & Stolzenberg, R. M. Intended childbearing and labor force participation of young women: Insights from nonrecursive models. *American Sociological Review*, 1976, *41*, 235-252.

Walker, K. E. Time spent by husbands in household work. *Family Economics Review*, 1970, *4*, 8-11.

Wallace, P. *Equal employment opportunity and the AT&T case.* Cambridge, Mass.: MIT Press, 1976.

Wallston, B. S., Foster, M., & Berger, M. I will follow him: Myth, reality, or forced choice. *Psychology of Women Quarterly*, 1978, *3*, 9-21.

Weil, M. W. An analysis of the factors influencing married women's actual or planned work participation. *American Sociological Review*, 1961, *26*, 91-96.

Weiner, B. *Theories of motivation.* Chicago: Rand-McNally/Markham, 1972.

Weiner, B., Frieze, I., Kukla, A., Reed, L., Rest, S., & Rosenbaum, R. M. *Perceiving the causes of success and failure.* New York: General Learning Press, 1971.

Weingarten, K. The employment pattern of professional couples and their distribution of involvement in the family. *Psychology of Women Quarterly*, 1978, *3*(1), 43-52.

Weitzman, L. J., Eifler, D., Hodaka, E., & Ross, C. Sex-role socialization in picture books for preschool children. *American Journal of Sociology*, 1972, *77*(6), 1125-1150.

Weller, L., Shlomi, A., & Zimont, G. Birth order, sex and occupational interest. *Journal of Vocational Behavior*, 1976, *8*, 45-50.

Wells, T. Equalizing advancement between women and men. *Training and Development Journal*, 1973, *27*, 20-24.

Whelpton, P. K., Campbell, A. A., & Patterson, J. E. *Fertility and family planning in the United States.* Princeton, N.J.: Princeton University Press, 1966.

Wiggins, J. E., Dill, F., & Schwartz, P. On "status-liability." *Sociometry*, 1965, *28*, 197-209.

Willis, R. A., & Willis, Y. A. Role playing vs. deception: An experimental comparison. *Journal of Personality and Social Psychology*, 1970, *16*, 472-477.

Winter, D., Stewart, A., & McClelland, D. Husband's motives and wife's career level. *Journal of Personality and Social Psychology*, 1977, *35*, 159-166.

Wirtenberg, T. J., & Nakamura, C. Education: Barrier or boon to changing occupational roles of women? *Journal of Social Issues*, 1976, *32*, 165-180.

Wolman, C., & Frank, H. The solo woman in a professional peer group. *American Journal of Orthopsychiatry*, 1975, *45*, 164-171.

Wyer, R. S., Jr. Behavioral correlates of academic achievement: Conformity under achievement and affiliation-incentive conditions. *Journal of Personality and Social Psychology*, 1967, *6*, 255-263.

Yankelovich, D. Turbulence in the working world — Angry workers, happy grads. *Psychology Today*, 1974 (December), 81-87.

Yankelovich, D. Work, values and the new breed. In C. Kerr and J. M. Rosow (Eds.), *Work in America: The decade ahead*. New York: Van Nostrand Reinhold, 1979.

Zuckerman, M., & Wheeler, L. To dispel fantasies about the fantasy-based measure of fear of success. *Psychological Bulletin*, 1975, *6*, 932-946.

Zytowski, D. G. Toward a theory of career development for women. *Personnel and Guidance Journal*, 1969, *47*, 660-664.

INDEX

ABOUT THE AUTHORS

VERONICA F. NIEVA is a Research Associate at the Urban Institute in Washington, D.C. She received her Ph.D. in Organizational Psychology at the University of Michigan in 1976. She has been doing research in the general areas of work and organizational behavior, on issues such as improving the quality of work life, organizational diagnosis and change, and equity in performance evaluation. She has coauthored *The New Plant* with Dennis N. T. Perkins and Edward E. Lawler, and has published articles on work and organizations, with a special focus on the conditions of women at work.

BARBARA A. GUTEK is Assistant Professor of Psychology at UCLA. She received her Ph.D. in Organizational Psychology at the University of Michigan in 1975. The area of women and work has been a major research interest; she has taught courses and published frequently in the area, often in collaboration with Veronica Nieva. She edited *New Directions for Education, Work and Careers: Enhancing Women's Career Development* (1979), and coauthored with Daniel Katz, Robert L. Kahn, and Eugenia Barton *Bureaucratic Encounters: A Pilot Study in the Evaluation of Government Service* (1975). She is currently researching sexual harassment and sexual interest at work.